The
Princeton
Review

MEDICAL SCHOOL ESSAYS THAT MADE A DIFFERENCE

By The Staff of The Princeton Review

Random House, Inc.
New York
www.PrincetonReview.com

The Princeton Review, Inc
2315 Broadway
New York, NY 10024
E-mail: bookeditor@review.com

ISBN-13   978-0-375-76571-1
ISBN   0-375-76571-9

Publisher: Robert Franek
Editor: Michael Palumbo
Production Manager and Designer: Scott Harris
Production Editor: Christine LaRubio

Manufactured in the United States of America.

9 8 7 6 5 4 3 2

ACKNOWLEDGMENTS

This book would not have been possible without the contributions of several members of the Book Publishing team here at The Princeton Review, most notably Robert Franek, who was instrumental in the development of the *Essays that Made a Difference* series and an essential advocate for the creation of this book; Scott Harris and Christine LaRubio, who deserve an award for their patience as they transformed the manuscript into the book now in your hands; and Suzanne Podhurst, who merits special thanks for all the valuable input she provided along the way.

Other contributors include Adam Davis and Julie Doherty, who were particularly helpful as the manuscript took shape in the final days of the book's production, and Andrea Kornstein, who provided much administrative support. A thank you also goes to Bill Fox for his insight during the production of this book.

We gained much helpful information, including trends in modern medicine and different ways to approach the personal statement, from Malaika Stoll, author of *The Best 162 Medical Schools*. The authors of *Planning a Life in Medicine*—John Smart, MS; Stephen Nelson, Jr., MD; and Julie Doherty (once again)—also deserve special mention. Their overview of the application process, in particular, was helpful as we sought to give premeds an idea of what to expect each step of the way.

Gratitude is also reserved for the three medical school admissions officers—Lorna Kenyon, Megan Prince, and Jennifer Welch—who kindly set aside time to speak with us about the particulars of their institution's admissions process.

The folks most vital to this book, of course, are the contributors—41 amazing students who took time out of their busy lives to stay in touch and answer questions. To each student who participated in this project: Many thanks for your patience, hard work, and generosity. We commend you for having the guts to lay it all out there for the benefit of future generations of medical school applicants.

—Michael Palumbo

ACKNOWLEDGMENTS

CONTENTS

INTRODUCTION

WHY DID WE PRODUCE THIS BOOK?

Too many freaked-out premeds with outstanding academic records, enviable MCAT scores, and impressive experiences outside the classroom experience frustration with their medical school personal statement. Given the task of boiling down their desire to be a doctor to a single page of prose, many don't even know where to start. This book is designed to show that there are many different ways to approach the personal statement and that, if a student reflects on what's most important in his or her life, he or she will indeed have something to write about. Our evidence is enclosed herewith: actual personal statements that got living, breathing premeds into medical school.

The personal statements in this book display a range of creativity and sophistication with the written word. Some are so good they may intimidate you; others may hardly impress you. We think you'll find, as we have, that the most memorable ones illuminate their writers. They're believable and perhaps relatable—but above all else, they're sincere.

Of course, personal statements don't stand alone; they have a place within the larger admissions context. In this book, we give you the whole picture with the college GPA; graduate school GPA, if applicable; extracurriculars; hometown; race; and Medical College Admissions Test (i.e., MCAT) scores of the student who wrote each personal statement we feature. Some students were also generous enough to provide essays they wrote for secondary applications. Finally, we include a list of admissions decisions for every single applicant whose personal statement you'll read. In this way, we hope to provide you with an understanding of the relative selectivity of the medical schools that the students in this book applied to and the admissions context within which the personal statement functions. Sure, you can find the average MCAT scores and GPAs of last year's freshman class in most college guides, but what you'll find here are the profiles of individual applicants who are currently enrolled in, or have recently graduated from, U.S. medical schools.

HOW CAN THIS BOOK HELP YOU?

The early chapters of this book are primarily a guide to medical school admissions and the writing that med school applications entail, with some extra information that you may find helpful as you decide whether or not to pursue a career in medicine. These chapters will fill in any gaps in your knowledge and make you a well-informed premed.

The personal statements, secondary essays, applicants, and admissions results in this book are presented without commentary. Among the personal statements and secondary essays, not every sentence is eloquent, nor every comma perfectly placed. However, they all passed the ultimate test for medical school application soundness: Their authors gained acceptance into at least one of the medical schools to which they applied. Ideally, these personal statements and secondary essays will inspire you, supply you with paradigms for narrative and organizational structures, teach you ways to express yourself that you hadn't yet considered, and help you write exactly what you wish to communicate.

This book should also help prepare you to encounter both success and failure in the admissions process. You're going to be a bit perplexed when UCSF accepts, Penn waitlists, and Mt. Sinai rejects a student in the book. As you'll see, even wunderkinds—we've profiled plenty of them—get denied admission to top-flight schools. In fact, very few of the students you will encounter in this book got into every medical school to which they applied. So what should this mean to you? It means that failure is a part of life, even when you've busted your hump working on whatever it was that ultimately failed. But even if you do get a rejection letter, there's no reason to feel completely bereft: a few fat envelopes are probably wending their way to you.

WHY'D THEY DO IT?

Why *would* current medical school students and recent grads allow us to publish their personal statements, test scores, grades, and biographical information? They realize the value their stories have for prospective medical school students. After all, gaining admission to medical school is no small feat. Many said they were honored to have been chosen for publication and to have been given the chance to help the next generation of medical school students.

WHERE'D THEY GET IN?

Students with personal statements published in this book received offers of admission from the following U.S. medical schools:

Albany Medical College

Baylor College of Medicine

Boston University, School of Medicine

Brown University, Brown Medical School

Case Western Reserve University, School of Medicine

Cornell University, Joan & Sanford I. Weill Medical Center

Creighton University, School of Medicine

Duke University, School of Medicine

Emory University, School of Medicine

George Washington University, School of Medicine and Health Sciences

Johns Hopkins University, School of Medicine

Loma Linda University, School of Medicine

Loyola University of Chicago, Stritch School of Medicine

Mayo Clinic College of Medicine, Mayo Medical School

Medical College of Georgia, School of Medicine

Medical College of Wisconsin

Meharry Medical College, School of Medicine

Michigan State University, College of Osteopathic Medicine

New York University, Mount Sinai School of Medicine

New York University, NYU School of Medicine

Northwestern University, Feinberg School of Medicine

Ohio State University, College of Medicine and Public Health

Oregon Health & Science University, School of Medicine

Pennsylvania State University, College of Medicine

Rush University, Rush Medical College

Saint Louis University, School of Medicine

Southern Illinois University, School of Medicine

State University of New York—Downstate Medical Center

State University of New York—Stony Brook University, School of Medicine

State University of New York—University at Buffalo, School of Medicine and
Biomedical Sciences

State University of New York—Upstate Medical University, College
of Medicine

Temple University, School of Medicine

Thomas Jefferson University, Jefferson Medical College

Tufts University, School of Medicine

Tulane University, School of Medicine

UMDNJ, New Jersey Medical School

UMDNJ, Robert Wood Johnson Medical School

University of Alabama—Birmingham, School of Medicine

University of California—Irvine, College of Medicine

University of California—Los Angeles, David Geffen School of Medicine

University of California—San Diego, School of Medicine

University of California—San Francisco, School of Medicine

University of Cincinnati, College of Medicine

University of Illinois at Chicago, UIC College of Medicine

University of Iowa, Roy J. and Lucille A. Carver College of Medicine

University of Kentucky, College of Medicine

University of Maryland, School of Medicine

University of Massachusetts, Medical School

University of Minnesota—Duluth, Medical School

University of Minnesota—Twin Cities, Medical School

University of North Dakota, School of Medicine and Health Sciences

University of Pennsylvania, School of Medicine

University of Pittsburgh, School of Medicine

University of South Alabama, College of Medicine

University of Southern California, Keck School of Medicine

University of Virginia, School of Medicine

University of Wisconsin—Madison, School of Medicine and Public Health

Virginia Commonwealth University, School of Medicine

Wake Forest University, School of Medicine

Washington University in St. Louis, School of Medicine

West Virginia University, School of Medicine

Yeshiva University, Albert Einstein School of Medicine

After considering the information for applicants who were accepted to a given medical school, you'll start to get an idea of what you will need—in terms of academic competitiveness, personal statement quality, extracurricular experiences, etc.—to gain admission to it. Even if you do not plan to apply to the same schools as the students included in this book, the quality of the students' personal statements and the overall strength of their applications can be used to measure your own writing and credentials.

THE PARTS OF THIS BOOK

Chapter 1

Following Directions: A Brief Overview of the Medical School Application Process

Before we get down to the business of your personal statement and secondary essays, we place them both in the context of your application; we also place your application in the larger context of the medical school admissions process.

Chapters 2–4

Getting Personal: Primary and Supplemental Essays
Having Heart: What Really Makes an Essay Tick
They're, Their, and There: Grammar and Writing Tips

These three chapters address how to write a great personal statement and first-rate secondary essays for admission to medical school. There's no magic recipe, of course; nevertheless, if you follow our advice about what to put in and what to leave out, we're very confident that you'll end up with memorable pieces of writing that will differentiate you from the applicant pool at large and make you a more competitive candidate.

Chapter 5

Making Ends Meet: Financial Aid Overview

Your basic financial aid options are laid out here. We present good strategies to adopt and common pitfalls to avoid.

Chapter 6

Being a Doctor: Things You Should Know

Is medicine the right career for you? This chapter presents a discussion of modern medical practice and current trends in medicine.

Chapter 7

Q&A with Admissions Officers

This part of the book consists of interviews with three medical school admissions professionals—two from allopathic schools and one from an osteopathic school. Read about what they do and don't like to see in applications, how *their* admissions office works, and just how much the personal statement and secondary essays are worth at their school. We think you'll find their opinions intriguing; they also lend a human perspective to the sometimes harrowing medical school admissions process.

Chapter 8

Real Personal Statements and Secondary Essays

This part of this book contains 41 actual, unexpurgated personal statements written and submitted by real medical school applicants to a variety of schools. Each student profile is broken down into manageable chunks. The name of the student[1] and a photograph (if he or she provided one) come first. We then offer a short paragraph summarizing the major accomplishments and activities the student highlighted on his or her applications. Next, we provide statistical information which appeared on the student's apps and a list of schools to which the student applied. Below that you will see the *unedited* personal statement that the student wrote for his or her American Medical College Application Service (AMCAS) primary application.[2] For any non-AMCAS schools to which the applicant applied, he or she would have had to prepare an additional application or applications, which may not have included the personal statement shown.[3] It is not uncommon,

1   Ten students wished to have their profiles listed anonymously. Their profiles can be found at the end of the chapter.

2   A list of medical schools participating in AMCAS for the 2006 entering class can be found at www.aamc.org/students/amcas/participatingschools.htm. Please note that the schools participating in AMCAS changes somewhat annually—schools on this list may not have been participating when a given applicant applied to medical school.

3   All osteopathic schools participate in the American Association of Colleges of Osteopathic Medicine (AACOM)'s Application Service (AACOMAS), discussed in chapter one of this book. Some allopathic schools also do not participate in the AMCAS, though the number of schools in that category has steadily decreased over the last decade. *Medical School Admissions Requirements*, a book annually published by the American Association of Medical Colleges (AAMC), provides contact information for non-AMCAS schools.

however, for premeds to use their AMCAS personal statement for a non-AMCAS primary application if the prompt is general enough.

Four students profiled in this book also shared one or more essays written as part of a secondary application. Secondary essays are always written for a specific school, in response to prompts that are more explicit than those found on primary apps. Though chances are you won't encounter the exact essay prompts that these students received, these real-life examples can help to demystify this part of the application. The particulars of primary and secondary applications are discussed in more detail in chapters one and two of this book.

In this section, we did not group the applicants into any categories or organize them by school; you will find them in alphabetical order by first name. The location of the page listing each applicant's admissions decision(s) can be found at the end of his or her profile. While you read, you may want to consult the medical school profiles on our website, www.PrincetonReview.com. In each school profile, you will find information about students who applied in the most recent academic year, including the average MCAT score and average college GPA of the entering class, as well as the school's acceptance rate. We also provide admissions requirements and suggestions for each school, as well as a description of its admissions process.

CHAPTER 9

Where They Got In

This is an index of the admissions decisions each student received. Below the name of the student is the name of the medical school he or she decided to attend. Try putting yourself in the position of the admissions officer; you may be surprised by some admissions results! This index is also alphabetized by the student's first name.

EDITOR'S NOTE

Though it goes without saying, *don't* plagiarize the personal statements and essays in this book. Your response must be in your own words. We encourage you to note themes, structures, and words that you like, but draw the line at copying paragraphs, sentences, or even phrases. There's a chance you'll get caught, and then you wouldn't get into medical school at all. Penalties notwithstanding, plagiarism is simply wrong, so don't do it.

CHAPTER 1

FOLLOWING DIRECTIONS: A BRIEF OVERVIEW OF THE MEDICAL SCHOOL APPLICATION PROCESS

A VIEW TO ADMISSIONS

If you want to be a doctor—whether you aspire to do reconstructive surgery, administer anesthesia, or treat cataracts—your first steps are clear: Fulfill your premed requirements and go to medical school.

You probably already know that medical school admissions are a challenging enterprise. Those who've succeeded, however, are often quick to point out that it is a small price to pay for the rewards reaped. You also have some help in the form of this book. In this chapter, we'll guide you through each step of the medical school admissions process, describing the hurdles you'll have to leap and the potential pitfalls. There are seven key components to the process, and all are worth separate and special consideration, as admissions committees will carefully assess your performance on each one. They are as follows:

1. GPA and academic performance in college

2. MCAT score(s)

3. Extracurricular preparation

4. Letters of recommendation

5. Primary application (AMCAS or other)

6. Secondary application

7. Interview

Medical schools share a general application process, but individual schools can vary significantly in how they evaluate candidates. Here are some across-the-board commonalities: Every admissions committee does an initial evaluation by way of some type of admissions index. This is a system that assigns a set of points or category ranking to each applicant based mainly on his or her GPA, MCAT scores, and other objectively quantifiable elements from the primary application. For example, a certain number of points might be assigned to a candidate who has to work more than 20 hours a week to pay his or her way through college. This index is most commonly used in the first round to eliminate low-performing students from further consideration. It may also be consulted in later rounds for decisions between close candidates, but this is less common.

If a student's application achieves the initial minimum index, the admissions committee then reviews his or her subjective criteria—the extracurricular preparation, letters of recommendation, and essays submitted with the primary and secondary applications. Most top schools also consider subjective aspects of a student's academic record in this phase, such as the type and difficulty of courses taken, GPA trends, special academic projects undertaken, and the reputation of the major or school attended. Students who pass this more subjective evaluation are then offered interview spaces. After the interview, the interviewers' impressions are prepared for the student's file and final admissions decisions are made, either on a case-by-case basis or with groups of applications being ranked by committee vote.

Gaining admission to medical school is never an easy task, but in some years it can be significantly more competitive. In the "easiest" years, two out of three students who apply are accepted; in other years, it's one out of two; in the most difficult years, it's one out of three. Of course, many more potential medical school students are lost during the undergraduate years than during this stage. In 2005, roughly one-third of the students admitted to Washington University in St. Louis— a school that enrolls about 6,500 undergraduates—had expressed some interest in the school's premedical program. Only about 125 of Washington students, however, apply to medical school each year.[1] Though attrition rates vary by school, fulfilling premedical requirements is one of the most difficult things to do as an undergraduate—those who do so successfully should congratulate themselves!

Depending on who you are and what your preparation has been, you may find the challenges of medical school admission relatively easy, or you may find them unexpectedly difficult. One often-cited motto for minimizing procrastination is: **Plan and do first those things which scare you.** If thinking about any aspect of the admissions process gives you anxiety just by thinking about it, you need to plan ahead and start working toward a solution now, rather than later. If you are anxious about maintaining your undergraduate GPA, find courses, majors, and universities that will allow you to highlight your abilities. Seek help from your school's tutoring center. If letters of recommendation scare you, go to your professors' office hours and get to know them. Become a Research Assistant. If it is the MCAT that concerns you, start taking sample tests. If it is the interview, you can conduct mock interviews at your career services center and take humanities courses that will improve your verbal communication skills.

1 Erin Fults, "Wash U's Pre-Med Mortality Rate," *Student Life*, April 18, 2005, http://www.studlife.com/media/paper337/news/2005/04/18/Scene/Wash-Us.PreMed.Mortality.Rate-928167.shtml?norewriteandsourcedomain=www.studlife.com.

PRE-GAME HUDDLE

You may often feel pressure to be the perfect premed, but don't get caught up in competitiveness. You should minimize self-doubt and focus on your own goals. There is no set path to achievement, so embrace your individuality and be kind to yourself and others along the way—how you get there is just as important as actually getting there. Remember: You aren't alone in your endeavors. Take comfort in your friends and be on the lookout for any useful tools and tips you can pick up along the way. Learn what you can from those who have gone through this process before you and the books—such as this one—written about their experiences. If you reach out to well-chosen classmates, mentors, and friends, you can build an effective support team, whose members can motivate and encourage you along the way.

THE PREMEDICAL TIMELINE

The traditional medical student is one who prepares for and applies to medical school during college, entering a program directly upon graduation from his or her undergraduate institution. Although there is no prescribed order in which students should complete the academic requirements for medical school (which are primarily entry-level courses), most premeds do so during the first few years of college. That said, **you can arrange your premed courses in any way that accommodates your schedule. If you feel that your academic record will suffer if you follow the standard timetable, don't adhere to it!** Think creatively and find your own path.

The requirements are the same for students who are considering allopathic or osteopathic medicine. The following is an outline of a *typical* premedical curriculum for a traditional, full-time undergraduate student:

FRESHMAN YEAR

Academic:

- One year of general chemistry

- One year of calculus

- One year of biology

- One semester of English

- Introductory major requirements (optional)

Extracurricular:

- Explore all the various specialties of medical practice.

- Begin a health-care-related volunteer job or internship.

- Research academic societies, premed clubs, and other student organizations and consider joining one.

Other:

- Visit your school's premed advisor, review course requirements, and create a premedical game plan.

- Continue investigating medicine. Is it right for you? Develop personal and academic goals. Write them down.

- Build relationships with professors who can later serve as mentors, offer you the opportunity to participate in research, or write recommendations on your behalf.

SOPHOMORE YEAR

Academic:

- One year of organic chemistry

- Other introductory major requirements

Extracurricular:

- If you had a positive experience your freshman year, continue with the same extracurricular activity; if you didn't enjoy it or were not sufficiently challenged, begin a new one immediately.

Other:

- Toward the end of the year, begin researching medical school programs.

- Continue seeking relationships with professors and begin a list of those who might write your recommendations.

JUNIOR YEAR

Academic:

- One year of calculus-based physics

- Upper division major course work

Applications:

- Begin drafting your personal statement in early spring.

- Request applications from non-AMCAS medical schools in April.

- Collect letters of recommendation to send in September of your senior year.

MCAT:

- Take the April MCAT. This is the best month to take it, if you have a choice*.

SUMMER BEFORE SENIOR YEAR

Applications:

- Complete primary medical school applications. You may start this process as soon as April and, ideally, you should complete it by June or July ("in the J's"). As the vast majority of medical schools review applications as they come in and assign interview spots on a rolling basis, your chances of scoring an interview are significantly higher if you apply early. If you want to be considered seriously for a position, you'll want to submit all application material no later than September. Your chances of acceptance go down *steadily* after the J's and *rapidly* after September.

- Research financial aid options.

MCAT:

- Premeds who did not take the MCAT in April or want to retake the exam take the August MCAT*.

---

* The MCAT has traditionally been offered twice a year, once in April and once in August. In 2007 the test will move to a computer-based format and will be administered 20 times a year, in four windows of five days each. As of this book's printing, the 2007 test dates have not yet been determined. Premeds should still aim to take the computer-based test (CBT) in April—or May, if applicable—so that they receive their scores by June. (AMCAS begins accepting applications on June 1 and the vast majority of medical schools read apps on a rolling basis.) CBT scores will be available 30 days after the test date. For the most current test-date information, visit the official MCAT website at www.aamc.org/students/mcat/ or The Princeton Review's Med Schools & Careers homepage at www.princetonreview.com/medical/default.asp.

Senior Year

Academic:

- Finish remaining premed requirements.

- Finish remaining major/university requirements.

- Take upper-division or graduate-level courses in medically related subjects such as physiology, histology, pharmacology, and anatomy, if you have time. This will allow you some breathing room during the first two years of medical school.

Applications:

- Do more comprehensive research about the medical schools to which you applied.

- Complete secondary applications and send in letters of recommendation between September and January.

- Submit FAFSA.

- Prepare for interviews and wait for invitations to interview. Interviews typically take place in the fall, winter, and, at some schools, early spring.

- Interview and wait for letters!

Bear in mind that this list represents only the minimum requirements for admission to most medical school programs. Some medical schools ask applicants to take additional courses as prerequisites to their programs. If you have your heart set on a certain medical school program, you should do research about its prerequisites.

THE NOTORIOUS GPA

Your undergraduate academic performance will be the most important factor in your admissions decisions. In 2005, the average GPA for medical school applicants was 3.48; the average GPA for students who successfully matriculated was 3.63.[2]

Since your GPA is an average of all your grades, you don't need to perform at a B-plus/A-minus (3.33/3.67) level in *all* your classes, though that would be ideal. If your average science subject (biology, chemistry, physics, and math) GPA— what AMCAS calls BCPM—is around 3.35, you can still be accepted to medical school. Chances are, however, that you will need the GPA of your other course work to compensate.

While medical schools do evaluate the rigor of science courses, they first look for students with high grade point averages (3.5 or above). Therefore, unless you are extremely talented in science, it is better to take all the prerequisite courses in college. Even if you took AP Biology and were able to pass out of the introductory course, you should take first-year bio with all the other premeds and receive a high mark.

Most medical schools will evaluate an applicant's GPA in the context of his or her entire academic history. Medical schools look favorably on students who overcome adversity to achieve as well as students who come from disadvantaged or minority backgrounds. A demanding work schedule of more than twenty hours per week during college may also receive special consideration. Also of importance, particularly for top-tier medical schools, is the quality of the college or university attended. Some allowance may be made for lower grades at a top public, Ivy League, technical university. **Admissions officers, however, are most impressed by** *sustained periods of high GPA.* Think of your premedical curriculum as a *marathon*, not a series of sprints followed by walking. Shoot for consistent, strong performance in all your academic work.

---

2 Association of American Medical Colleges, "MCAT Scores and GPAs for Applicants and Matriculants, 1994 – 2005," AAMC Data Warehouse, http://www.aamc.org/data/facts/2005/2005mcatgpa.htm (accessed March 9, 2006).

MCAT ON A HOT TIN ROOF

The MCAT is a standardized exam administered by AMCAS, designed to test the general critical thinking abilities and introductory science knowledge of medical school applicants. Since there is a wide range of difficulty in curricula at U.S. colleges, the MCAT helps medical schools to contextualize or "normalize" an applicant's GPA, evaluating his or her basic knowledge and critical thinking abilities on a standard measure. The MCAT is also designed to serve as a barometer for how a student will perform in medical school, though it is not always very successful in that endeavor.

Virtually all U.S. and Canadian allopathic and osteopathic medical schools require the MCAT. You should, if possible, sit for the test in the spring of your junior year. Most medical schools have rolling admission policies, so earlier test dates, as long as you've finished your prerequisite course work, are better. Of course, not all applicants' academic schedules realistically allow them to take the April test.

The test attempts to be culturally neutral, indifferent to a student's real-world background, skills, and environmental influences. In that sense, the MCAT has major limits as a tool for evaluating an applicant's unique abilities. Fortunately, most students can do well on it, regardless of background, with a program of advanced preparation. It is far more a test of your preparation technique and test-taking skills than it is of your innate learning, verbal, or critical-thinking abilities.

But what is it? The MCAT is a five-and-a-half hour, multiple-choice, passage-based test designed to determine your ability to *rapidly apply basic sciences and verbal knowledge.* The test is passage-based, meaning that students must read and then answer a set of conceptual questions that follow each passage. It is divided into four sections: biological sciences, physical sciences, verbal reasoning, and the writing sample. It is not so much a test of your basic science knowledge as it is a test of your ability to interpret and apply the information you've learned in your prerequisite course work. By the time you have finished your prerequisites, you have already learned everything you need to know for the MCAT. Unfortunately, **success in premed course work does not translate directly into success on the MCAT.** Premedical students are generally exposed to the information tested on the MCAT over the course of several years—many never learn to retrieve it quickly, some never integrate it, and, most importantly, none ever have *all* of it at the forefront of memory at the same time, ready to be called upon at a moment's notice.

Therefore, it is imperative to design an effective method of preparation early on.

As you're reading a book published by The Princeton Review, you're correct in assuming that we're a little biased as to how we think you should study for the MCAT. The short answer here is that, for most people, taking a course to prepare for the MCAT is worth both the time and the money. MCAT scores are heavily weighted on your medical school application—at some schools, they are weighed as heavily as undergraduate GPA. A class forces you to study in a reasonable way, cover the material efficiently, and get plenty of practice. It also gives you the resources to shore up any gaps in your academic preparation. The MCAT is a tedious and wretched business; it's nice to have a class full of fellow sufferers who can make you feel less alone in your pain. Simply put, an investment in studying for the MCAT is an investment in your future, and the more you invest, the better you'll likely do.

There are three ways to get the forms you need to register for the MCAT. You can request them at the AAMC website (www.aamc.org), pick them up from a premed advisor, or contact the MCAT CBT program office* at the following address:

MCAT CBT Program Office

1000 Lancaster Street

Baltimore, MD 21202

INVEST IN EXTRACURRICULAR ACTIVITIES

Extracurriculars are a key component of one's medical school application. Most schools carefully review students' postsecondary nonacademic experiences to learn more about personality and interests. Qualities that cannot be measured by GPA and MCAT scores—such as humanity, maturity, and leadership—are often measured by one's prolonged involvement in an extracurricular activity.

You're probably saying, "Wait, where do I find the time for that?" Thankfully, **extracurricular activities are not necessarily time-consuming. On average, the time commitment is *four hours a week*.** This means that no matter how busy you are, you shouldn't have too much trouble fitting an extracurricular activity into your schedule.

Look at it this way: the more extracurricular activities you participate in, the more admissions index points—points that can mean the difference between your applications being accepted or denied—you might earn. The maximum number of admissions index points you can earn is four—one for each year of extracurricular activities. As you want to get as many points possible, you should participate in four years' worth of extracurricular activities: four hours of extracurriculars a week, for four years. You might continue with an extracurricular that you were involved in during high school. In this scenario, many schools award credit for the time you were involved as a high school student, particularly if the activity was medically related.

It is important to emphasize, however, that you should not approach extracurricular activities as something you must do in order to meet an admissions index number. Students who are passionate about medicine often find volunteer and internship opportunities to be rewarding, life-enhancing, and interesting experiences. In addition, sustained commitment to a well-chosen extracurricular activity can demonstrate qualities that medical schools find desirable, such as leadership ability, altruism, and maturity. On top of that, extracurricular activities often provide excellent material for personal statements and secondary essays. They are also generally discussed in your interview, so you should be able to talk about why you chose a given activity and what you have taken from it.

If you have questions about how much a certain extracurricular program, such as a summer internship, might be valued on your application, consult your premed advisor.

LETTERS OF RECOMMENDATION

In most cases, medical schools request of applicants either a minimum of three recommendations or a premedical committee letter. The latter can be a letter written by the undergraduate premedical committee specifically recommending you, or it can be a letter that summarizes your achievements and suitability for medicine and lists your class rank and comments various faculty members have made about you.

If you are a student who is still in school and you have access to pre-health advising, your letters will probably be handled by that office, and at least one of your letters will probably be from the pre-health advisor. If your school does not have a premedical committee or you are a returning adult, you may have to take care of all the requests and letters yourself.

Letters of recommendation for medical school work same way other such letters do—**you will have much better luck if you approach your potential recommender with a copy of your resume, transcript, and personal statement.** Make an appointment to speak with each potential recommender and explain why you are applying to each school on your list and make your case.

As a rule of thumb, a strong application file will contain at least one letter from a professor in the sciences and one letter from a professor outside the sciences. Even if you have been out of school for a while, you should try to get at least one letter from a former professor. During your undergrad years (or your post-bacc program) you should build relationships with faculty members so they can write something meaningful about you. Don't ask for a letter from someone famous unless they know you pretty well. Name-dropping is not considered to be particularly attractive in a prospective medical student.

Although many returning adults feel awkward approaching professors they might not have spoken with in several years, most are pleasantly surprised to discover that, for the most part, professors do tend to remember their students, and most are happy to write letters of recommendation.

As with all aspects of your application, it is good to submit a well-rounded set of recommendations, including letters from people who can attest to your personal qualities, as well as your academic abilities. Aside from the obligatory faculty recommendations, you may wish to submit additional recommendations from supervisors you had at research, volunteer, or professional positions, who can discuss your nonacademic strengths, such as compassion, dedication to service, and professionalism. Both current and former students should also consider asking for letters from doctors with whom they have worked or volunteered. Those applying to an osteopathic school must submit a letter of recommendation from a doctor of osteopathy (DO). Unless a medical school specifically limits the number of recommendations you can send, you can send up to double the number they request. More than that, however, would be overkill. While you should definitely consider nonacademic supervisors as a source of recommendations, do not send letters from family, friends, or graduate students.

HOW TO APPLY

There are 142 accredited allopathic medical schools that confer the MD degree—122 in the United States, 3 in Puerto Rico, and 17 in Canada—and 19 accredited osteopathic medical schools that confer the DO degree. The main difference between allopathic and osteopathic programs is the latter usually have a greater focus on preventative medicine, holistic healing, and patient care skills. They also incorporate training in "manipulation," a traditional form of healing that is intended to promote musculoskeletal health. An advantage to osteopathic schools is that admissions standards are generally less stringent than they are for allopathic schools, which can be very enticing to older applicants or students who lack a perfect academic record, but nonetheless have a strong desire to be a doctor. However, those interested in entering a specialized allopathic medical field or engaging in clinical medical research will find that attending an osteopathic school severely limits certain choices. The moral herein: do your homework before applying.

Whether applying to allopathic schools, osteopathic schools, or both, it is a good idea to **apply broadly—the typical premed applies to *ten to twelve* schools. In competitive states, such as California, the average is often as high as 20.** Make sure to include "safety" schools where you will most likely be accepted. In addition to admissions competitiveness, there are many factors to consider when evaluating medical school programs, including: location, reputation, affiliated teaching hospitals, pre-clinical and clinical curriculum, teaching methodology, and student life.

Most allopathic medical schools use the AMCAS application, a standardized form handled by the AAMC. The six medical schools in Ontario, Canada, use the Ontario Medical School Application Services application (www.ouac.on.ca/omsas/index.html) and the seven medical schools at the University of Texas use their own central application service (www.utsystem.edu/tmdsas). For some schools, you will need to request a specific application.

In the spring of 2001, the AAMC switched to an entirely Web-based AMCAS application. This online application is available directly from www.aamc.org and costs $160 for the first school you apply to and $30 for each additional school. If you have significant financial hardship, you can apply directly to AMCAS for a fee waiver on their services.

When you begin the AMCAS application you will be prompted fill in your undergraduate course work and grades, your work experience and extracurricular activities, and the personal comments section, where you'll have exactly one typewritten, single-spaced page to explain your life and convince admissions officers that you should be one of the chosen few. Needless to say, this part of the application takes time and patience—we will address it in more detail in the following chapters.

You will also need to prepare transcript requests for every postsecondary school you ever attended, even if you only took one class there or the credits transferred elsewhere. You can download official transcript request forms as part of the online AMCAS application. Undergraduate colleges will send your transcripts to AMCAS, who will use them to verify the information on your application. AMCAS begins accepting transcripts on March 15 each year and completed applications on June 1. It will take a couple of weeks for AAMC to process everything, at which point you'll receive a "transmittal notification." You can contact AAMC to check the status of your application (you can reach them on the Web at www.aamc.org or by phone at 202-828-0600).

When you are choosing which schools to apply to, make sure that you check in-state residency requirements. Although many allopathic schools are private, there are quite a few public schools that receive free money every year from out-of-state applicants they are prohibited from accepting into their programs. It doesn't matter how qualified you are; if you aren't a state resident, you can't get in.

Osteopathic schools use their own internal system, AACOMAS, which in many respects works exactly the same way as AMCAS: You can download a paper application from their website, fill one out online at www.aacom.org, or call 301-968-4100. Like the AMCAS application, the AACOMAS application takes some time to fill out, so make sure you get started early. It also includes a personal statement, but it's even shorter than the AMCAS's—you only have half a page to explain why you want to be an osteopathic physician. You will also need to get a recommendation from a DO, a fact that takes some applicants by surprise. If you are serious about osteopathic school, search for a mentor DO as early as possible. One of the nice things about AACOMAS is that all osteopathic schools use it—you don't have to worry about tracking down additional applications. Because osteopathic schools are private institutions, they don't have residency requirements (although some may have tuition breaks for residents of particular states). If you are interested in studying osteopathic medicine, investigate all of the colleges and choose based on your interest in the program and living conditions in the area.

Another rule of thumb, regardless of the schools you apply to, is to apply as early as you can in the process. In general, premedical students begin the application process in the spring semester of their junior year, or approximately a year and a half before they want to enter medical school. The vast majority of medical schools engage in some type of rolling admissions, which means that they read and evaluate applications as the folders arrive. However, they will not begin evaluating an applicant until all of his or her admissions materials (*e.g.,* application, transcripts, MCAT scores) have been received. In practical terms, this means that if you take the MCAT in the spring and get your applications in by late June, you will have a distinct advantage over someone taking the test in the summer, who may not have their application materials submitted until early September. Each year, students are accepted with summer test scores and applications that arrived late in the process. Unfortunately, there are also large numbers of students who are not accepted but would have had a decent chance had they applied earlier. Basically, you should try for every possible advantage. Turning in your application early can certainly help to give you an edge. Also, procrastinators take note: AMCAS is serious about its deadlines. If an application or transcript is late, you'll get it back.

ROUND #2: SECONDARY APPLICATIONS

If you take the MCAT in the spring, you will get a short breather after submitting your primary applications. Traditionally, premeds take advantage of this time with a well-deserved vacation. But keep the phone handy during this leisurely interlude; only a few weeks after you submit your primaries, medical schools will start mailing secondary applications.

Most schools send secondary applications indiscriminately, meaning that every living, breathing candidate who submitted a primary application will get a secondary. The main reason schools send out secondary applications without reviewing the primary application first is that they charge fees, ranging from $35 to $120 per school, for the privilege of filling one out. And while there are a few student-friendly schools that will review GPA and MCAT scores before sending a secondary application, in most cases you will receive a secondary application even if you have no chance of acceptance. If you find that the cost of sending back secondaries becomes prohibitive, you should call the schools and request fee waivers, especially if you were already eligible for a waiver from AMCAS.

Needless to say, spending countless hours filling out secondaries for schools that would decline to interview applicants based on their primary applications is a source of irritation for many. Keep this in mind and don't have false hopes that a secondary application means any more than it does. The types of questions you'll find on secondary applications are discussed in the following chapter, *Getting Personal: Primary and Supplemental Essays.*

THE ART OF THE INTERVIEW

To many admissions committees, the interviewer's opinions matter even more than recommendations, partly because recommendations often come from unknown sources. Again, if you consider the expense and hassle involved in setting up a personal interview for every possible admit, you have an idea of how much medical schools value the process. The interview is a chance to get a real sense of the candidate as a person, and the school's opportunity to hear a medical professional's first-hand evaluation of an applicant.

For highly desirable applicants, the interview will not be a deal-breaker unless something dramatically bad happens. For top-tier candidates, the interview is primarily an opportunity for the medical school to confirm credentials and verify that the actual person roughly matches the impressive application. Even if they don't dazzle their interviewers, top applicants are still very likely to be accepted.

For students who have high potential but are not at the top of the stack, in other words, for the average applicant, the interview is an important opportunity to make a positive, distinctive impression on the admissions committee. Therefore, it is important to spend some time preparing for the interview by reviewing sample questions and rehearsing answers. You might also spend some time reading the newspaper or science magazines, as your interviewer may ask you about current issues in medicine. Even if you are naturally charming and charismatic, resist the temptation to wing it in the interview.

Regardless of which category you fall into, simply by being invited for an interview, you officially join the ranks of "desirable" applicants. Remember: it would be too costly and time-consuming for medical schools to interview all possible candidates; therefore, it is only the most promising who are invited. That said, **about 50 percent of interviewed candidates are not offered admission— you have to use every advantage you can.** The earlier you interview, the sooner the admissions committee can begin evaluating you for a position. Whenever possible, you should take the earliest interview date you are offered. As a rule, don't put off or delay interviews unnecessarily.

Nonetheless, you will want to control travel costs by scheduling interviews for schools that are in similar geographic regions within the timeframe of a single trip. Schools understand students' desire to minimize costs and will often accommodate changes. If you receive an interview request from one school and have applied to another school in the same area, you may consider calling the second school and asking politely if they are planning to interview you. Explain that you have another interview at a school in the area and were wondering if you should also be planning to visit their campus. In that case, schools are often happy to let you know whether they will be able to interview you in the same timeframe.

Interviewees often have the option of staying with a current medical student the night before the interview. If you are comfortable with new people and short on cash, this option is a good way to save some money and get to know more about the school. Be sure to ask your host for his or her honest opinion of the strengths and weaknesses of the school. A friendly host may also be able to offer a couple last-minute interview tips. If, however, you would feel stressed or are unwilling to sleep on someone else's sofa, look for accommodations on or near campus. The key is to be prepared, even if it costs a few extra bucks. Your future self will thank you.

CHAPTER 2

GETTING PERSONAL:
PRIMARY AND SUPPLEMENTAL ESSAYS

THE PERSONAL STATEMENT

The AMCAS and AACOMAS applications both feature a personal comments section, also referred to as "the personal statement" or "the essay." It is the first and best opportunity you have to speak directly to admissions officers. Don't underestimate its power to make a strong, positive impression on an admissions committee. Whether you're a budding wordsmith or have daily nightmares about the written page, it presents an opportunity to give your application a voice—*your voice*. It is your chance to convince the committee that you are more than the sum of your academic record and that you deserve a shot at an interview.

Neither AMCAS nor AACOMAS will provide you with a specific prompt for your personal comments. They will, however, provide topics to consider. These topics typically concern your motivation for a medical career and the experiences, situations, and ideas that have influenced your life and academic career and are not mentioned elsewhere in your application. Considering this, most personal statements tend to utilize one or more of the following basic themes:

- A life-changing personal experience with medicine, as a patient or as a person close to a patient, which led to an interest in a career as a doctor.

- A relationship with a mentor, or another inspiring individual.

- The decision to pursue a medically related career.

- An experience that challenged or changed your perspective about medicine.

- A challenging personal experience and its effects on your life.

- An insight into the nature of medical practice or the future of medical technology, and your perceived relation to this insight.

No one theme is inherently better than another—there are excellent personal statements written using commonplace themes and poor ones written using extraordinary themes. The best, however, tend to focus on a single theme supported by a few well-chosen, illustrative examples.

When brainstorming ideas for your personal statement, consider events that have strongly influenced or affected you. You've probably had a number of experiences that have affirmed or challenged your sense of purpose, or led you to reconsider a long-held opinion. Think about how these moments have shaped you. Make a list of them and begin to look for a connection between them. What have you learned in the past few years? How have you and your perspectives changed? What part of medicine was not like you expected it to be? What has been the most difficult thing for you to accept? What has been the most enlightening?

Whichever topic you choose will require thorough care and consideration. For example, you may decide to write about a complex, tragic experience that challenged your faith in medicine, such as the death of a loved one. When writing this, you could simply retell the story, explaining what happened, how you felt about medicine before the event, and how you felt after. A better approach, perhaps, would be to consider the deeper issues related to this experience. This approach might explore how the health care system functions on the individual level, what preventive care was missing from your loved one's experience, or it might define the lack of technology or science that could have provided a solution to your loved one's problem. You could discuss the physical aspects of the health care setting, describing the hospital room, ambulances, other patients, and the nursing staff. You might also discuss the positive aspects of the experience, such as the influence of a trusted doctor or nurse. In addition, you could explain how this experience affected other parts of your life, what you did and didn't do as a result of it, and how it might impact you as a medical student or a doctor.

The main point is: **whatever you say, it shouldn't be simple.** Medicine is a complex, interdisciplinary, and wholly human profession. Though you should have a clear subject and theme—they might even be "well-worn"—take the time to write something truly heartfelt and original. The goal isn't to rewrite history but to suggest that, if given the chance, you could change it for the better.

AN ANGLE ON SECONDARY APPLICATIONS

Unlike primary applications, secondary applications ask specific questions about your goals, experiences, and personal views on a wide range of topics. This is not a time to get lazy, so don't rely on copying and pasting boilerplate responses from a previous draft of your personal statement. **Your secondaries will be read to see how they compliment what you have already said in your primary**

application. You may have an opportunity to highlight achievements or experiences that received less attention in your primary application. You should not, however, force subject matter that does not pertain to the question or questions asked. At the most basic level, your secondary is another test to see whether you can adequately understand and follow instructions—this time, the school's specific directions.

As you write your secondaries you can refer briefly to themes in your personal statement, but you should focus more on new material. If, for example, you wrote in your personal statement about a primary care experience, you may want to point out some research experience in your secondary application, showing that you are an even broader applicant than your initial application suggested—just make sure not to bring in new material that in any way casts doubt on your original statements.

If given enough room on certain questions, you may want to follow the thesis, body, and conclusion structure that you would use for a longer essay. Don't, however, try to squeeze in extra words by using a font more than a point smaller than your AMCAS application. The admissions committee will notice and you'll come across as a rule bender, which isn't the most ideal image to portray.

POTENTIAL QUESTIONS

Secondary questions run the gamut from personal to political to pointless. If you want to see what to expect, you can contact your premed advisor as they often keep a file with the previous year's secondary applications. Here are a few questions from recent apps:

- "Write a short autobiography of your life. You should include childhood and elementary school experiences, all the way to college."

- "Compare and contrast managed care and traditional fee-for-service medical care."

- "Describe a challenge or obstacle you have overcome, and what you learned from the experience."

- "Describe an instance where you helped someone in need."

- "Describe your greatest accomplishment."

STRATEGIZE AND PRIORITIZE

As you begin to receive secondary applications, there are several different approaches you can take. Some students focus first on the schools that they would most like to attend. Other students realize that their last secondaries will be better written than their first. Thus they hold off sending secondaries to the more competitive schools until they've sent out a few to the less competitive ones. Still other students reply first to schools whose secondaries ask questions to which they can easily give solid answers. This allows them to work their way up to the more difficult applications. Finally, a few students practice writing secondary essays even before they get their first ones, so that they're ready to respond to their top choices first. In many cases, schools reveal what type of student they're looking for in the type of secondary questions they ask. Therefore, the stronger the answers you have for their questions, the more likely it is that you have the characteristics they're looking for in an applicant.

Ultimately, only you know which approach will work best for you, so trust your instincts. If you want to make sure that you are not wasting time and money by filling out secondary applications for particular schools, research their admissions requirements *before* you write them checks.

CHAPTER 3

HAVING HEART: WHAT REALLY MAKES AN ESSAY TICK

GUIDANCE, IF NEEDED

Writing a personal statement is a unique experience. In fact, it is something of a genre of its own. Even if you're an English major and have written 101 papers on the writings of famous authors, you might find yourself tongue-tied when attempting to pen the story of your life thus far. **A good way to get an idea of how to approach your personal statement is to read other students' attempts.** Later in this book we reproduce 41 personal statements and 10 secondary essays written by real medical school applicants. Your premed advisor also may have some examples of exemplary personal statements on file. For an even wider perspective, you might consider reading law or business school applications to see what students in other disciplines have written about themselves (our own *Law School Essays that Made a Difference* and *Business School Essays that Made a Difference* are good resources for this task).

THE SECRETS TO YOUR SUCCESS

The keys to success when approaching your personal statement are compression and clarity. As it's extremely difficult to write about anything important in a page or less, assume that you'll be spending a lot of quality time with your computer. To get started, you can try a couple of different approaches to get your fingers moving:

CLUSTERING

Get a large blank piece of paper and write down a few words to describe what has led you to apply to medical school. You can also jot down some interesting, sad, or memorable experiences and try to link them to your interest in medicine. You don't have to write these items in any particular order, just scatter your thoughts across the page. After you have several topics to work with, see if you can spot any patterns. Some of the topics will probably be interrelated. Next, generate longer descriptions of the words you wrote. For example, try to explain what you meant by "intellectual challenge." Was there a particular class you took? A paper you wrote? After you have some ideas on paper, try to pull them together based on the patterns of relationships you see between the topics. When writing your personal statement, **it is often more effective to let the reader draw conclusions than to spell things out.** Relate how you felt while treating a patient and let the reader see that you are compassionate. Don't write, "That experience demonstrates my compassion." The key is to show, not tell—imply, never spell out.

Free Writing

This is particularly helpful if you find that you're having trouble figuring out where to start. All you have to do is sit down and force yourself to write about anything that comes to mind. Don't worry about punctuation or grammar—just write for several pages. Take a break and look back at what you wrote. Most of the time, you'll be surprised to discover the beginnings of an idea. Make sure to keep a notepad with you and by your bed so you can jot down ideas as they arrive.

Talk, Talk, Talk

If you have serious writer's block, you can talk into a tape recorder or bribe a friend to write as you speak. If you go the latter route, have your friend write down what he or she thinks is interesting or important as you explain why you want to go to medical school. You shouldn't expect to generate your essay in this way, but you will be able to produce some material that you can start writing about.

THREE APPROACHES

There are many different ways to structure the personal essay, but here are three basic approaches that can be used alone or in combination:

"My History in School"

This essay focuses on college experiences. It works well for people whose grades are fairly high and who want to emphasize their growth during college. If you go this route, you should write about your development, specialties, and strengths. **The best essays of this genre usually have specific examples—it helps to have a specific class, professor, paper, or experience that crystallizes your experiences and ties into your goals.** One of the benefits of this essay is a built-in chronology and organizational structure.

"My Life History"

In this essay, focus on a few events or main ideas that illustrate the qualities you can bring to medicine. If your whole life clearly leads up to being a physician—even if it didn't seem that way at the time—this can be a good choice. One of the pitfalls of this genre is that it can free you to ramble and lose clarity. As you give a brief overview of your life, you should concentrate your paragraphs around individual ideas.

"The Story"

This is often the most effective genre if it's done correctly. It has the potential to be the most fun for admissions officers to read; it's also the most likely to be coherent and cohesive. Focus on one or two stories that illustrate your key points. You don't have to go overboard with adjectives or turns of phrase to write an effective narrative. Just pick a couple of moments that clearly define why you want to be in medicine.

ROADMAP TO GREATNESS

Great personal statements are, well, personal. They're also on topic—*i.e.,* medically oriented. And all your application essays should be well organized, thoughtful, clear, honest, and unique. It's a tall order, but essays that feature all these qualities can make your application truly memorable. As you write your essays, keep the below points in mind. Where does your essay shine and where can it be improved?

Personal

The best personal statements are those that tell a real story from your real life. Adding an original, intimate component will make your statement stand out among the thousands seen by admissions officers every year. Though you may feel like you have the same experiences as every other premed, that is never the case. Everyone takes their own path. Take time to think back on your life and review your experiences; you'll likely come up with many small (or large) ways in which you are an original person.

MEDICALLY ORIENTED

A good personal statement clearly explains why an applicant is interested in a medical career. In fact, the central theme of the essay should demonstrate the applicant's interest in or commitment to medicine. If you choose to write about an experience that is not directly related to health care, you'll need to immediately explain how that experience contributed to your desire to go to medical school or how it'll specifically inform your experience as a medical student.

WELL ORGANIZED

Choose one central theme and stick to it. Make sure your essay has a thesis statement or overriding purpose. Before you begin writing, organize your essay into clear paragraphs, with a beginning, middle, and end. Organization makes your points understandable and is essential in a great personal statement.

THOUGHTFUL

Take the time to develop a theme for your essay. Pick out some memorable experiences that relate to the theme and explore each one. Why did that experience affect you? How does it pertain to medicine and the type of physician you want to become?

CLEAR

Don't try to outshine other essays by using fancy words and terminology, and never underestimate the power of a short declarative statement. If you use a flowery or overwrought writing style, you may muddle your main point. Though you should certainly try to vary sentence structure and word choice throughout the essay, resist the temptation to pull out your thesaurus and replace adjectives with bigger, more impressive variations. Simpler and shorter sentences are often the clearest way to convey your message; after all, it worked for Hemingway.

HONEST

Admissions committees are quick to distinguish between an essay that describes a real personal experience and those that describe an exaggerated or contrived event. In addition, your interviewers will occasionally follow up on the things you said in your personal statement, asking you further questions about the experiences you described. It doesn't pay to be dishonest. What's more, there's no reason to be. If you feel like something you have to say is inadequate or uninteresting, consider why that is the case rather than masking it with a synthetic emotion. For example, if you worked in the oncology ward of a hospital for two years but found yourself generally uninspired by the job, don't pretend that the experience was life-changing or moving just because you think that's what an admissions committee wants to hear. Instead, consider what your reaction to the situation says about you or medicine. What could have been improved? Why weren't you able to make an emotional connection with the patients? How did the shortcomings of that experience inform your view of medicine? The answers to your questions may not always be the "right" ones; however, if you take the time to reflect and carefully consider your experience, you will ultimately find a satisfying, original, and thoughtful response.

Unique

Admissions essays have a tendency to sound the same. Knowing this, some applicants try to make their essay stand out by telling jokes, writing in the third person, inserting heady intellectual quotations or commentary, or telling a story from a very unusual perspective (*e.g.*, a patient or a child). While you do want your statement to be unique, you don't need to resort to such gimmicks. Remember, a good story shines through every time—a classic tale of content over style. Make your essay special by telling a personal story in a personal way. Why is your essay about *you* and not about any other medical school applicant? What qualities are special about you or the circumstances you are describing? Bring your own voice, perspective, and experiences to the story to give it a truly unique and memorable flavor.

Finally, you can make your essay unique by occasionally using powerful, original language, as long as it is not overdone. You might start with a great opening line that catches the reader's attention, expressing an original sentiment or thought.

THE BENEFITS OF PEER PRESSURE

Writing is an ongoing process of drafts and revisions. If you've been taking mandatory writing-based humanities courses, you know how long it can take to craft a perfect paper. (And, to be brutally frank, the paper never will be perfect. "Perfect" is a subjective evaluation about and by you. How could something like that ever be perfect?) To improve your essay's quality, seek out a small circle of reviewers to help in the revision process.

The first person to recruit should be someone with an *admissions background*, such as your premed advisor, who can tell you whether the essay is addressed appropriately to your medical school audience. The second reader should be someone who *knows you very well* and can analyze the content of the essay based on what they know about you and your passions. The third reader should be someone with an *English or composition background* who can identify whether your statement is appropriately organized, grammatically correct, and tells a compelling story. If you think you're particularly weak in your insights about medicine, in your personal introspection abilities, or in your composition abilities, you might think about recruiting more than one of a particular reader type.

When looking for readers, start by asking people who are in your immediate circle. In particular, you may have trouble finding a composition reader. If you don't know anyone who's a great writer and willing to spend an hour carefully critiquing your essay, you'll need to specifically recruit someone for the job. Humanities TAs and paid writing tutors, who will review your essay for grammar, syntax, organization, and content, are good bets.

QUESTIONS FOR YOUR ADMISSIONS READER:

- Does my personal statement compliment my application?

- Is my interest in medicine and medical school evident?

- Are there any other aspects of my premedical experience that I should address?

QUESTIONS FOR YOUR PERSONAL READER:

- Have I forgotten to include any important aspects of my background or personality?

- Does this essay reflect me as a person?

- Do I represent myself well?

QUESTIONS FOR YOUR COMPOSITION READER:

- Is my essay well structured?

- Is there a central theme?

- Are my ideas expressed well?

- Do I use proper vocabulary?

With hard work and good editing, you will eventually recognize your personal statement as a well-crafted testament to your desire to attend medical school. When this time comes, *leave it alone*—further tinkering will only reduce its impact and originality.

DOS AND DON'TS

- **Do** focus on a single theme or thesis. Elaborate on your theme through details, opinions, and experiences.

- **Do** outline your theme and main points before you start writing. Aim for an organized, direct statement.

- **Do** tell a personal story, rather than make generalizations.

- **Do** write about something medically oriented.

- **Do** start your essay with a solid, attention-grabbing sentence.

- **Do** end your essay with a strong conclusion.

- **Do** spend time on your personal statement—it isn't a "throw away" part of the application.

- **Do** proofread carefully.

- **Do** spell check and spell check again.

- **Do** have three different reviewers, but not many more than that.

- **Don't** list all your awards and achievements, or try to include everything you have ever done on a single page.

- **Don't** be overly philosophical or abstract (a common mistake).

- **Don't** be self-aggrandizing or try too hard to impress the admissions committee; tell a real story and let the details speak for themselves.

- **Don't** use clichés or resort to attention-getting gimmicks to stand out. Use real, honest detail to make your personal statement unique.

- **Don't** lie or exaggerate.

- **Don't** use too much detail. Aim to be succinct and direct.

- **Don't** be too controversial. Avoid topics that may raise eyebrows.

- **Don't** make negative statements unless you can show how they lead to a positive counter-argument.

- **Don't** use the word "I" too often. If you state an opinion, the reader will assume it's yours. Tell a story and let the details speak for themselves.

CHAPTER 4

THEY'RE, THEIR, AND THERE: GRAMMAR AND WRITING TIPS

PUTTING THE PIECES TOGETHER

Remember: Good writing is writing that's easily understood. You want to get your point across, not bury it in words. Make your prose clear and direct. **If an admissions officer has to struggle to figure out what you're trying to say, there's a good chance he or she might not bother reading further.** Abide by word limits. We can't recommend highly enough that you read *The Elements of Style*, by William Strunk Jr., E. B. White, and Roger Angell. This little book is a great investment. Even if you've successfully completed a course or two in composition without it, it will prove invaluable and become your new best friend—and hopefully also your muse.

GOOD GRAMMAR = GOOD FORM

You should strive to make your writing 100 percent grammatically accurate. Think of each essay you write as a building. If it doesn't have structural integrity, medical school admissions officers will tear through it with a wrecking ball.

Let's face it: You can write the most rip-roaring yarn this side of Clive Cussler, but without grammatical accuracy, it'll fall apart. **Though a thoughtful essay that offers true insight will undoubtedly stand out, it will not receive serious consideration if it's riddled with poor grammar and misspelled words.** *It's critical that you avoid grammatical errors.* We can't stress this enough. Misspellings, awkward constructions, run-on sentences, and misplaced modifiers cast doubt on your efforts, not to mention your intelligence.

GRAMMATICAL CATEGORY	WHAT'S THE RULE?	BAD GRAMMAR	GOOD GRAMMAR
ISPLACED ODIFIER	A word or phrase that describes something should go right next to the thing it modifies.	1. Eaten in Mediterranean countries for centuries, **northern Europeans** viewed the tomato with suspicion. 2. **A former greens keeper** now about to become the Masters champion, **tears** welled up in my eyes as I hit my last miraculous shot.	1. Eaten in Mediterranean countries for centuries, **the tomato** was viewed with suspicion by Northern Europeans. 2. **I was a former greens keeper** who was now about to become the Masters champion; **tears** welled up in my eyes as I hit my last miraculous shot.
RONOUNS	A pronoun must refer unambiguously to a noun and it must agree in number with that noun.	1. Although **brokers** are not permitted to know executive access **codes, they** are widely known. 2. The **golden retriever** is one of the smartest breeds of dogs, but **they** often **have** trouble writing **personal statements** for law school admission. 3. Unfortunately, both **candidates** for whom I worked sabotaged their own **campaigns** by accepting **a contribution** from illegal **sources**.	1. Although **brokers** are not permitted to know executive access **codes, the codes** are widely known. 2. The **golden retriever** is one of the smartest breeds of dogs, but often **it has** trouble writing **a personal statement** for law school admission. 3. Unfortunately, both **candidates** for whom I worked sabotaged their own **campaigns** by accepting **contributions** from illegal **sources**.
UBJECT/VERB GREEMENT	The subject must always agree in number with the verb. Make sure you don't forget what the subject of a sentence is, and don't use the object of a preposition as the subject.	1. **Each** of the men involved in the extensive renovations **were** engineers. 2. Federally imposed **restrictions** on the ability to use certain information **has** made life difficult for Martha Stewart.	1. **Each** of the men involved in the extensive renovations **was** an engineer. Federally imposed **restrictions** on the ability to use certain information **have** made life difficult for Martha Stewart.
ARALLEL ONSTRUCTION	Two or more ideas in a single sentence that are parallel need to be similar in grammatical form.	1. The two main goals of the Eisenhower presidency were a **reduction** of taxes and **to increase** military strength. 2. **To provide a child** with the skills necessary for survival in modern life is **like guaranteeing their** success.	1. The two main goals of the Eisenhower presidency were to **reduce** taxes and to **increase** military strength. 2. **Providing children** with the skills necessary for survival in modern life is **like guaranteeing their** success.
OMPARISONS	You can only compare things that are exactly the same.	1. The **rules** of written English are **more stringent than** spoken **English**. 2. The **considerations** that led many colleges to impose admissions quotas in the last few decades **are similar to the quotas** imposed in the recent past by large businesses.	1. The **rules** of written English are **more stringent than those of** spoken English. 2. The **considerations** that led many colleges to impose admissions quotas in the last few decades **are similar to those** that led large businesses to impose quotas in the recent past.
ASSIVE/ CTIVE VOICE	Choose the active voice, in which the subject performs the action.	1. **The ball was hit by the bat.** 2. **My time and money were wasted** trying to keep www.justdillpickles.com afloat single-handedly.	1. **The bat hit the ball.** 2. **I wasted time and money trying to** keep www.justdillpickles.com afloat single-handedly.

NAVIGATING THE MINEFIELD

Besides grammatical concerns, premeds should keep in mind the following points while writing their admissions essays:

DON'T REPEAT INFORMATION FROM OTHER PARTS OF YOUR APPLICATION

That is, don't repeat information from other parts of your application *unless* you can spin it to elucidate previously unmentioned facets of your personality and perspectives. The admissions staff already has your transcripts, MCAT score, and list of academic and extracurricular achievements. The personal statement is your *only* opportunity to present all other aspects of yourself in a meaningful way. Even if you don't mind wasting your own time, admissions officers will mind if you waste theirs.

IN GENERAL, AVOID GENERALITIES

Admissions officers have to read an unbelievable number of boring essays. You'll find it harder to be boring if you write about particulars. It's the details that stick in a reader's mind. As Ludwig Mies van der Rohe wrote, "God is in the details."

DON'T GO ON AT LENGTH ABOUT YOUR GOALS

Face it: You have only an imprecise idea of what medical school will be like. Everyone's goals change through the years. Your goals are especially likely to change because medical school will change you. So leave the seventy-five-year plan out of your personal statement.

MAINTAIN THE PROPER TONE

Your essay should be memorable without being outrageous and easy to read without being too formal or sloppy. When in doubt, err on the formal side.

DON'T TRY TO BE FUNNY UNLESS WHAT YOU HAVE TO SAY IS ACTUALLY FUNNY

An applicant who can make an admissions officer laugh never gets lost in the shuffle. No one will be able to bear tossing your application into the "reject" pile if you garner a genuine chuckle. But beware! Only a select few are able to pull off humor in this context.

Stay Away from Anything Even Remotely Off-Color

Avoid profanity. It's not a good idea to be irreverent in admissions essays. Also, there are some things admissions officers don't need (or want) to know about you, so keep those things to yourself.

Circumvent Political Issues if Possible

Admissions officers don't care about your political perspectives as long as your viewpoints are thoughtful. They don't care what your beliefs are as long as you are committed to the preservation of human life. The problem is that if you write about a political issue, you may come across as the type of person who is intolerant or unwilling to consider other viewpoints. In medical school (and certainly in your career as a medical practitioner), you'll occasionally be challenged to defend a position with which you disagree—and you don't want to seem like someone who is so impassioned that you are incapable of arguing both sides of an issue. If you opt to write about politics, be very careful.

Consider Your Audience if You Want to Write about Religion

As a general rule, don't make religion the focal point of your essay unless you're applying to a medical school with a religious affiliation. Don't misunderstand us—religion is not taboo. It's *totally fine* to mention religion in any personal statement; just make sure to put it within the context of the whole, dynamic person you are.

Put the Fraternity Bake Sale Behind You

The same goes for the juggling club juggle-a-thon and the like. It's definitely worth noting on your resume if you were the president of your sorority or of any such institutionally affiliated organization. That said, achievements in a Greek organization or any club or student group are not the kind of life-changing events that have made you the person you fundamentally are today. **Make sure what you write about has had an actual impact on your life (and better yet, on the lives of others).**

No Gimmicks, No Gambles

Avoid tricky stuff. You want to differentiate yourself but not because you are some kind of daredevil. Don't rhyme. Don't write a satire or mocked-up front-page newspaper article. Gimmicky personal statements mostly appear contrived and, as a result, they fall flat, taking you down with them.

EXCUSES, EXCUSES...

"MY MCAT SCORE ISN'T GREAT, BUT I'M JUST NOT A GOOD TEST TAKER."

Don't dwell on a low MCAT score in your personal statement. If there were extenuating circumstances, you can briefly mention them or you can include a separate note in your application. If there were no such circumstances, it's best to avoid mention of your score.

There's a reason for the test being taken before entrance to medical school—it's a primer, the first of many tests that you will take as a medical student. If you don't take tests well and the MCAT confirms it, don't make excuses for it; instead, resolve to do better.

Consider also that a low MCAT score speaks for itself—all too eloquently. It doesn't need you to speak for it too. The MCAT may be a flawed test, but don't argue the unfairness of the test to admissions officers who use it as a primary factor in their admissions decisions. We feel for you, but you'd be barking up the wrong tree there.

"MY COLLEGE GRADES WEREN'T THAT HIGH, BUT . . ."

This issue is a little more complicated than the low MCAT score. If your grades fall below average acceptance criteria to most medical programs, or if there are certain anomalous periods of low achievement on your transcript, it's probably best to offer some form of explanation—especially if you have a good reason for lower performance, such as illness, pregnancy, or a demanding work schedule. Medical school admissions committees will be more than willing to listen to your interpretation of your college performance, but only within limits. Keep in mind that medical schools require official transcripts for a reason. Members of the admissions committee will be aware of your academic credentials even before they read your essay.

If your grades are unimpressive, the best strategy is to offer the admissions committee something else by which to judge your abilities. Many admissions committees say that they are willing to consider students whose grades or MCAT scores fall slightly below the average acceptance criteria, particularly if they've demonstrated extraordinary altruism or service to the community. Again, the best argument for looking past your college grades is evidence of achievement in another area, whether it is your MCAT score, extracurricular activities, overcoming economic hardship as an undergraduate, or career accomplishments.

CLICHÉS

"I'VE ALWAYS WANTED TO BE A DOCTOR."

A great personal statement should clearly illustrate the applicant's commitment to and interest in medicine. Even so, avoid throwaway lines and generic statements that could be repeated by any other premed. Many students who choose to study medicine truly feel the decision is the result of a long-term life calling, but making such statements will not distinguish you from the crowd. Instead, focus on illustrating *how* you have demonstrated that commitment to medicine academically and through your activities.

"I WANT TO BECOME A DOCTOR TO HELP PEOPLE."

Let's be clear: If you really want to spend your life saving lives, then by all means write about it. Just keep in mind that many other people will go this route as well. Although some of these people really *do* want to save lives, way down in the cockles of their hearts, most just say it because they want to look good and are motivated by less altruistic desires to attend medical school.

Here's the rub: Many essays about saving lives and healing will appear bogus and insincere. Even if you're heartfelt, your essay may get tossed into the same pile as all the insincere ones. Admissions officers will take your professed altruistic ambitions (and those of the hundreds of other applicants with identical personal statements) with a sizeable grain of salt. The key is to demonstrate your commitment to public service through examples of the work you have done. If you can in good conscience say that you're committed to a career in the public interest, you must *show* the committee something tangible on your application and in your essay that will allow them to see your statements as more than hollow assertions. ***Speak from experience, not from desire.*** This is exactly where those details we've already discussed come into play. If you can't show that you're already a veteran in the good fight, then don't claim to be. While medical schools value altruism and philanthropy, there are many other worthy reasons to study medicine, such as the intellectual challenge, a love of science and research, and the ability to participate in one of the most dynamic professional fields while making a positive contribution to society. Be forthright. Nothing is as impressive to the reader of a personal statement as the truth.

READY, SET, WRITE!

Hopefully what you've read here will help guide you through the process of writing a great personal essay and stand-out secondaries. Though there's no magic recipe, we're confident that if you follow our advice about what to put in and what to leave out, you'll end up with a memorable personal statement that will differentiate you from the larger applicant pool and make you a more competitive candidate. Take our word for it and give it your best shot.

CHAPTER 5

MAKING ENDS MEET: FINANCIAL AID OVERVIEW

MAKING FRIENDS WITH MONEY

Few people enjoy the process of thinking about and researching financial aid. As no one requires them to do it, most manage their school finances poorly. With a little effort, you can avoid the mistake of putting this issue off until the last minute and avoid taking out big loans to pay for medical school. Though you may not want to put in any time on financial issues, think about it this way: **if someone were willing to pay you $10,000 for a week or two of your time, you probably wouldn't hesitate to take the job.** But with financial aid planning, you could save far more than $10,000 if you take just a few days to research and consider your options.

For specialized tasks that you don't enjoy, get help. Ask a parent who's good at managing the family funds or see a financial planner. Every medical school has a financial aid officer who's usually happy to give advice over the phone, even to prospective students. Most current medical students don't talk to financial aid officers nearly as much as they should, perhaps because they are afraid of dealing with money issues or thinking about displeasing topics such as debt. You'll quickly overcome your fears simply by taking proactive steps, talking to the helpful experts at your medical college (or prospective medical college), and making a plan.

WHAT IS FINANCIAL AID?

Financial aid is money given or loaned to students to help cover the gap between their and their families' resources and the amount needed to pay for an education. Some schools and independent foundations offer scholarships, grants, and fellowships to students based on their academic performance or other factors. In most cases, however, medical students receive financial aid awards based on their demonstrated financial need.

Given the large price tag of a medical education, almost everyone is eligible for at least some financial assistance. To apply for financial aid, you will need to file an application for medical school admission and a standardized need analysis form. Generally, med schools require you to submit the Free Application for Federal Student Assistance (FAFSA) as well as their own financial aid forms. The FAFSA is available via the Web at www.fafsa.ed.gov.

FINANCIAL ASSISTANCE:
YOUR BASIC OPTIONS

Medical school ain't cheap, and the majority of medical students need some form of financial assistance to help cover schooling costs. Students usually fund their education through one or more of the following:

LOANS

Taking out student loans is the most common form of covering medical educational expenses. Medical students may participate in subsidized federal loan programs (Stafford loans), as well as proprietary loan programs through private schools, associations, and financial institutions (Bank of America's Education Maximizer Loan, Key Bank's MedAchiever Loan). As we'll discuss shortly, each has different terms and conditions, and you will save thousands by finding one that's best suited to your needs.

SCHOLARSHIPS AND GRANTS

Qualified students can receive "free money" in the form of scholarships or grants from the school they're attending. The amount can vary significantly from school to school. In addition, some private sources of scholarship money are available for medical students, though these resources are limited and harder to locate. Check to make sure that any third-party grants or scholarships will offset your loans and not your school-based grants. If they offset your school-based grants, third-party awards will not lower your overall costs; they'll just save your school some money.

Though scholarships and grants are generally awarded to students who display both financial need and academic prowess, federal service programs, such as the National Health Service Corps, can cover the entire cost of a medical education in exchange for several years of service in the military or in underserved communities. These programs can be particularly excellent choices for students with primary care practice interests. Be sure to investigate them thoroughly to understand the options they provide.

SAVINGS

Though it's unlikely that you'll have extra money after your undergraduate years, those lucky few who were thinking ahead may have some savings to help cover the cost of med school. **If you're an undergrad, ask your financial advisor if there are any savings programs they would recommend.**

TEACHING ASSISTANT/RESEARCH ASSISTANT FELLOWSHIPS

Some institutions will cover a significant portion of a student's tuition in exchange for his or her services as a graduate research assistant or as a TA to undergraduate classes. Availability of this type of opportunity varies by institution and is usually limited to a small subset of students.

DON'T GO IT ALONE

Finding viable financial aid options is near impossible without help. To get more information on the variety of available loans, scholarships, and grants, you will need to dedicate some time and resources to researching these topics. Here are some of the best places to start looking:

FINANCIAL AID BROCHURES

Request a financial aid brochure from at least three prestigious, private medical schools. Most will send one to you at little or no cost. Expensive colleges typically do the best job finding and explaining financial aid options to help struggling students and parents offset their high annual tuition. Review these brochures to acquaint yourself with the wide range of financing tools available to you.

INTERNET

The Internet is one of the cheapest and most efficient ways to get information about scholarships and loan programs. In fact, it is usually more effective than private aid search services, which differ greatly in quality. A number of independent websites can help you locate free money and financing options. Official financial aid sites provide useful information, eligibility requirements, and forms.

BOOKS AND PUBLICATIONS

There are several good books published on the topic of financial aid and scholarships. The Princeton Review's *Paying for College Without Going Broke* and *Paying for Graduate School Without Going Broke* are among the best and most comprehensive guides on the market.

PRIVATE CONSULTANTS

Financial aid options are so vast and confusing that it can be difficult to navigate the terrain alone. Consider seeking the help of a professional, such as a certified financial planner (CFP) or certified public accountant (CPA), who can help you create a viable, long-term financial strategy. Many CFPs, as well as the more expensive CPAs, can also handle your annual tax returns for a low fee.

HOW MUCH?

By any standard, medical school is extremely pricey. Tuition and fees generally represent the most sizable expense, especially for students attending private institutions. Even students at public schools may discover that the cost of their education is far from reasonable, given living expenses, equipment, transportation, and incidental costs. How much can you expect financial aid to cover? When determining your eligibility for financial aid, schools factor in the following:

- Tuition and fees

- Room and board

- Supplies, including lab equipment

- Medical and licensing exams

- Transportation to and from school or hospital

They do NOT generally include:

- Family expenses for married students or student-parents

- Relocation expenses

- Debt or other financial obligations

When you consider these factors, you can actually begin to determine what you will have to pay to attend medical school.

A LITTLE HELP FROM THE FAMILY

In most cases, your *expected family contribution* (EFC) is calculated using the federal methodology, which takes into consideration the income and assets of both the student and parents, then subtracts taxes, standard living expenses, and asset protection allowances (in the case of the parents, this depends on the age of the oldest parent). If more than one family member is attending college, the parent contribution is divided into equal portions for each student. The basic formula for determining financial need is:

Financial Need = Costs of Education – Expected Family Contribution

This formula, however, can be more complicated in reality. **Many students are surprised to hear that their parents' income is factored into their financial aid package, especially if the student has already graduated from college and has been living independently for several years.** All U.S. Department of Health and Human Services programs, as well as most institutional loans, grants, and scholarships, consider students dependent by default, regardless of their age or whether they actually receive financial support from their family. U.S. Department of Education (ED) programs, however, consider students independent; parental contributions are not factored into ED calculations.

Your financial aid package will fluctuate every year, based on changes in your and your family's life and finances. If, for example, one of your siblings graduates from college, you may be eligible for less financial aid the following year.

MORE ON LOANS AND SCHOLARSHIPS

LOANS

Most students take out loans to pay for medical school and in 2004 the average medical student graduated with $115,218 of school-related debt.[3] Since doctors are, on average, the highest paid professionals in the United States, most schools assume that students will be able to deal with the consequences of a significant amount of debt. You should be aware, however, that student loans vary widely with regard to interest rates, terms, repayment plans, and deferment options.

Federal Loans:

Loans offered through the federal government are generally attractive to students because they offer lower interest rates than commercial student loans. Medical students who demonstrate financial need are eligible for Stafford (Subsidized and Unsubsidized) Student Loans and Federal Perkins Student Loans from the federal government. These programs differ with regard to interest rate, repayment method, borrowing limits, deferment options, fees, application procedures, and eligibility requirements.

State Loans:

If you plan to attend medical school in the state in which you are a resident, you may be eligible for need-based state loans. State loans have lower interest rates than commercial loans and are generally available to minority or disadvantaged students. Some states also have service programs that grant full tuition in exchange for service in disadvantaged communities after graduation.

Institutional Loans:

Many schools offer their own loan programs for medical students. However, the amount of money available, interest rates, and repayment methods vary greatly by institution. While some schools have a great deal of money to offer students, others have none. **If you're offered a loan through your medical school, you'll need to carefully evaluate whether that loan is better than something you could find through a federal, state, or private source.**

---

3   Includes premed borrowing. American Medical Association, "Medical Student Debt," Medical Student Section (MSS), http://www.ama-assn.org/ama/pub/category/5349.html (accessed Feb. 1, 2006).

Private Loans:

Students can also get loans from banks or private lending institutions. The federal government does not subsidize these loans. Many private loans are not very good options, as they have high interest rates and strict repayment plans. But terms and conditions vary, and a private loan may be very helpful in a pinch.

In addition to loans from traditional lending institutions, some private foundations, corporations, charities, and associations make *charitable loans* to medical students. These loans may have lower interest rates or other benefits over traditional private loans. Charitable loans are usually designed to assist a certain segment of the population, such as minorities or students with disabilities. To find the best option or to locate a good private source for which you qualify may take some research.

Popular Loan Programs:

- The Access Group (www.accessgroup.org) offers the Medical Access Loan, Medical Residency Loan, and Dental Access Loan.

- Bank of America (www.bankofamerica.com/studentbanking/) offers Maximizer loans for medical students and residents.

- Citibank (www.citiassist.com) offers CitiAssist loans.

- Key Education Resources (www.key.com/education) offers the MedAchiever Loan for full-time students in allopathic or osteopathic school and the Alternative DEAL for students pursuing dental or postdoctoral dental degrees.

- Sallie Mae (www.salliemae.com) offers the MEDLOANS program, sponsored by the AAMC.

- TERI (www.teri.org) offers the Health Professions Loan for allopathic medicine, osteopathic medicine, and dentistry.

SCHOLARSHIPS

Though they're considerably harder to come by, some students are eligible to receive scholarships, which are awarded to cover tuition costs. Scholarships are administered, like loans, through federal funds, state funds, private institutions, and associations. Usually, scholarships are either merit- or need-based, and aimed at helping students of a particular demographic.

Federal Scholarships:

The U.S. Department of Education and the U.S. Department of Health and Human Services have some limited funds available for medical students. Usually the awards are need-based, but they also consider other factors. Scholarships for Disadvantaged Students (SDS) are awarded through the U.S. Department of Health and Human Services. These scholarships are reserved for students from disadvantaged backgrounds, who are extremely financially needy. You can obtain more information about these from your school's financial aid office.

Institutional Scholarships:

Most medical schools have some proprietary funds, which they award to qualified students based on merit or a combination of merit and need. Through these scholarships, students receive what amounts to a discount on their tuition. These funds often come from an endowment and involve specific criteria, such as a student's ethnic background or research interests.

Obligatory Scholarship/Service Options:

A number of federal scholarships are available to students who are willing to serve in organizations such as the Army, Navy, or National Health Service Corps upon graduation. The service "repayment" process usually begins after residency and is usually directly proportional to the number of years of support. Most programs cover up to $25,000 of tuition cost annually, as well as a monthly stipend for living expenses. On top of that, the subsequent service experience can be in a very desirable training environment. Students should be prepared, however, for a seven- to ten-year-long service commitment after leaving the classroom. For those who require more independence, these programs may not be ideal; for those with an interest in community service, however, they are an option to carefully consider. Some examples of obligatory scholarship/service programs are described below.

- National Health Service Corps

    If you're interested in primary care medicine, you have the option of participating in the National Health Service Corps (NHSC), a scholarship program that covers a medical student's tuition and expenses and offers a monthly stipend. In return, students are obligated to work in Health Manpower Shortage Areas, such as rural communities, assigned by the NHSC. Again, the number of years a recipient is required to serve is directly proportional to the number of years he or she received support, usually about four to seven. These scholarships are very competitive. For more information, visit their website at http://nhsc.bhpr.hrsa.gov.

- Armed Forces Health Professions Scholarships

    The Army, Navy, and Air Force operate scholarship programs for students training in professional health fields. Students who participate in these programs spend forty-five days on active military duty each academic year, usually during summer, or when the school's schedule permits. Upon completion of residency, scholarship recipients must serve a year as a medical officer for every year of support they received. The minimum number of years served is three. In exchange for their service, students receive full coverage of their tuition and fees, reimbursement for books and supplies, and a monthly stipend. These scholarships are very competitive as well, but can be tremendously rewarding. Dr. Stephen Nelson, a pediatrician and MCAT tutor for The Princeton Review, describes his experience: "I funded my medical school through the Health Professions Scholarship Program. I am now completing my pediatric residency while on active duty in the Air Force and will be spending next year as a Flight Surgeon (deploying with a fighter wing, doing operational medicine, flying in the jets), and then will start my pediatric neurology fellowship. I owe the Air Force four years of service after residency for my medical school training, and will incur an additional three years of commitment for my fellowship (since my fellowship is three years). Do not think that military scholarships will prevent you from doing the residency that you want, because the military trains physicians in all specialties. Furthermore, because you do your residency on active duty, you make about $15,000 per year more than your civilian colleagues. As a fellow, you may receive about $45,000 per year more than your civilian counterparts. Also, you gain many unique experiences that they will never have, such as: going on medical missions to other countries, military transports of patients to other hospitals/ states/countries, medical care in field environments, and many other unique benefits. During medical school you hold the rank of Second Lieutenant (Ensign in the Navy) and after graduation are commissioned to the rank of Captain (Lieutenant in the Navy). I highly encourage anyone who has an interest in serving his or her country to explore this option."

- Army National Guard

   Medical students can be commissioned as Second Lieutenants in the Army National Guard through the Medical Student Commissioning Program. While in medical school, these students train sixteen hours per month and two weeks annually. Upon graduation, they are promoted to the post of Captain in the medical corps. In exchange for this service, the Army National Guard covers roughly $6,000 to $28,000 of students' annual fees. For many medical students, Guard duty is the difference between significant and insignificant debt by the end of medical school. It is also less time-intensive than the service options listed above.

EVALUATING YOUR FINANCIAL AID PACKAGE

After you receive an offer of admission from a school, you will be offered a financial aid package to help cover your estimated need—as determined by the FAFSA—through a combination of loans, scholarships, grants, and/or employment. If you have other options, **don't automatically accept everything in the aid package (or any of it, for that matter).** Don't automatically accept the school either, even if it's your first choice. Before you start packing, you need to think about how you'll pay for your education. Is the offer sufficient to accept? How will you cover the difference? When you're finished with medical school, what will your debt be? What is the interest rate and repayment schedule? If you have more than one offer, you should compare the two options carefully. If one school makes you a great offer but you have your heart set on another, use the difference between the two packages as bargaining leverage. Students in the enviable position of having multiple acceptances can save thousands to tens of thousands of dollars by negotiating better financial aid packages.

FINANCIAL AID PITFALLS

While today's financial aid programs make it possible for almost everyone to pay for higher education, there are some common pitfalls that can inhibit your ability to participate in loan programs—especially low-interest and subsidized loans. Watch out for the following problems:

MISSING DEADLINES

Like all aspects of your application, the earlier you submit your financial aid materials, the better. Financial aid deadlines are strongly enforced. Keep careful records and be sure to send everything *on time*.

POOR CREDIT HISTORY

As long as you have good credit, you can borrow money to pay for your education. However, if your credit is bad when you start medical school, you may be ineligible for loans, even high-interest loans. If you have a bad credit rating, get started on credit repair now. In this case, you may need to seek professional assistance. There are a number of credit-rating repair services, but beware: some are scams. Get a referral to a reputable agency from a certified financial planner. Even if you don't have bad credit, you should check your credit rating before applying for financial aid. Sometimes even a few late payments on your car or credit card will show up in your credit history.

DEFAULTING ON UNDERGRADUATE LOANS

If you've not met your undergraduate loan payments, you'll have a hard time qualifying for medical school loans, especially federal loans. **Before you apply for aid, try to clear up any problems with your undergraduate student loans.** Again, you may want to seek professional assistance from a financial planner. If you have undergraduate loans and are still in school, talk to financial aid officers about deferment options.

SMART MONEY

Hopefully this chapter will help you to better understand and successfully navigate the murky world of medical school finances. By cultivating good financial habits now, you can not only secure funding for your degree, but also get an early start on providing for your family, buying a home, caring for your aging parents, and, eventually, saving for your own retirement. Think of today as the first day of the rest of your financially secure life.

CHAPTER 6

BEING A DOCTOR: THINGS YOU SHOULD KNOW

THE MEANING OF AN MD

Before you apply to medical school, you should carefully consider the following questions:

Do you want to spend your life helping others?

Doctors heal people, save lives, and help others—often through direct, face-to-face interactions. According to a recent survey of medical school students, "helping others" is the primary motivation for pursuing an MD. If this is your motivation, you're in good company. However, there are other altruistic careers out there and they all involve less schooling and less debt than medical school. **The desire to help others should be one, but not the only, reason for becoming a doctor.**

Do you enjoy working hard?

Medicine is an incredibly challenging field. This was the case a hundred years ago when doctors worked to fight yellow fever, polio, and influenza, and it is the case today as health professionals try to prevent and treat heart disease, cancer, and AIDS while dealing with the constraints of managed care. So consider medicine only if you know you want tremendous challenge in your professional life. As you read this chapter, think about whether the challenges involved in practicing medicine are the ones that appeal to you. For example, a physician who is 20 years out of medical school is still expected to be familiar with the latest medical developments. A commitment to lifelong learning is one of the challenges of practicing medicine.

It should also be noted that doctors don't just work hard; they work long hours—most put in about 60 hours a week.

Are you interested in science and health issues?

If you enjoyed some aspects of your science courses—few people enjoy all aspects of premedical course work—and you find yourself drawn to health issues, there's a good chance that you will enjoy studying and practicing medicine. Although medicine has changed significantly over the years, its roots remain in basic science.

Do you like working with different people?

With the exception of a few fields, medicine involves working with people, many of whom may be very different from you. If science interests you but working with people does not, you may wish to consider an advanced degree other than an MD; chances are it will involve less debt. You might also look into an MD that allows you to do only research.

The above should give you an idea of what it has been and is currently like to be a doctor. But what will it take to be a doctor in the world of tomorrow? Although it will depend a great deal your on specialty, geographic region, and employment situation, the main criteria will be whether or not you feel compelled to be a doctor—*is practicing medicine your calling?* Consider the following:

Compassion—a critical part of healing

Advocacy—for your patients and for those without health care

Leadership—in improving health care at the team, hospital, and policy level

Lifelong learning—there will always be more to know

Interpersonal skills—communication with patients and among providers is key

Negotiation—to work around bureaucratic constraints

Grasp—of increasing amounts of medical knowledge and of a health care system in flux

If you feel the C.A.L.L.I.N.G. acronym describe qualities and desires that you have, congratulations!—you should have what it takes to become a successful and adaptable doctor. The more you know about what to expect, the more prepared you can be for it when it arrives.

PATIENT CARE

Most doctors spend their time seeing patients and generally work in one of three situations: solo, as part of a group practice, or as an employee of a hospital or organization. The most common reason people go to the doctor is for some sort of check-up or test. Other common reasons for doctor visits are respiratory, gastrointestinal, and psychological complaints. **An important responsibility of the primary care physician is to identify potentially serious issues during routine examinations.** On the other side of the spectrum, doctors with highly specialized training—*e.g.*, oncologists, cardiologists, and surgeons—are charged with saving and improving the lives of those affected by serious medical issues. In 2000, the following were the ten most common causes of mortality in the United States[4]:

1. Heart diseases

2. Malignant neoplasms (cancer)

3. Cerebrovascular diseases (stroke)

4. Chronic lower respiratory diseases (e.g., emphysema, asthma, bronchitis)

5. Accidents

6. Diabetes mellitus (diabetes type 2)

7. Influenza and pneumonia

8. Alzheimer's disease

9. Nephritis, nephrotic syndrome, and nephrosis (kidney disease)

10. Septicemia (blood poisoning)

Note that all of the above except Alzheimer's are preventable. As such, it is important for the modern physician to be well-versed in preventative medicine.

---

4   Centers for Disease Control and Prevention, "The Most Common Causes of Death in the United States," Health, United States, 2002 With Chartbook on Trends in the Health of Americans, http://www.cdc.gov.

COMPENSATION

A survey of physicians in various medical specialties yielded the following results[5]:

Specialty	Average Annual Salary (in USD)
Anesthesiology	265,753
Cardiology	283,298
Cardiovascular Surgery	558,719
Colorectal Surgery	263,199
Dermatology	199,028
Emergency Medicine	197,000
Endocrinology	160,085
Family Practice	142,516
Gastroenterology	250,574
General Surgery	261,276
Hematology	249,298
Internal Medicine	148,206
Nephrology	233,824
Neurology	186,653
Neurosurgery	438,426
Obstetrics/Gynecology	238,224
Ophthalmology	246,823
Oral and Maxofacial Surgery	208,340
Orthopedic Surgery	346,224
Otorhinolaryngology (ENT)	254,978
Pediatrics	143,754
Plastic Surgery	266,047
Psychiatry	142,610
Pulmonary Medicine	188,956
Radiology	286,361
Rheumatology	155,164
Urology	248,236
Vascular Surgery	359,339

5   Medical Resource Group, "Physician Salary Survey Results," Medical Education Guide, http://www.studentdoc.com/salaries.html (accessed March 13, 2006).

The figures listed above don't account for residents, who are notoriously over-worked and underpaid. **Many residents continue to work more than 100 hours per week.** Currently, a number of organizations, including the American Medical Association (AMA) and American Medical Students Association (AMSA), are pressing for more legislation to protect residents from extreme working conditions. Why are residents required to work so hard? In part, it's because hospitals depend on residents as a cheap source of labor, since they are paid much less than other physicians and somewhat less than nurses and other health professionals.

PRESTIGE

Almost universally, being a doctor carries prestige. Doctors are thought by the general public to be smart, well educated, hardworking, caring, and dedicated. **Even in this era of managed care and malpractice lawsuits, doctors are well respected.** You should consider the degree to which having a prestigious career is important to you. Other health professions, although perhaps less glamorous, also involve healing and helping others.

TRENDS IN MEDICINE

Several trends of the past few decades are likely to continue well into the twenty-first century. These trends have implications for you, the aspiring doctor. They will impact the nature of your work, the structure of the organization in which you work, your salary, the relationship you have with patients, and, above all, the quality of the health care you deliver.

In the sections to come, we'll consider the following trends (with a disclaimer that predicting the future is difficult) affecting medicine in the twenty-first century:

- Development of new technology

- Increased health care costs

- Evolution of health care delivery and payment systems

- Greater reliance on primary and preventive care

- More guidelines for patient care

- Better gender and ethnic diversity among physicians

- An aging patient population

- The emergence of new ethical issues

- Changes in academic medicine and medical education

Note that the above list is by no means complete. Many of the trends listed are interrelated and they are not necessarily presented in order of importance.

NEW TECHNOLOGY

Health care has improved during the past few decades largely due to technological advancement and there are more exciting developments on the horizon. The term *technology* is often used broadly. In the health care arena, it means the development of new drugs, procedures, techniques, and means of communication that, if used correctly, have the potential to improve diagnosis, care, and patient outcomes.

Medications and Procedures:

The increase in life expectancy over the past few decades is partially due to improvements in medications and procedures. For example, the death rate due to heart disease is declining because of better drugs (hypertension, heart, and cholesterol medications) and surgical techniques.

Laboratory Techniques:

Often, improvements in laboratory tools or techniques lead to important discoveries. For example, better tools allowed the human genome to be mapped.

The Internet:

The Internet can allow a patient to arrive at the doctor's office well-informed about his or her illness. On the other hand, the Internet houses a great deal of misinformation. The physician who is Web-savvy can guide patients to informative websites and Web-based support groups. The Internet is invaluable for research.

Telemedicine:

Telemedicine is defined by the American Telemedicine Association as *"the use of medical information exchanged from one site to another via electronic communications to improve patients' health status."*[6] The sharing of radiographic images and patient information via computer between physicians is an important current application. In the future, we may see telemedicine bringing the expertise of specialists to rural or other remote areas.

Other Computer Applications:

Computerized database systems are used for billing and patient records. Some physicians take advantage of software programs made for hand-held devices. These can be used for note-taking, reference, or even patient management. Not surprisingly, it is often the younger doctors (and medical students) who are the most comfortable with computer technology. An understanding of relevant computer applications can give you an advantage when it comes to working with older, more experienced doctors; in addition to learning from them, you will have something to contribute.

HEALTH CARE COSTS

The United States spends more money per capita on health care than any other country in the world. Some believe that the U.S. offers the best medical care in the world, thereby justifying the cost. Others assert that, according to indicators such as life expectancy and infant mortality, the U.S. lags behind other industrialized countries. Regardless, the amount annually spent on health care in this country is rising. In 2003, 15.3 percent of the U.S. Gross Domestic Product (GDP) was spent on health care. By 2014 that percentage is expected to reach 18.7.[7] There are many theories as to what is causing this escalation—hospital consolidation, inefficient spending for inpatient care and hospital bureaucracy, the cost of prescription medication, the prevalence of expensive technology, and a lack of incentive programs are all commonly invoked reasons. Two are discussed below.

6   American Telemedical Association, ATA News and Resources, http://www.atmeda.org/news/ definition.html (accessed March 13, 2006).

7   National Coalition on Health Care, "Health Insurance Cost: Facts on the Coast of Health Care," Facts About Health Care, http://www.nchc.org/facts/cost.shtml (accessed March 13, 2006).

Technology:

As discussed earlier, technological advances usually serve to improve health care and health outcomes. Technology, however, is often cited as a major cause of rising health care costs. When new tools are developed and advertised, hospitals and physicians may feel pressure to purchase and use them, sometimes even if the benefit of the new device is questionable. Someone ultimately pays for such purchases, and thus we see rising health care costs. It is important to remember, however, that technological advances can also serve to reduce costs. By preventing illnesses and reducing the spread of disease, new vaccines (anti-influenza, for example) lower the costs of treatment for society overall. New surgical instruments and the development of medications in pill form facilitate the use of outpatient procedures instead of expensive hospital stays.

Incentives:

Patients are generally far removed from the cost of their care, and therefore have little incentive to keep costs down. Employers and the government—not patients themselves—foot most of the bill for health care, creating a system of "third-party payers." Some believe that since patients don't pay much for their own health care, they overuse it, thereby driving government and employer health care expenditures up.

As a physician, you'll undoubtedly feel pressure to keep health care costs down. In many practice settings, insurers scrutinize doctors on the basis of the cost of the tests and treatments they prescribe. For example, primary care doctors are sometimes encouraged to limit referrals to specialists. All doctors may be monitored for "overuse" of expensive tests and equipment. Physicians face difficult decisions as they attempt to provide excellent care at a lower cost: if a patient has a slim chance of benefiting from an expensive treatment, should that treatment be employed? The physician must balance the cost of treating with the risk of not treating.

HEALTH CARE DELIVERY SYSTEMS

One of the most important trends of the past few decades has been the replacement of simple fee-for-service plans by the growth of the managed care industry.

Fee-for-Service:

Before managed care, health care was delivered on a "fee-for-service" basis. Medicare (federally funded health insurance for those over 65 years of age) remains a fee-for-service program. Under a fee-for-service system, doctors and hospitals perform a service—a check-up, an operation, etc.—and charge a fee for the service. Typically, the patient's health insurance company pays this fee. The patient pays the health insurance company monthly premiums or, if the patient has health benefits from his or her employer, the employer pays the monthly premiums. The insurance company calculates monthly premiums based on how much it pays out to hospitals and doctors each year for all people enrolled in the insurance plan.

Managed Care:

Managed care was introduced as a response to rising health care costs, and has succeeded in slowing the rate at which health care costs are rising. Thus, the trend towards managed care will probably continue. Although managed care is often thought to be synonymous with Health Maintenance Organizations (HMOs), an HMO is, in fact, just one of many systems for managing care.

Managed care usually involves set monthly premiums that are lower than those in fee-for-service plans, and this makes those paying the premiums (usually employers) happy. How do managed care organizations keep their premiums down? It's simple—by keeping their financial outlays down. Under managed care, expenditures are typically controlled through several mechanisms:

- Participants in a managed care plan agree to use doctors and hospitals that are part of the plan, and these providers are either paid yearly salaries or charge reduced fees for services rendered.

- Primary care physicians serve as "gatekeepers" in limiting the use of expensive medical specialists. (Many patients find that nurses and other health care professionals are responsible for a large amount of their care, and that they usually have less access to physicians.)

- Guidelines and regulations are implemented that attempt to limit the use of expensive tests and equipment in unnecessary situations.

- Inpatient care is reduced and there is greater emphasis on outpatient services (care that does not involve an overnight hospital stay).

Managed care has generated discontent among some patients and providers. Patients are often frustrated by red tape, the inability to choose one's doctor, short visits, long waits, obstacles to seeing specialists, and limitations on coverage. Many doctors object to managed care because the cost-cutting mechanisms can compromise patient care; their salaries and autonomy are also reduced in these arrangements.

There can be some advantages, however, to working for a managed care organization. For one, doctors are often salaried, which means that they earn a specified amount each year and their income does not depend on finding clients. Doctors also tend to work fewer hours a week, which is probably good for both doctors and patients. For better or for worse, being a doctor in the twenty-first century is likely to involve practicing in a managed care environment of some form.

Uninsured:

A discussion of health care delivery would be incomplete without mention of the uninsured. At least 15 percent of people in the United States have no health insurance. The U.S. is unique among industrialized nations in that respect, and it's not exactly something to be proud of. Individuals without health insurance tend to seek medical care—typically through an emergency room—only after a health problem has become really serious. This is obviously bad for the patient, who, with early treatment, might have avoided serious complications. It's also costly to society, because prevention and early treatment are less expensive than late intervention. Most people—physicians and nonphysicians alike—believe that everyone should have access to health care. However, there is less agreement on how universal access should be achieved and funded. Doctors must speak out to ensure that this issue is addressed as soon, and as equitably, as possible.

GREATER EMPHASIS ON PRIMARY AND PREVENTATIVE CARE

Most observers predict that as managed care grows, primary care physicians will continue to play a very important role, and the demand for primary care doctors will remain relatively high. In addition, **it has become increasingly clear that investing in preventative care is more cost-effective than treating advanced illness.** Therefore, there has been a growing emphasis on encouraging preventative treatment.

Gatekeepers:

Before the days of managed care, if a person discovered an odd-looking spot on his skin, he could go directly to a dermatologist and be reimbursed by his insurance company for the visit. An important tenet of managed care has been the requirement that enrollees see a primary care physician prior to visiting a specialist. Family practice, pediatrics, internal medicine, geriatrics, and ob/gyn are typically considered primary care fields. The primary care physician serves as a "gatekeeper," presumably reducing unnecessary visits to expensive specialists.

Without the training of a specialist, however, the primary care physician may not be equipped to judge the seriousness of some conditions. Missing a pre-cancerous skin lesion, for example, may cause hardship for the patient later on. On the other hand, if a primary care doctor refers *all* patients with skin lesions to the dermatologist, the system has failed because each patient required two doctor visits rather than one.

Integrated Approach:

A benefit of this emphasis on primary care is that, in theory, patients develop a long-term relationship with their primary care doctor, who is better able to understand the social, economic, and community-related issues associated with their health. The primary care doctor presumably has an understanding of all physiologic systems. This comprehensive knowledge facilitates diagnosis or at least allows the physician to make the initial decision about what steps will lead to diagnosis. Primary care physicians are well-positioned to address behavioral changes, such as exercise programs, that aid in the prevention of disease.

Prevention:

Several of the major causes of morbidity (illness) and mortality (death) in the U.S. are preventable. Emphysema, for example, is often the result of heavy smoking. The most common type of diabetes is linked with obesity. We have learned that the spread of HIV can be reduced through educational programs and behavioral interventions. The high death rate in this country due to violent crime is often attributed to the prevalence of handguns, a situation that could be addressed through legislation. Advances in genetics could potentially revolutionize preventative medicine by allowing physicians to identify people who are going to get sick before they show any symptoms of disease.

Prevention is preferable to treatment for the obvious reason that, with prevention, illness is reduced or eliminated altogether. Whether prevention efforts are cost-effective depends upon the disease, its prevalence, and the technology employed. For example, mammography is helpful in detecting breast cancer at a treatable stage and can potentially prevent mortality and reduce the high costs associated with treating end-stage cancer. It's sensible and cost-effective to offer mammograms to women above a certain age. However, it's probably unreasonable to encourage women in their 20s to have annual mammograms because breast cancer at that age is rare and can be difficult to spot on a mammogram.

GUIDELINES FOR PATIENT CARE

The doctor-patient relationship, the belief that each patient must be considered individually, and the principle that doctors should be allowed to use their best judgment when providing care are all fundamental to medicine. Do these ideals conflict with the recent trend of using guidelines in clinical medicine?

Evidenced-Based Medicine or Cookbook Medicine?

Doctors vary tremendously in their approach to medicine and disease treatment. This is why, in serious illness, a second opinion is usually recommended. In recent years, there has been increased use of Evidenced-Based Medicine (EBM) in clinical practice. EBM employs *scientific evidence* for the purpose of standardizing and improving patient care. Quantitative indicators such as rate of reduction of disease are typically used to evaluate procedures and treatments. The goal of EBM is to establish guidelines for clinical decision-making based on the results of studies, particularly randomized clinical trials, which are generally considered the most accurate type of study.

Some doctors worry that the trend toward EBM de-emphasizes physician judgment, results in strict guidelines for treatment, and amounts to "cookbook medicine." In fact, this hasn't been the case. EBM, with its population-based approach, actually complements the one-on-one tradition of medicine by allowing doctors to defend their decisions with data. However, there are many diseases and clinical situations for which the literature fails to provide clear evidence. In some cases, the risks and benefits of a particular therapy vary depending on the study examined.

Cost Consciousness:

Occasionally, guidelines that dictate clinical care are based on cost-cutting objectives rather than on sound medical evidence. Such "guidelines" may compromise patient care. Going back to our mammogram example, an HMO might encourage physicians to recommend mammograms to all women over 50, when research suggests that mammograms are highly beneficial for women in their 40s as well. It is the physician's ethical responsibility to give his patient honest and up-to-date medical advice (in this case, to recommend mammograms after age 40). At the same time, the physician may want to support the cost-cutting goals of his employer. This is the type of conflict that doctors face in the current era of cost-consciousness. There are no easy answers, but familiarity with medical evidence and the rules of the organization should allow you to make informed and responsible decisions.

DIVERSITY AMONG PHYSICIANS

Increased diversity among physicians is a positive trend and may result in better patient care for the following:

Women:

Approximately 48 percent of entering medical students are women.[8] There are outstanding female physicians in every imaginable medical field. Women are especially well represented in pediatrics and ob/gyn, but less well represented in surgical subspecialties. Several theories and generalizations have been put forth to help explain why women are more attracted to some fields than others, including: people tend to be interested in fields that have personal relevance; once there is a critical mass of women within a field, it becomes a more welcoming environment for other women; and women tend to avoid fields with the very longest residencies.

Female doctors are having an important influence on the medical field. In general, female physicians tend to spend more time with patients than their male counterparts and tend to emphasize the psychological and emotional issues related to illness. Furthermore, female physicians have begun to promote a reduction of the hours that physicians work, leaving more time for family and personal life.

Minorities:

The medical profession is slowly becoming more ethnically diverse, as increased numbers of nonwhite medical school graduates enter the workforce. This increase in diversity reflects the changing demographics of the U.S. population, better and more widely available educational opportunities, and active minority recruitment on the part of medical schools that recognize that it is extremely important to have a physician population that represents the population it serves. If this trend continues, we will someday have a physician workforce that is representative of the population at large. In 2005, underrepresented minorities made up 15 percent of entering medical school classes.[9]

---

8   American Medical Association, "Matriculants by Race and Ethnicity within Sex," AAMC Data Warehouse, Oct. 15, 2005, http://www.aamc.org/data/facts/2005/2003to2005detmat.htm (accessed March 13, 2006).

9   American Medical Association, "Matriculants by Race and Ethnicity Within Sex," AAMC Data Warehouse, Oct. 15, 2005, http://www.aamc.org/data/facts/2005/2003to2005detmat.htm (accessed March 13, 2006).

Aging Population

In 2000, the median age in the U.S. was 35.3 years, up from 32.9 in 1990.[10] As the population continues to age, the demand for medical care will increase—older Americans, on average, require more doctor visits per year. This contributes to rising health care costs. Because Medicare covers almost all individuals over 65, government expenditures on health care are expected to rise steadily. The paperwork involved in treating a patient with Medicare is also notoriously time-consuming.

An older population will cause growth within certain fields, such as geriatrics, internal medicine, orthopedics, and cardiovascular medicine. The incidence of chronic disease, meaning disease that is long-lasting and often incurable, will increase. In situations such as these, physicians will often be called upon to provide palliative care that addresses symptoms rather than the underlying disease. Physician-researchers will be encouraged to find treatments for conditions that afflict the elderly, such as Alzheimer's disease.

This increase in the patient population has also led to fears of a physician shortage. The U.S. government actively encourages students to consider medicine.

Ethical Issues

Physicians have always dealt with important ethical issues related to life and death. As a physician in the twenty-first century, some of your ethical dilemmas are likely to involve the conflict between saving money and saving lives. Consider the following scenario:

You're a pediatrician, seeing a patient you've never seen before. The patient is a very ill six-year-old girl without health insurance. Do you treat her, knowing you'll hear about it later? Or do you send her to the free clinic across town, even though it will entail a long bus ride for the sick girl?

With an older patient population, ethical issues about end-of-life care will become increasingly relevant. For example:

Your patient is 80 years old and suffers from terminal lung cancer, which has spread to his brain. There are no cures for him at this stage, so your care has been

10   Robert Longley, "U.S. Median Age Highest Ever," About.com, http://usgovinfo.about.com/library/weekly/aa051801a.htm (accessed March 14, 2006).

focused on keeping him comfortable. He can't breathe on his own, is incoherent, and has been more or less motionless in the hospital for one week. His daughter doesn't want you to remove life support. What do you do?

The rule of doctor-patient confidentiality can be another source of ethical dilemmas. Consider this situation:

You've been treating a young man in the hospital for a lung infection. During his hospital stay, he was tested for HIV and the test results were positive. He's unwilling to discuss the matter, doesn't want medications that will help his HIV symptoms, and appears to be in denial. Do you have a responsibility to alert the man's wife?

There is an increasing emphasis on the ethical and emotional issues of doctoring in medical school curriculums, and some top programs require course work in patient treatment and medical ethics. Unfortunately, some medical schools barely address ethics, leaving you on your own to learn about and think through important ethical issues. A mentor, someone whose opinion you respect, can serve as a resource for sorting out ethical questions. If you feel strongly about a particular issue, you should consider getting involved by writing, attending conferences, or engaging in dialogue about it.

CHANGES IN ACADEMIC MEDICINE AND MEDICAL EDUCATION

Most medical schools are directly affiliated with teaching hospitals. Three advantages to this arrangement are:

- Medical students have an opportunity for hands-on learning.

- Patients are treated by expert physicians and benefit from the latest technology.

- The academic environment coupled with clinical facilities provides an ideal setting for research that ultimately pushes medicine forward and improves care.

Academic medical centers throughout the country are having a tough time financially, leading some experts to question their future viability. Although medical school tuition seems incredibly high, it does not cover the complete cost of a medical education; academic medical centers have historically depended on income from clinical activities to subsidize medical education costs, research activities, and the management of a teaching hospital. As discussed earlier, the shift toward outpatient medicine has resulted in reduced earnings for hospitals. For academic medical centers, this means less revenue to cover their high costs. As more and more academic medical centers face financial crisis, there will be pressure to either cut costs or raise revenue significantly. We might see academic medical centers restrict their patients to those who can pay higher fees, or we may see an increase in government funding or medical school tuition.

In response to the changes in medicine and health care described above, most medical schools are attempting to revise their programs of study. Some of the revisions we see are:

- Less time spent in lecture. Educators recognize that in this age of technology and information, there are simply too many facts to learn. Rather than inundate students with massive amounts of information, some medical schools hope to teach students general concepts that will prepare them for a lifetime of learning.

- More clinical problem-solving during the first two years. With all that we now know and all the treatment options available today, physicians must be thinkers and problem-solvers. In fact, several top-tier medical school programs have converted to entirely problem-based programs of study, greatly reducing class time and creating more opportunities for group and independent work.

- Greater emphasis on health economics, health care management, public health, and patient care. Doctors should understand the interdisciplinary nature of health care and the forces that affect medicine. Furthermore, doctors in almost every specialty are required to interact with the public with sensitivity and candor—traits that don't come naturally to every person and were previously disregarded in medical programs.

- Better training in outpatient medicine, with the use of outpatient clinics and doctors' offices for clinical rotations of outpatient facilities.

With at least 11 years of post-high school training required, becoming a physician takes longer in the U.S. than anywhere else in the world. This is costly to society. Some people predict that, as a result of financial pressures, the amount of schooling required to become a doctor will be reduced. For the time being, however, you have a long—but exciting—road ahead of you.

A VERY BIG ADVENTURE

Expect a period of massive and fantastic change in medicine over the next 15 years. If you apply yourself, deal effectively with the tasks at hand, and focus on patients and solutions by following your best knowledge and instincts, there's no reason why you won't be able to contribute to this new and adventurous era in medicine.

CHAPTER 7

Q & A WITH ADMISSIONS OFFICERS

We asked admissions officers at two allopathic schools and at one osteopathic school about medical school applications, personal statements, and secondary essays. They told us what they like and don't like to read, the number of applications they read each year, and just how much the personal statement and secondary essays count. The following professionals dedicated their time to answering our questions:

- Megan Price, Director of Admissions at Edward Via Virginia College of Osteopathic Medicine

- Lorna Kenyon, Director of Admissions and Student Records at the Ohio State University College of Medicine and Public Health

- Jennifer Welch, Director of Admissions at State University of New York Upstate Medical University

For ease of reading, we introduce each officer's response to the questions we asked with the name of the institution she serves.

SUBJECT MATTER & WRITING

Which themes continually appear in personal statements?

VCOM: Reasons for pursuing a degree in (osteopathic) medicine, including: life events and experiences, steps taken to present a competitive medical school application, and explanations for deficiencies in the application.

Ohio State: We see expanded discussions of applicants' involvement in the medical field, from their first interest in medicine to shadowing experiences to specific examples of patients who have had an impact on their lives. We also see detailed outlines of research, community service, and volunteer experiences.

State University of New York Upstate: The story of the loss or illness of a loved one, and how this experience has influenced the applicant's decision to become a doctor.

If your school requires essays as part of its secondary application, what are common topics that students address?

VCOM: VCOM includes three essays as part of the Secondary Application:

- What qualities do you feel you bring to VCOM that would enhance the overall climate of our college?

- Osteopathic medicine is a distinct practice with parallels to allopathic medicine. Why do you desire to enter the field of osteopathic medicine?

- There are many problems facing health care in America today. Describe what you feel are the most important and what you, as an osteopathic physician, would do to help find the solutions.

We also offer a fourth essay that is directed towards our reapplicants:

- Did you submit an application to VCOM last year? If so, please explain how you improved your application.

Ohio State: We ask the applicants how they define altruism and to give examples of when they exhibited altruistic behavior. They are also asked to describe their motivation for a career in medicine.

State University of New York Upstate: Not applicable.

What writing tips would you offer to your applicant pool?

VCOM: Write from the heart. Be careful not to make the statement too choppy after edits (this often occurs when the initial statement is over the size limit). Try not to write a creative writing essay.

Ohio State: Provide insight into who you are as a person that is not available in other parts of the application. Whatever you decide to write about, provide some discussion as to how this would make you a caring physician.

State University of New York Upstate: Please do not have run-on sentences or use a quote as the intro to your personal statement—I don't care about Robert Frost, I want to know more about you. Please be sure to spell physician correctly, if you really want to be one. Spend a great deal of time proofing your essay. Do not rely only on spell check, but please use it. If it doesn't look like a person put a great deal of time, thought, and energy into their application, the admissions committee won't be inclined to do so.

Which grammatical mistakes make you cringe?

VCOM: Poor spelling and punctuation.

Ohio State: Improper use of verb tenses.

Who should edit a student's personal statement and essays?

VCOM: Premed and academic advisors, faculty members, and physician mentors.

Ohio State: The student should write and edit his or her own statement and essays. Premed advisors are a good source of information and would be helpful. The applicant should not use a service to write their personal statement or essays.

State University of New York Upstate: Someone who is knowledgeable and does not know the applicant well. Does that person come away with a sense of who you are? Was it clear?

What do you not like to read in a personal statement or essay?

VCOM: It is unimpressive when an applicant copies their personal statement for one of our secondary application essays. While the topics may overlap, the lack of creativity is disappointing.

Ohio State: Our Admissions Committee does not find definitions or ideals of what a physician is or should be useful. The applicant should treat the personal statement and essays separately and not cut and paste the same text for all.

State University of New York Upstate: Please do not reiterate your academic record, GPA, MCAT scores—I can see them for myself. I want to know more about a student on a personal level, who they are, what they are all about, etc. I would also stay away from the "I" factor: "I did this" and "I did that." Be truthful and sincere in your personal statement. Don't try to be someone that you are not or tell us what you think we want to hear; we want to get to know more about the "real" you.

What do you love to read in a personal statement or essay?

VCOM: With regard to our secondary application essays, I love to read why the applicant is applying to VCOM.

Ohio State: The Admissions Committee enjoys reading the responses of applicants whose true passion for helping people and genuine interest in medicine shine through no matter the topic.

State University of New York Upstate: Personal stories about applicants, what makes them unique, what sets them apart from the other applicants, what they are passionate about.

Which topics or styles bore you?

VCOM: We prefer not to read personal statements that are written in a creative-writing format; we want information displayed in a more factual and heartfelt manner.

Ohio State: Talking about how great our college is or repeating information found in print or on the Web is not useful to us.

State University of New York Upstate: Don't try to impress upon us what a genius you are. Confidence is good, but overconfidence can be a turnoff. Let your experiences and achievements speak for themselves. View the essay as our chance to get to know you as a person and as a future physician.

What kinds of experiences would you like students to write about more often?

VCOM: Why they want to practice medicine, what field they are considering post-graduation, and international clinical experiences.

Ohio State: Any experience in which the student was actively involved, exhibited altruistic behavior, or grew as a person.

Which topics would you consider risky? When are such topics effective?

Ohio State: Occasionally, some applicants sound as if they are making excuses for poor grades, MCAT scores, etc. These explanations can be effective when there were circumstances that they were able to overcome. Other risky topics include adversity such as an abusive relationship, substance abuse, a dysfunctional family, etc. If these issues have been dealt with and overcome, they can be effective topics.

State University of New York Upstate: Sometimes students will talk about, let's say, having been captain of their volleyball team or something totally unrelated to the field of medicine and, by the end of the essay, you're left wondering why this information was included at all. Think about the point you're trying to make and be sure that your message is conveyed to the reader. Also, avoid blanket statements and generalizations about people and certain professions. You never know who will be sitting on the Admissions Committee and what their career path has been.

While not a topic, using humor can be risky. If it's used correctly, it can make your essay more creative and interesting. More often than not, however, you come off as silly, which leaves the reader questioning your sincerity and maturity.

Which topics would you advise students to avoid addressing?

Ohio State: We would not want to restrict a student from addressing a topic which he or she felt compelled to write about since all information provided is used to assess whether or not the student is a good match for our program.

What's an example of a ridiculous achievement that you've seen referenced in a personal statement or essay?

Ohio State: Unless a student is simply trying to fill an application with activities and achievements, they list achievements that they feel are important.

State University of New York Upstate: "At age four I was reading human anatomy books for fun . . ."

INSIDE THE ADMISSIONS OFFICE

Do you have an overall mission statement that you follow when looking at personal statements, essays, and applications in general?

VCOM: Yes. The Mission of the Edward Via Virginia College of Osteopathic Medicine is to prepare osteopathic primary care physicians to serve the rural and medically underserved areas of the Commonwealth of Virginia, North Carolina, and the Appalachian region and to provide scientific research that will improve the health of all humans.

Ohio State: We use the previous year's entering class profile as a guide; we also look for evidence of altruism and professionalism.

State University of New York Upstate: We truly see the personal statement as the one place where we really get to know the student, the one place where they become more than just their numbers—it is our opportunity to see who they are and what they are all about.

How many personal statements do you and your staff receive? How many secondary essays? How much time do you spend reading each application? Each personal statement and essay?

VCOM: This year we will receive over 2,200 primary applications. We read the personal statement for all primary applications. We anticipate receiving over 600 secondary applications. Our secondary includes three essays. We spend 10-20 minutes on each application during a review session.

Ohio State: About 4,000 personal statements and about 5,800 secondary essays (we have two essay questions on our secondary application and we receive about 2,900 secondaries each year). On average we spend 5 to 10 minutes reading each application, including the personal statement and secondary essays.

State University of New York Upstate: Each AMCAS application has a personal statement, which we read; this year there were 3,800. We do not require secondary essays. Each application is reviewed at least twice and we do a thorough screen each time. The time varies—some can take 15 minutes to read and others can take half an hour.

What work experience do you require of the people who review applications? Are there any particular qualities you look for in a reader?

VCOM: In general, we restrict application review to senior administration. These individuals include our President, Dean, Vice President for Student Services, and Director of Admissions.

Ohio State: Previous admissions experience is essential. Fairness, compassion, and the ability to read between the lines are a few of the qualities that are useful.

State University of New York Upstate: Training and admissions experience.

Do you use an academic or other index initially to sort applications into "for sure," "maybe," and "long shot" piles? If not, how do you do your initial sorting?

VCOM: Yes. We place an extremely strong emphasis on the science GPA. We work with a minimum of 2.75 but our average science GPA is 3.4. We closely screen all applicants with a science GPA under 3.2.

Ohio State: We use a combination of grades, test scores, and experiences to sort applications into "invite to interview," "possibly interview," and "do not interview" groups.

State University of New York Upstate: We used to use a matrix that sorted applications based on GPA and MCAT scores, but now we review each application by hand once it is complete. There are so many variations in applications—e.g., lower MCATs with a really high GPA from an Ivy League institution, inconsistent MCATs, grad work and post-bacc course work, low verbal scores for ESL students; I worried about fairness. Reviewing each application by hand makes it more consistent.

If you have not already explained this, what is the process that each application undergoes, from receipt to decision? How many hands does it pass through on the way?

VCOM: When we review an AACOMAS application, we look at up to three categories of information—requirements, academics, and extracurricular activities. With regard to requirements, we want to ensure the applicant has completed or will complete their undergraduate degree before matriculation; that the applicant has completed or will complete the course requirements before matriculation; and that the applicant has a recent MCAT score (within the last three years). If the requirements have not been met, we send notification that we will be unable to proceed with the application for the current cycle. If the requirements have been met or will be met before matriculation, we look at the academics. We want to ensure that the GPA meets our minimum. If the minimum GPA has not been met, we send notification that we will be unable to proceed with the application for the current cycle. If the minimum GPA has been met, we take a closer look at the GPA and MCAT score. We review the academic and nonacademic portions of the AACOMAS application concurrently because we feel the extracurricular activities are just as important as the academic background. For a candidate to be competitive, it takes a range of nonacademic activities that speak to his or her interest in becoming a physician. We are not particular about what form these activities take. However, it is important that these activities reflect the candidate's passion for medicine and capacity for studying. Candidates [who] present a competitive AACOMAS application will be invited to submit a secondary application. Note: Not all of our candidates receive this invitation. Once the application is complete, we screen the application again to determine whether or not the candidate will be invited to Blacksburg for an interview.

Ohio State: When verified applications are received from AMCAS electronically, an e-mail is sent from our admissions office to the applicant providing them with access information to a personalized status page and the secondary application. From this status page, the applicant can track receipt of reference letters and view their application status in real time. Applicants are notified through the status page of their invitation to interview (if applicable) and of the Admissions Committee decision. The page is interactive, which allows the applicant to: confirm or reschedule an interview date; accept an offer of admission or withdraw; or accept or decline a scholarship award online. Applications are reviewed upon receipt of the AMCAS application, the secondary application, and MCAT scores, and pass through about four or five sets of hands. Applicants are invited to an on-campus interview about one month in advance of their scheduled date. Interviewed applicants receive an admission decision within two weeks of their interview date.

What steps do you take to recognize and prevent plagiarism? Do you have an institutional policy regarding plagiarism?

Ohio State: It would be very difficult to know if someone plagiarized his or her personal statement or essay responses. If it were discovered that any part of an application was plagiarized, it would be taken very seriously. Our students are required to sign a medical student honor code and conduct themselves in a professional manner.

THE INFLUENCE OF THE ESSAY

If you have an applicant with lower numbers (MCAT and GPA) but a great personal statement, what do you do? If the personal statement is unimpressive but the student's grades or MCAT scores are great, what then? Is it possible for a personal statement to change your mind about a candidate? And what kind of influence can secondary essays have?

VCOM: We place a strong emphasis on the science GPA as it is the best predictor of performance in our program. We do utilize the personal statement to learn about the candidates' passion for medicine. The personal statement and secondary essays can sway our decision to invite a candidate in for an interview.

Ohio State: If one part of an application is weak, we review the rest of the application materials to determine if the student will be invited to interview or not. There have been some instances where applicants wrote about inappropriate topics in the personal statement, which caused our Admissions Committee to believe they were not appropriate for our program. Responses to secondary essays can have a similar influence; they are used to provide additional information not found elsewhere in the application.

State University of New York Upstate: Yes, I think that the personal statement can have a huge impact on an admission decision, both positive and negative.

How is your decision affected by a perspective or opinion (expressed by an applicant in a personal statement or essay) with which you categorically disagree? What happens if you find the content offensive?

VCOM: All communications should show a well-thought-out point of view. We will likely not penalize a candidate for having an opinion that we merely disagree with. However, if we find content in a personal statement or essay offensive or unimpressive, then that can prevent a candidate from receiving an invitation for an interview.

Ohio State: If an interview is granted, more questioning will occur to determine how the student would handle situations in a patient care setting. They would most likely not be invited to interview if the content was more than a difference of values.

State University of New York Upstate: One applicant stated that "people are only sick because they choose to be." The thought of someone one day treating patients with this belief is scary. If your grades and MCATs are borderline, this only makes one more reason not to consider you further.

The low GPA/MCAT score explanation: When is this necessary? Unnecessary? How often does this change your mind? (Have you ever received any ridiculous explanations that you'd like to share?)

VCOM: Because we place such a strong emphasis on the GPA, we look for the candidate to provide an explanation for a low GPA. Reasonable explanations include: working full-time during college; a traumatic event or serious illness; the illness of a family member; or the birth of a child. We do not appreciate candidates who blame their performance in a class on the professor, or candidates who do not take appropriate personal responsibility for weaknesses.

Ohio State: It could be useful if there was an unusual dip in grades or if there was an unusual incident during the MCAT exam administration. One low grade does not necessarily need to be explained. Rarely do explanations for grades or MCAT scores change the Admissions Committee members' minds—the interview typically brings out other strengths and/or weaknesses; grades and MCAT scores are a part of the total application presented.

State University of New York Upstate: I think it is absolutely necessary to put something somewhere if you need to explain your scores. The last paragraph of the personal statement or a separate note to the admissions committee works fine for me. I just think it is really important for the student to clarify the reasons why something might be "off"—please don't leave what was going on in your life at that time up to my imagination or the imagination of 20 admissions committee members!

GENERAL APPLICATION QUESTIONS

If an element on the application is marked "optional," is it truly optional? If a candidate opts not to complete that part of the application, is his or her candidacy weakened?

VCOM: We do not include any optional portions on our application.

Ohio State: If applicants do not complete "optional" questions, their candidacy won't be adversely affected. Not completing other parts of either the AMCAS or secondary application denies us essential information, which could impact the outcome.

State University of New York Upstate: Yes, it is truly optional—it makes no difference to me.

Do applicants send extra material to you? If so, which materials are helpful? How much is too much?

VCOM: We only require two letters of recommendation—one from a premedical committee or science faculty member and one from an osteopathic physician. Some applicants also submit letters from supervisors, academic advisors, or allopathic physician mentors; we welcome these recommendations.

Ohio State: Yes. Information updating their application between the time they submit the AMCAS application and the time of the interview is helpful. Sending grades at the end of each term and complete manuscripts of research is not necessary.

State University of New York Upstate: Yes, additional information can be sent, but it can get out of hand. A LOR [letter of recommendation] from someone that the applicant shadowed, a supervisor, or an advisor is helpful, but a letter from a doctor that did your surgery when you were nine is not helpful. Also, please do not send videotapes, DVDs, CDs, 3" e-ring binders, or complete manuscripts—an abstract is fine. I do encourage applicants to send updated information in, particularly if they are interviewing in the spring and they submitted their AMCAS application the previous summer.

Do you regard or consider candidates who fulfilled their premedical requirements via a post-baccalaureate program rather than a premedical curriculum in college differently? If so, how? Is it beneficial for a student to complete premedical requirements within a particular channel? If so, which is preferable?

VCOM: We do not regard candidates who fulfilled their premedical requirements via a post-baccalaureate program differently.

Ohio State: No. We do, however, discourage applicants from completing the prerequisites at a two-year community college.

Do you find that students with a particular major (biochemistry, for example) are particularly well prepared for the challenges of medical school? If so, which major(s)?

VCOM: We do not hold any preferences regarding our candidates' undergraduate major. Consequently, for the Class of 2009 admissions cycle, we added an additional six hours of science as an entrance requirement. We feel this will better prepare our candidates, regardless of their major, for our medical school curriculum.

Ohio State: We don't. A strong science aptitude, regardless of major, will prepare students for the medical school curriculum.

Does coming from a specific, underrepresented-in-medical-school field (French, for example) help someone? Hurt someone?

Ohio State: We view these students as bringing much-needed diversity to the class.

How are nontraditional applicants viewed by the admissions office? What questions might you ask yourself while reading a nontraditional student's application that you wouldn't ask while reading a traditional student's application?

VCOM: We accepted a number of nontraditional applicants into our program this year. If a candidate has been out of the classroom for several years, we want to ensure that he or she is prepared for our curriculum.

Ohio State: Nontraditional applicants are viewed similarly as the nonscience applicants—they will bring a different level of diversity to the class. We try to determine how long they've been interested in a career in medicine. Is this a recent decision with no experience to back it up? What is their motivation?

Do you have a descending degree of importance that you assign the different application requirements? Is the MCAT score, for example, the most important measure of ability? Where do the personal statement and essays fall?

VCOM: We first consider the science GPA, then the essays, then lastly the MCAT.

Ohio State: We do not rank or assign percentage values to the different parts of the application.

State University of New York Upstate: I would say that grades and MCAT scores account for the largest part (about 65 to 70 percent) of each decision, followed by the personal statement, then extracurriculars—clinical, research, and service experiences.

If you had the option of doing away with the AMCAS (or ACOMAS) personal statement, would you? What about secondary application essays?

VCOM: We heavily weight the personal statement and essay responses. Thus, we would not support a decision to eliminate these portions of the applications.

Ohio State: Absolutely not! Although we change the secondary essay questions periodically, we will continue to use them to obtain additional information not found in other parts of either application. We use the personal statement and secondary essay questions to assist us in gaining insight into the applicant's thought processes, motivation, and commitment to a career in medicine.

State University of New York Upstate: No—I really value the personal statement. To me, it is the only place where the applicant truly becomes more than their "numbers." I want to learn something about the kind of person they are, what they are passionate about, what they value, and how they came to the decision to pursue medicine as a career. We do not require an additional essay.

Official Disclaimer!

Our editors aren't asleep on the job.

The following personal statements and secondary essays appear exactly as they did for medical school admissions officers. We only changed their layout so that they fit on the pages of this book. Because we have not edited them, you may find errors in spelling, punctuation, and grammar. We assure you that we found these errors as well, but we thought it would be most helpful for you to see what the medical school admissions officers saw—not what they could (or should) have seen. We recommend that you carefully proofread your own personal statement and secondary essays, but, should you miss an error, take comfort in the fact that others (accepted applicants, even!) sometimes did too.

CHAPTER 8

REAL PERSONAL STATEMENTS AND SECONDARY ESSAYS

ADAM DOUGLASS MARKS

Adam speaks Spanish and volunteered several summers in South and Central America. After college he worked as a research assistant at the Centers for Disease Control and Prevention in Atlanta, Georgia. He was an Eagle Scout and plays jazz saxophone.

Stats

MCAT: Physical Sciences, 12; Verbal Reasoning, 12; Writing
  Sample, R; Biological Sciences, 13

Undergraduate overall GPA: 3.79

Undergraduate science GPA: ~3.65

Undergraduate college attended: Kenyon College

Undergraduate graduation year: 2001

Gender: Male

Race: Caucasian

Applied To

Emory University, School of Medicine

Medical College of Georgia, School of Medicine

Ohio State University, College of Medicine and Public Health

State University of New York—University at Buffalo, School of
  Medicine and Biomedical Sciences

University of North Carolina—Chapel Hill, School of Medicine

University of Pittsburgh, School of Medicine

University of Virginia, School of Medicine

University of Wisconsin—Madison, School of Medicine and Public
  Health

AMCAS Personal Statement

It has been my experience that only a few memories stay with you through everything else. The details of most events blur, but certain special moments become a permanent part of who you are. When I think of the time I spent in Guatemala, I remember the lightning storms that came down the Toliman Mountains. As I was there during the rainy seasons, every day brought rain in one form or another, but rarely thunderstorms. On a few nights, however, walking back from the community hospital, I would see lightning playing off the mountains, silently at first, and then with increasing volume until I was running full tilt for the volunteers' dormitory, trying to escape the thundering sky.

I had come to Guatemala to familiarize myself with the daily activities of a doctor. Summers of volunteering and working in hospitals had given me the basic outline of what doctors did, but I felt that I had yet to understand what it really meant to be a physician. I hoped that working with medical teams in the rural highlands of Guatemala would give me a deeper insight into the profession. So, I went out with the teams, driving for an hour or two on mountain roads to the coffee plantations where the villages were located. I helped organize the temporary day-clinic, telling patients where to wait (Espera aqui, por favor), and asking them to tell the doctor their symptoms (Porque esta en la clinica hoy?). In the first few weeks, I derived a great deal of satisfaction from knowing that I was helping these people, that my work was bettering their lives. I felt good about myself, and was heartened by the thought that this feeling of satisfaction could be obtained by practicing medicine.

When I was not working, I spent time with the other workers and volunteers at the church in the town of San Lucas, where the medical program was based. One of the priests there was Father Carter, who had grown up in Guatemala, left for America to train as a priest, and then had returned to San Lucas. He was a big man who spoke two Mayan dialects in addition to Spanish and English, and he was a favorite among the local townspeople. He would often give talks to the visiting teams of doctors and medical students who came to work for a few weeks in the Toliman area. His talks usually started with a description of the "wrong" kind of help that he had seen during his years in San Lucas. He told of the people who came to San Lucas with the attitude of "helping these poor people." "This attitude," Father Carter would continue, "is dangerous for several reasons, the most of important of which is that it fosters a separation between you and those you serve. Such a separation can lead to a feeling that the people you help are themselves helpless, and allows you a position of superiority." Instead of seeing oneself as helping the people of Guatemala, Father Carter encouraged the medical teams and visiting volunteers to remember that they were working *with* the people, to bring about a better future for everyone. At the end of his talk, Father Carter would always urge us to recognize that "in serving others, you serve yourself."

Of all my experiences that summer, Father Carter's talk had the most profound effect on me, and like the lightning storms, is one of the first things I remember when I recall my time in Guatemala. I saw clearly in myself this feeling of superiority against which Father Carter had warned. I can vividly remember the way I analyzed my actions in the weeks following Father Carter's talk, and how my attitude separated me from the patients with whom I interacted. I struggled to overcome this attitude, and in my last few weeks, I felt that I was working towards something of value rather that undergoing just another summer experience. I still struggle with my tendency to think in terms of charity, and of giving to the poor less-fortunate. However, I left Guatemala with a clearer understanding of myself, and how medicine would give me a way to help myself and others in a meaningful way.

See page 250 to find out where this student got in.

BRANDON DEVERS

Brandon worked two summers at the National Institutes of Health (NIH) and conducted research at the National Institute for Neurological Disorders and Stroke (NINDS), where he was awarded the Exceptional Summer Student Award. After his sophomore year, he worked at the National Human Genome Research Institute (NHGRI). He also played varsity football for four years, volunteered as a tutor for Horton's Kids, and coached a youth basketball team.

Stats

MCAT: Physical Sciences, 12; Verbal Reasoning, 12; Writing Sample, N; Biological Sciences, 11

Undergraduate overall GPA: 3.60

Undergraduate science GPA: 3.55

Undergraduate college attended: Princeton University

Undergraduate graduation year: 2005

Gender: Male

Race: African American

Applied To

Baylor College of Medicine

Duke University, School of Medicine

Johns Hopkins University, School of Medicine

Stanford University, School of Medicine

University of California—Los Angeles, David Geffen School of Medicine

University of California—San Francisco, School of Medicine

University of Kentucky, College of Medicine

Washington University in St. Louis, School of Medicine

AMCAS Personal Statement

When I was twelve, riots broke out in my city after a white police officer shot and killed a black teenager. I remember my parents waking me up around midnight to inform me that they had to leave immediately and did not know when they would be back. It was my responsibility to watch over my younger siblings, wake them up in the morning, feed them breakfast, and make sure that we were all ready for our carpool to school. I can still picture my parents emerging from downstairs clad in full riot gear. They were wearing bulletproof vests, carrying guns, and each had a protective helmet in hand. That was the first time I remember thinking to myself that I may never see my parents again. While I was overcome with this dread and confusion, I also knew that I had three younger siblings who were depending on me. That experience not only taught me the value of responsibility, but also engraved in me a deep respect for life. Not only was I twelve and facing the fact that my parents could die at any moment, I also came to the realization that my parents were actively putting their lives at risk to protect the lives of others. This was very inspiring and it influenced my views on life, personal interactions, and civility. I believe that this and similar early experiences not only helped shape me into the person I am today, but have also led in part to my interests in medicine, especially my desire to help others.

While my early environment and experiences instilled in me an interest in serving more than just myself, my later experiences with medicine linked this desire to serve and help others with a profession that fulfilled these interests. After undergoing shoulder surgery, I was invited to shadow the surgeon who had operated on me for a week to observe his rounds and surgeries. I remember the anticipation I felt dressing up in nurse's scrubs and stepping into the operating room. Although I observed surgeries repeatedly for three straight days, I never lost interest in the experience. I was captivated by each surgical procedure and the explanations that accompanied them. Yet, the most rewarding experience throughout the week was visiting the patients afterwards in the recovery ward. Just being a part of that experience and witnessing the joy and appreciation of the patient and his or her family upon recovery was amazing. I also noticed how adamantly the families thanked the surgeon and that he knew each family member's name. I believe that this type of personal interaction and the establishment of a trustworthy relationship with the patient and his or her family are imperative in practicing quality medicine. While this experience exposed me to the direct and individual service a doctor can provide for his or her patients, later experiences also showed me that medicine can provide the opportunity for service on a more global level in a group oriented setting.

This past summer I worked at the National Human Genome Research Institute (NHGRI). It was exiting to be at the forefront of genomics research during these times of rapid discovery, insight, and technology development. I was especially interested in projects and meetings concerning gene discovery and therapy directed towards improving medical treatments for a variety of disorders such as cystic fibrosis. While the experience itself was rewarding and educational, I was also impressed by how brilliant and interesting the people I was working for were. Yet, what impressed me the most was how they all worked together.

Furthermore, although I was the least experienced member of the group, they all listened intently to my opinions and suggestions during meetings and small conferences. While being an athlete has always taught me the value of teamwork, this experience taught me its importance and applicability in the real world. I believe this concept of teamwork is critical in the medical profession. While each doctor is intelligent and possesses his or her own personal skills and talents, the advancements in health care that we enjoy today did not stem from one or several different individuals working alone. Instead, they reflect the vast network of health professionals working together to gain insight and knowledge from one another with the common goal of improving medicine and health care in general. As a doctor, I would strive to establish networks and consult with other physicians, as this interaction is invaluable from both a health care and academic standpoint. Thus, my experience at the NHGRI helped to reinforce my value of teamwork and further define the type of medicine I want to practice. Although these two experiences exposed me to two distinct sides of the medical profession, they both taught me that the primary interest of the medical field is the service of others. These experiences, among others, resonate strongly with my interests and goals, which were engrained in me at an early age. It is important to me that I am able to lie down each night and know that I have actually helped someone and improved the quality of his or her life. This may occur through direct patient care or simply through the establishment of a worthwhile doctor patient relationship.

See page 250 to find out where this student got in.

CAELAN JOHNSON

As an undergrad, Caelan did psychiatric neuroimaging research. She graduated with general honors and with departmental honors from her school's Neuroscience and Spanish departments. During her post-baccalaureate year, she worked a tutor and volunteered at a pediatric hospital. The following year she worked as a pediatric dental assistant.

Stats

MCAT: Physical Sciences, 8; Verbal Reasoning, 11; Writing Sample, P; Biological Sciences, 12

Undergraduate overall GPA: 3.64

Undergraduate science GPA: 3.51

Undergraduate college attended: Johns Hopkins University

Undergraduate graduation year: 2003

Gender: Female

Race: Caucasian

Applied To

Case Western Reserve University, School of Medicine

Loyola University Chicago, Stritch School of Medicine

Northwestern University, Feinberg School of Medicine

Rush University, Rush Medical College

Southern Illinois University, School of Medicine

University of Chicago, Pritzker School of Medicine

University of Illinois at Chicago, UIC College of Medicine

University of Iowa, Roy J. and Lucille A. Carver College of Medicine

University of Wisconsin—Madison, School of Medicine and Public Health

Washington University in St. Louis, School of Medicine

AMCAS Personal Statement

My inspiration to pursue medicine came from an aunt who completed an MD/PhD when I was in grade school. She visited us often and spent hours describing the remarkable things she learned. Now, as a retinal surgeon and mother of four, she illustrates the joys and challenges of balancing a family with practicing medicine. As an adult, I see her path as something for which numerous experiences in my life have prepared me: academic, cultural, work- and family-related, and others. I put a lot of thought into pursuing medicine, and am extremely motivated to become a physician. The field of medicine integrates many of my academic and personal interests, such as human biology, anthropology, and helping people understand and address issues regarding health and living.

The art of communication has always intrigued me. I spent my childhood in culturally diverse areas of Wisconsin, Illinois, and Ohio, and I continue to have a deep desire to learn how other cultures communicate. I enjoy poetry, in both English and Spanish, and editing, and I have received literary honors and awards for excellence in both Spanish and English. More importantly, however, I view communication as an essential tool for problem-solving. Through various jobs, travels, and life experiences I have noted that improved communication not only solves problems but can preclude them as well. After completion of my two months at Escuela Internacional in Salamanca, Spain, I decided that I want to incorporate Spanish fluency into my career. I would love to work with the largely underserved Midwestern Hispanic population in a healthcare setting, to help improve the quality of their care.

The development of the brain has also interested me; because I have taught, counseled and observed children, I have considered the fields of child psychiatry, pediatrics, and pediatric neurology. From the age of fifteen, I worked with children at a day camp in Illinois. By my fifth year there, I ran the camp when the Director was gone, took charge of disruptive campers, and interacted regularly with parents, who can be the most challenging aspect of working with children. I dealt with discipline problems and learned about diplomacy in delicate situations, reprimanding without adding to the problem, and motivating kids to behave. My recent experiences shadowing the attending physician on the schizophrenia service at the Johns Hopkins Hospital showed me that some of the same problem-solving skills I utilized at camp are essential in medicine. This year I will continue to interact with children and parents as a dental assistant in a pediatric practice in Illinois.

Through my work with children, I have come to see the importance of education in everyone's life. Assisting in a Spanish class at Baltimore City College High School and volunteering at Mt. Washington Pediatric Hospital helped me realize my ideal role would be a mix of teacher, social activist, and healthcare provider: a physician. I found that I was less interested in teaching kids about a specific subject than in making sure they knew how to deal with other people, make good decisions in life, communicate with those around them, and take care of themselves. I also discovered that I couldn't ignore my love of Neuroscience. During the year I focused on Spanish, I still read every brain-related article I could find and really missed my science coursework. It was while studying in Spain that I resolved that the best way for me to pursue my interests in Spanish and Neuroscience and meaningful interaction with people would be through medicine. When I returned to Baltimore, I renewed my double major status, and have thoroughly enjoyed courses like psychopharmacology and general biology.

As a part of the Neuroscience curriculum, I worked on a few studies as a research assistant doing volumetric analysis of structural MRI data at the Johns Hopkins University School of Medicine. What I love most about the systems approach to the brain is that it ties back into how we communicate, on numerous levels. Each element of communication, such as emotion, speech production, word recognition, sensory cues, and cognition has its own area, but they are all connected, and the information must be passed on to the body so that it can respond appropriately. The communication between physician and patient is analogous to that between the brain and the body in that the physician must effectively convey her knowledge for the patient to use and benefit from it. I want to be a physician in order to use my knowledge of language and science to creatively help people deal with their health and life issues. Medical school will give me the education I need to achieve this goal, and the opportunity to continue to grow in my understanding of others and myself.

See page 250 to find out where this student got in.

COLLEEN KNIFFIN

Colleen volunteered for a year with a medical service organization in Africa before attending college. While in school, she continued to work in the medical field and held a job as a patient care technician at a local hospital. She also oversaw a campus-wide mentoring program, organized an annual conference on volunteer service, and ran freshman orientation.

Stats

MCAT: Physical Sciences, 11; Verbal Reasoning, 10; Writing Sample, S; Biological Sciences, 12

Undergraduate overall GPA: 3.77

Undergraduate science GPA: 3.70

Undergraduate college attended: Wheaton College (IL)

Undergraduate graduation year: 2003

Gender: Female

Race: Caucasian

Applied To

Baylor College of Medicine

Loma Linda University, School of Medicine

University of California—Davis, School of Medicine

University of California—Los Angeles, David Geffen School of Medicine

University of California—San Diego, School of Medicine

University of Illinois at Chicago, UIC College of Medicine

University of Minnesota—Duluth, Medical School

University of Minnesota—Twin Cities, Medical School

University of Southern California, Keck School of Medicine

AMCAS Personal Statement

I remember waking that morning to the rooster's crow just as the sun peaked over treetops of the rain forest. By that time, the small Ghanaian village was already bustling with activity as people left to work in the cocoa fields. I fumbled in the folds of my mosquito net until I found the opening and slid my feet onto the cold cement floor. Locating some clothes stacked on the floor of my perpetually dark mud hut, I dressed quickly and made my way to the mission compound, greeting each villager along the way with "Daayo" ("good morning" in Twí).

I soon found the doctor that I was shadowing during my two month stay in the village (the second portion of a five month program with the medical non-profit organization, Mercy Ships). Dr. Gurling introduced me to a young African who had stepped on a thorn a week earlier. Following his tribal practice, the boy had packed the large wound with mud, leading to an infection. Dr. Gurling, who needed to see other patients, asked if I would care for the boy. I gathered antiseptics and knelt down to clean the wound. Between winces of pain, the patient flashed me beautiful smiles of gratitude. I fought back tears of joy as he hugged me when I finished. If the doctor or I had not been there to help, the boy's foot would have become dangerously infected. My tears flowed from the knowledge that I had given a gift that the boy may not otherwise have received—health.

There is something significant about providing healthcare. Even more extraordinary is offering health to those who would otherwise be helpless. Someday, whether by traveling again to a small Ghanaian village or by volunteering weekly in an inner city clinic, I want to be involved in giving health to those in desperate need. Obtaining that ability is one thing that greatly excites me about becoming a physician.

From another experience with Mercy Ships, I can recall the lines, a thousand people long, on the pier next to the hospital ship. During this screening week the Africans would wait for days hoping to get a doctor's appointment. Had that ship not been there, many would have suffered to their death. But, because a handful of doctors used their vacation time to volunteer in Africa, those otherwise hopeless people were given health. I want to be involved in that type of medical work.

There are many other ways to bring relief to suffering and desperate people. Doing social work or lobbying for the underprivileged offer good alternatives. So then, "Why medicine?" you may ask. "Why accrue a huge educational debt and dedicate many years in medical training?" I struggled with this question for a while myself and, after much introspection, have formulated two answers.

First, my passion for providing desperate people with healthcare is conveniently supported by both my aptitude and affinity for scientific study. Throughout high school and college biology and chemistry classes have been my most rewarding and enjoyable academic pursuits. I love the sense of achievement when I finally understand how a complicated chemical reaction progresses. While my classmates are preparing to graduate from college and "been done with school", I feel I have only sipped from the ocean of information that I want to learn. There is so much to know about the structure and function of the human body.

Second, through my hospital work experience I witnessed the profound emotional effects that can be made on people by simply healing their body. I remember realizing this during one night in particular. I was bathing an elderly woman who was very sick and quite delirious. As I changed her diaper I recall wondering why I was at a job where so much of my work was not even comprehended by those I was helping. It smelled bad. I was tired. I wanted to go home. A few moments later, however, as I rubbed lotion into her feet, the elderly woman opened her eyes, grasped my hand, and gave me that same unforgettable look that I had seen on the African boy. She smiled because I had tended for her physically and, being near death, she cared about her health above all else. The gleam in the woman's eyes, however, also revealed that through my corporeal touch, I had ministered to her emotionally as well. At that moment I realized the strong impact that one can have on people, emotionally as well as physically, who are desperate for medical attention. This experience confirmed my desire to provide healthcare above any other type of social service.

I recognize that I hold lofty ideals of serving those who would otherwise receive no care. However, these dreams are also balanced by a comprehension of the difficult realities of medicine. Through my job at the hospital I learned that overnight shifts are not easy. There is endless paperwork. Decisions need to be quick and correct despite stressful conditions. And most importantly, patients do not often offer the "grateful African boy" smile.

These truths, although they have not frustrated my dreams, have caused me to realize the amount of discipline, dedication and unshakable vision that will be required to achieve my goals. I am ready for the challenge.

See page 251 to find out where this student got in.

DAN NAYLOR

Dan volunteered for two-and-a-half years on a research project that examined the relationship between a "Western" — i.e. high sugar, high fat, low fiber — diet and the chronic low-level inflammation characteristic of a number of disease states. He also worked for a year at a lab that focused on iron absorption and metabolism research. At school, he was a member of the University of California Marching Band for four years and achieved many leadership positions within the group. He was also a leader in the music program of a religious fellowship for a year. He shadowed a local pediatrician for a semester and worked at the biosciences library on campus.

Stats

MCAT: Physical Sciences, 11; Verbal Reasoning, 10; Writing Sample, Q; Biological Sciences, 14

Undergraduate overall GPA: 3.46

Undergraduate science GPA: 3.38

Undergraduate college attended: University of California — Berkeley

Undergraduate graduation year: 2004

Gender: Male

Race: Caucasian

Applied To

Boston University, School of Medicine

Case Western Reserve University, School of Medicine

Dartmouth College, Dartmouth Medical School

Drexel University, College of Medicine

Duke University, School of Medicine

George Washington University, School of Medicine and Health Sciences

Georgetown University, School of Medicine

Harvard University, Harvard Medical School

Johns Hopkins University, School of Medicine

Loma Linda University, School of Medicine

New York Medical College

New York University, NYU School of Medicine

Northwestern University, Feinberg School of Medicine

Oregon Health & Science University, School of Medicine

Pennsylvania State University, College of Medicine

Stanford University, School of Medicine

Thomas Jefferson University, Jefferson Medical College

Tulane University, School of Medicine

University of California—Davis, School of Medicine

University of California—Irvine, College of Medicine

University of California—Los Angeles, David Geffen School of
Medicine

University of California—San Diego, School of Medicine

University of California—San Francisco, School of Medicine

University of Chicago, Pritzker School of Medicine

University of Michigan, Medical School

University of Vermont, College of Medicine

University of Southern California, Keck School of Medicine

Vanderbilt University, School of Medicine

Yale University, School of Medicine

AMCAS Personal Statement

The shrill sound of the whistle echoed through the tunnel, and nervous anticipation quickly turned to excitement as we rushed onto the field. After hours of practice learning and refining the skills necessary to put on a dazzling performance with the University of California Marching Band, I finally high-stepped into Memorial Stadium for the first time, and was suddenly surrounded by tens of thousands of fans. The long, exhausting days of training and a spirit of dedication to the university showed their value in a performance that left those in the stadium cheering with pride and appreciation.

I devoted countless hours over the next four years to this entirely student-run organization. I served through numerous leadership roles, involving everything from leading musical rehearsals and interacting with big financial donors at fundraising events, to performing first aid duties such as bandaging light wounds and calling 911 for band members in life-threatening situations. On a campus of over fifteen times the number of people living in my rural hometown, the band was an effective way to develop a sense of belonging. However, the transition to college was less successful than I had hoped. I found myself caught up in the new experiences of living with hundreds of people my own age, band-related commitments and a part-time job. With so many distractions, my grades suffered, and I ended my first year frustrated but motivated to improve. That summer, I excelled in my organic chemistry class, and having convinced myself that I could do well, I renewed my long-developing interest in becoming a physician. I decided to pursue a major in molecular and cell biology, and focused on learning more about the profession.

There is no single event in my life that I look back on and say, "This is when I decided to become a doctor." Though my mother is a clinical laboratory scientist, neither of my parents is a doctor, and they never specifically suggested that I become one. For me, the decision has been more gradual and natural. I've always loved investigating the world around me: I happily caught lizards in the front yard at five years old, and was looking at blood smears under my mom's microscope at age ten. During middle and high school, my reading interests centered on a number of books about veterinarians, neurosurgeons, and the deadly Ebola virus. More recently, I've confirmed my ability to think scientifically, perform detailed procedures, and produce accurate results in collaboration with other scientists during my internship and employment in a nutritional genomics laboratory at Children's Hospital in Oakland, California. We are attempting to elucidate the connection between a poor diet and low-level inflammatory conditions such as childhood obesity, diabetes, arthrosclerosis, and possibly even cancer. My own work consists primarily of observing gene expression in the tissues of mice chosen from inflammation-prone genetic backgrounds and fed a variety of unhealthy diets. Through this study, I hope to see evidence of an increase in inflammatory mediators brought on by the bad diets.

As a complement to my scientific interests, I've always been drawn to care for and motivate others. This has been most evident in my work with children at summer day camps in the eight years before college, during which I rose to become a senior leader in the last three years, and my people-oriented leadership in the Cal Band. I have also begun supporting and encouraging others with my interest in music, playing the guitar and singing at my church. It has been a natural, more personal extension of my ability to lead others than was expressed through the Cal Band. I have led musical worship regularly now for the college and high school groups, and for the adult religious services, attended by hundreds of people.

Hoping to acquire some grasp of the trials doctors face every day in the practice of their scientific and relational talents, I recently shadowed a pediatrician over the course of a semester. I became more clearly aware of the breadth of a doctor's responsibilities: the long days, extensive paperwork, and the daily confrontation with the heart-tugging trials of human life. And I resolutely accept them, because from the very first visit with this doctor, I began to see just how rewarding the profession can be.

"Dr. Wolffe" was a huge man with a heart to match. I followed him down the silent hallway into the examination room for the first time, and there sat a young Latina mother gently cradling her child, only a few weeks old. The doctor's evident confidence in his years of training and his commitment to medical science, complemented by his ability to truly care for someone, showed their value in the trusting smile on the face of that young woman. This and every other visit helped me realize that my lifelong attraction to the medical profession does not arise from a grand vision to rid the world of cancer or childhood obesity. Rather, it is my intention to use my growing knowledge and skills in concert with my concern for others to fight such problems, one person at a time.

See page 251 to find out where this student got in.

EDDIE SILVER

Eddie shadowed an orthopedic surgeon the summer before his senior year and was involved in one of the doctor's research projects. He also played on the varsity tennis team and intramural basketball team and worked at a Hillel Soup Kitchen.

Stats

MCAT: Physical Sciences, 11; Verbal Reasoning, 11; Writing
  Sample, Q; Biological Sciences, 9
Undergraduate overall GPA: 3.79
Undergraduate science GPA: 3.72
Undergraduate college attended: University of Pennsylvania
Undergraduate graduation year: 2006
Gender: Male
Race: Caucasian

Applied To

Thomas Jefferson University, Jefferson Medical College (early
  decision)

AMCAS Personal Statement

I want to dedicate myself to the study of medicine because I have a very strong interest in health, nutrition, and rehabilitative and preventative medicine, and believe that there is no better way for me to contribute to society. Over the past few years, the reading I have most enjoyed includes the latest medical and nutritional research, as well as issues in medical sociology. There is nothing that I would find more worthwhile than studying and practicing medicine.

Attending college in West Philadelphia has afforded me a glimpse into the vast economic disparities that plague our communities. As a director of Hillel's Sunday Night Soup Kitchen, I spend time with economically and socially disadvantaged individuals each week, and have experienced first hand the correlation between economic well-being and health, which has been thoroughly illustrated to me as a Health and Societies major at Penn. Volunteering at the soup kitchen has been both an educational and motivating experience. I have learned about some of the medical issues that face the working and non-working poor, including nutritional deficiencies, child health care needs, and prescription coverage problems. While it has been rewarding to participate in this food distribution program, I believe it would be even more satisfying to directly impact people's lives as a physician. I want to study medicine because of the dire need for quality health care for the economically disadvantaged, and hope to be a part of a generation of physicians who work towards lessening health and social disparities.

I credit my initial interest in health and nutrition largely to my passionate desire to succeed in sports. The abuse I have done to my body as an athlete made me a permanent fixture in my orthopedist's office throughout my high school and college athletic careers. My freshman tennis season in high school was over before it ever started due to hamstring tendonitis. After a frustrating year without tennis, I hit the courts as a sophomore determined to improve my game. That spring I had a successful campaign at number one singles, and spent every Saturday and Sunday working on my game for several hours a day. By the time I played the first national tournament of the summer, I had so thoroughly weakened my ankles that an awkward landing on my foot after an overhead attempt left me with two fractures and ligament damage in my left ankle. After a vigorous summer rehabilitation process, I again made it back to the courts, this time with such determination that I achieved my best national junior singles ranking of 138.

My college tennis career has only reinforced the reality that my body was not meant for hitting tennis balls eighteen hours a week. Each year I played through pain, and each summer I rehabilitated a severely weakened rotator cuff and a chronically inflamed biceps tendon. I credit my interest in fitness, strength training, rehabilitative medicine, nutrition, and my own resolve (some might say stubbornness) for my ability to compete in a sport for which my body was not designed. My experience as an athlete has reinforced my belief in the healing power of medicine. I also believe that this experience has helped me to develop my resolve, which should enable me to become a patient, understanding, and dedicated physician.

In the past, I combined my passion for tennis with my desire to help improve the lives of others through my involvement in Arthur Ashe's wheelchair tennis clinics. Helping this group learn to play tennis was most satisfying, and I became more optimistic about the ability to heal the body, mind, and spirit. After my sophomore year in college, I learned about the lives of children suffering from juvenile rheumatoid arthritis, as a counselor at Camp Victory. These experiences reinforced my desire to help others overcome their physical limitations and pain.

This summer I have become even more committed to pursuing a medical career. Volunteering in the Section of Orthopedic Surgery at St. Christopher's Hospital for Children,

I have watched my own pediatric orthopedist, Dr. Pizzutillo, and his partner, Dr. Herman, care for children debilitated by hip disease and scoliosis. Observing the very physician who repeatedly expedited my return from injury, and helping him document a study of growth plate ankle fractures in children has been especially interesting.

Please give me the opportunity to gain access to the medical knowledge that will enable me to help narrow the health divide plaguing our country, and assist my future patients in enjoying life to the fullest extent possible.

See page 252 to find out where this student got in.

ERIC RANDOLPH SCOTT

As an undergraduate, Eric participated in bioethics, philosophy, and interdisciplinary academic organizations. He volunteered at a local hospital, worked for the American Cancer Society, and worked with a mentor in the field of oncology. His was on several Dean's Lists, a member of Phi Beta Kappa, and a part of UVA's Echols Scholars Program. He took full advantage of his summers by doing laboratory research and taking summer classes. One summer, he studied comparative bioethics in London. He also participated in religious organizations, intramural sports, and political organizations.

Stats

MCAT: Physical Sciences, 11; Verbal Reasoning, 11; Writing Sample, R; Biological Sciences, 11

Undergraduate overall GPA: 3.70

Undergraduate science GPA: 3.83

Undergraduate college attended: University of Virginia

Undergraduate graduation year: 2003

Gender: Male

Race: Caucasian

Applied To

Boston University, School of Medicine

Dartmouth College, Dartmouth Medical School

Duke University, School of Medicine

Georgetown University, School of Medicine

Johns Hopkins University, School of Medicine

University of Chicago, Pritzker School of Medicine

University of Virginia, School of Medicine

Virginia Commonwealth University, School of Medicine

Wake Forest University, School of Medicine

Yale University, School of Medicine

AMCAS Personal Statement

The world is a harsh place. That is a position I think is indisputable. We all have challenges and obstacles we must overcome. Taking difficult classes, competing with your friends for precious few high grades, or overcoming shyness to approach faculty for recommendation letters. These are obstacles for many people. They are mere trivialities, however, with the proper perspective. The true struggles are those that threaten one's very life and well-being. Nature forces us to face countless difficulties each day; among them epidemics affecting multitudes, bodies wasting away leaving helpless loved ones, or the death of a child–the most innocent of us all. The suffering caused by these natural processes would certainly be sufficient, but there are also those sufferings inflicted on man by man. Combined, these evils can seem overwhelming. I believe it is each man's task to stem this tide of pain in whatever way they are capable.

I cannot claim that the origin of my desire to be a doctor is to help other people. I grew up in a hospital; my first memories are of doctors and hospitals. I had acute lymphoblastic leukemia, and was in and out of the hospital throughout my childhood. Many of these memories are not vague recollections of events, but vivid impressions of emotions–fear, pain, happiness, relief, and hope. For whatever reason I came out of this experience asserting that I wanted to be a doctor, a position I have maintained to this day. The ambition to be a doctor is not one that is discouraged by those around you. It is not hard to see why people are reluctant to leave the medical track, even when they find they are not suited to it. I do not believe I have remained in the track merely out of habit, however. In fact, I think it is almost miraculous the degree to which medicine is what I now desire to do.

My motivation now comes from several perspectives. The first is the pursuit of knowledge. Frankly, I love to learn and participate in the process of discovery. Science, history, literature, mathematics, and politics can all hold my attention. I do not think, however, there is anything more marvelous or contains more mysteries than the human body. Medicine allows me to pursue my desire for scientific knowledge. During my undergraduate years I have also developed a passion for philosophy. Chief among my interests in philosophy is ethics–how we should live our lives. The field of medicine is one that presents (and will continue to present) unique and serious issues that require answers. These problems are not merely abstract, but are faced daily by practitioners and must be answered to set social policy. I have a strong desire to participate in the dialogue to answer these questions. Finally, I have experienced the good that medicine can do. From my experiences as a patient, volunteer, and observer of medical professionals I have a sincere appreciation of the burden placed on a physician. Every visit a doctor makes in a day can dramatically change a life. Each visit is an opportunity to do good, however, and improve someone's quality of life. I cannot imagine a more gratifying life than doing such good on a daily basis.

There have been times I have questioned my resolve to be a physician. The most significant of these, I believe, occurred while I was studying in London. In an off-hand remark the head of admissions to St. Thomas medical school questioned the British policy of accepting students into medical school at the age of eighteen. She reflected: "Sometimes I wonder if what we're doing is right. We're taking our brightest, most creative students and turning them into human computer terminals." This affected me a great deal. I think she gave voice to a concern I had in the back of my mind. Is medicine just about memorizing and regurgitating at the appropriate time? Might a profession in academics be better than being an over-priced reference book? Having given the question thought I think the answer is no. The ideal practice of medicine is not reducible to diagnosis and distribution of drugs. Rather, proper care requires someone to care for the patient. Having experienced prolonged care I am confident the human aspect is not trivial. Receiving medical care can be a very scary thing, and any comforting can reduce the inevitable fear and anxiety. A kind look, pleasant small-talk, or the development of a trusting friendship can each help alleviate distress. A human being who cares is necessary for such relationships to occur, however.

Lastly, I want to be a doctor because I think I would be a good doctor. Despite my other motivations I do not think I could enter a profession that I could not excel in. I have the sincere belief I will be a good doctor, however. I believe I have the analytic and communication skills critical for success. Likewise, I have a temperament and a sympathetic outlook that I think are conducive to long-term success in the medical profession. I believe that to squander ability is wrong. I believe it is a moral imperative to use one's gifts in the proper ways. The medical profession is a proper way to harness potential. Though idealistic, I envision the good doctor as a model human being–using his reason to assist his neighbor in combating evils of the world. This is a vision I would like to have of myself.

Fundamentally the medical profession is based on healing and the reduction of suffering. I believe no other profession has an ethos as noble as that of the medical field. It is an ethos I could envision holding for my entire professional career. Likewise, I am motivated not only by the ends of medicine, but the means as well. The scientific and moral aspects of medicine are things that excite me. I think a good doctor should also understand why they hold their ethos, or they do not hold it at all. The justification for having such a creed is that to heal and relieve suffering are goods, some of the greatest goods men are capable of producing. To argue for the legitimacy of the state Thomas Hobbes claimed that a state of nature would be "solitary, poor, nasty, brutish and short." I believe life can still be that way for many. It is the moral task of each of us to try and eliminate that life not only for ourselves but also those around us. Those in the medical profession are uniquely qualified to aid this goal. By facilitating health, medicine facilitates man's growth, creation, and achievements. I hope I am given the opportunity to participate in such accomplishments.

See page 252 to find out where this student got in.

FAWN LANGERMAN

After earning her undergraduate degree, Fawn had a twelve-year career in engineering. Her first exposure to the medical field came as a volunteer at the Free Clinic of Greater Cleveland, where she screened people seeking HIV tests. Following that experience, she took a basic EMT class and worked Saturdays on an ambulance. To satisfy medical school prerequisites, she took 40 credits of biology, chemistry, and biological chemistry courses at Cleveland State University, where she maintained a 4.0 GPA. She worked full-time in an emergency room for a year before applying to medical school.

Stats

MCAT: Physical Science, 10; Verbal Reasoning, 12; Writing Sample, O; Biological Sciences, 10

Undergraduate overall GPA: 3.07

Undergraduate science GPA: 2.79

Undergraduate college attended: Cornell University

Undergraduate graduation year: 1990

Gender: Female

Race: Caucasian

Applied To

Case Western Reserve University, School of Medicine

Georgetown University, School of Medicine

Johns Hopkins University, School of Medicine

Ohio State University, College of Medicine and Public Health

Oregon Health & Science University, School of Medicine

University of Cincinnati, College of Medicine

AMCAS Personal Statement

The path less traveled is generally my path of choice. Some would say that the path most challenging is most intriguing to me. There is certainly plenty of data to support both statements; I am a female mechanical engineer and a female EMT. I chose Russian language to fulfill my high school language requirement. My idea of a good vacation is cycling and camping; the longer the mileage and the higher the hills to climb, the happier I am. But, most significantly and most obviously, I chose to leave a lucrative and intellectually easy career to start over, at 34 years old, in medicine.

The decision to leave engineering for a career in medicine did not come to me in a flash of insight or a vivid dream. It was founded gradually, after years of escalating interest in philanthropy coinciding with escalating frustration with the superficiality of the corporate world.

My path to medicine was non-linear and slow simply because it is quite intoxicating to be told repeatedly that you are the "best of the best," and "part of the next generation of corporate leaders." That my success was attained with so little sweat on my brow became more and more disconcerting to me. I began to change companies, hoping to find personal and emotional satisfaction, combined with effort commensurate with my success, in other corporate arenas. (I left GE, after 7 years, in 1997. I spent 2.5 years with a Tier 2 automotive parts supplier, .5 years with a small industrial manufacturer and then 2 years with larger industrial manufacturer.)

What I was seeking could not be found in the corporate world. In 1997, parallel with my first major job change, I went looking for an "extracurricular activity." Simply by chance I found the volunteer position at the Free Clinic of Greater Cleveland, and from that point on my life was changed. Sounds melodramatic, but it is quite true. My job was to screen people seeking HIV tests, in order to insure that they were educated about HIV risks and the AIDS disease. The standard final question, before taking the person to the phlebotomy area, was,

"Were you to test positive for the HIV virus, would you hurt yourself or someone else?" The volunteer training class taught me to listen to carefully to the answer of that question and, if that question were ever answered yes, to continue to listen and to bring in the Free Clinic psych services. The incidence of affirmative answer was quite low, but one day I came upon a potentially suicidal person. I spent almost an hour with her, just listening, and then spent another hour helping her transition to the psych services. About a month later she came back to the HIV testing area and gave me a hug; she told me that I had saved her life. I never saved anyone's life in an engineering capacity; I had never felt that I had had quite that strong of a personal effect on another human being via a job.

That was the first of countless positive interactions there, and in subsequent volunteer positions. I volunteered for six months in an ER and then for one year on a hotline. Volunteering can only take one so far, and my growing interest in the medical field led me to take an EMT-Basic class.

Upon completion I began my part-time medicine / full-time engineering life. As I progressed, it became more and more clear that I was spending my week looking forward to my Saturday ambulance work. The more that I saw of medicine and patients, the more that I wanted to learn about medicine, and about how it can help patients.

From that point, the path was clear. Compared to the amount of time that it took me to figure out that engineering had ceased to be personally, emotionally and intellectually fulfilling (five years), it took me a relatively short amount of time to sell my house, leave engineering, go back to school (biology and chemistry classes) and go to work in an emergency room (one year.) My emergency room job provides daily motivation for my career-change decision; as I watch and learn from the ER doctors and specialists, I grow more and more sure that my choice has been correct. This path feels right; I feel good about what I have the potential to do and I am excited to begin the journey of medical school!!

Thank you for your time and interest in my application.

See page 252 to find out where this student got in.

HEATHER NELSON

After college, Heather worked as a report analyst for a managed-care organization and trained in both acute- and long-term-care facilities to be a nursing assistant. She also got involved in an organization that took an interdisciplinary approach to health care, providing part-time care, nursing, general medicine, and public health services. She pursued interests outside of health care as well, including running, coaching a high school academic debate team, and volunteering with organizations such as Habitat for Humanity.

Stats

MCAT: Physical Sciences, 10; Verbal Reasoning, 10; Writing Sample, R; Biological Sciences, 11

Graduate school GPA: 3.90

Graduate school attended: University of Minnesota, School of Public Health

Graduate school graduation year: 2005

Graduate degree earned: Master of Public Health (MPH)

Undergraduate overall GPA: 3.80

Undergraduate science GPA: 3.60

Undergraduate college attended: Gustavus Adolphus College

Undergraduate graduation year: 2000

Gender: Female

Race: Caucasian

Applied To

Creighton University, School of Medicine

Emory University, School of Medicine

Medical College of Wisconsin

Pennsylvania State University, College of Medicine

Tulane University, School of Medicine

University of Illinois at Chicago, UIC College of Medicine

University of Minnesota—Duluth, Medical School

University of Minnesota—Twin Cities, Medical School

University of North Carolina—Chapel Hill, UNC School of Medicine

University of Pittsburgh, School of Medicine

AMCAS Personal Statement

With rising health care costs, limited access to care, and state budget reductions, individuals are slowly being cut out of avenues to maintain or protect their health. Even with new technology, genetic promises, and pharmacological advances, many preventable diseases are taxing health resources resulting in a trade off of care for those truly in need. The U.S. system cannot handle the burden of preventative programs nor can the public health infrastructure address current chronic health epidemics. Now, more than ever, a bridge between treatment and prevention needs to occur.

I have spent the past four years growing professionally and personally to come to the conclusion that physicians need to be that bridge. By combining an understanding of population distribution of disease from academic and industry angles, by gaining awareness of the physician's role within an interdisciplinary team, and by influencing individual health by direct patient care, a physician can become an agent in changing health care disparities while improving individual health. Through my experiences, I have worked hard to gain this knowledge and I believe I would be an excellent medical school candidate and, ultimately, a strong physician.

As a master's student in epidemiology, I have spent the past year learning the fine art of disease distribution for both chronic and infectious disease. Understanding the epidemiology of a disease helps me to understand the importance of tailoring policies and services to a population in order to best provide a high quality of care to my patient. My work as a research assistant in the Department of Otolaryngology at the University of Minnesota has helped put my public heath knowledge to work in a clinical setting. The study with which I am currently involved examines otitis media risk factor prevalence and intervention methods in an American Indian cohort. By understanding the disease picture from biological as well as demographical aspects of risk, I can identify the specific needs of a child, ensure proper diagnosis and prompt treatment, while providing beneficial preventative advice and education.

From an industry standpoint, I understand the role of the physician in the larger scheme of the health care system. As a report analyst for a division of UnitedHealth Group, I had the opportunity to work with HMOs, employers, medical directors, and pharmaceutical companies. Companies such as Medica and Schering Plough worked with us to establish disease management programs whereby physicians identified candidates for pediatric immunizations, mammography promotions, and hepatitis control. In conjunction with this exposure, my work as a nursing assistant has allowed me to see the interdisciplinary role of a physician within a clinical setting as a decision-maker. The physician surrounds themselves with experts such as pharmacists and physical therapists who provide data regarding the health of the patient; their job then is to integrate this knowledge using their own medical training as a guide to patient care.

With this role, though, comes a significant responsibility - the health and trust of the patient. The role is one of a communicator, a healer, and a trusted interface between science and the public. For two years, I have worked as a nursing assistant on a surgical intensive care unit at a hospital as well at a rehabilitation center for spinal cord injuries and stroke victims. The positions have increased my empathy and understanding of another human when faced with new physical, mental, and emotional challenges. I learned the fine art of a bedside manner, patience, compassion, and, more importantly, the skill of listening to the needs and desires of patients and their families. First hand I have seen the detrimental affects of poor health and I have felt the passion to help. One of my strongest memories is of an 80 year old man who had returned to the unit from a coronary artery bypass. The following morning, post surgery, the surgeon had been in along with the family and provided a promising prognosis. A half hour after his family left he went into cardiac arrest. Twenty minutes later, after numerous attempts at resuscitation, the resident pronounced him dead. An hour before all this, I had held this man's hand and I finally understood the delicate line we hold between life and death. After my shift, I cried but realized I wanted to be the person that was there to help save that man and also be the person to prevent others from going through that experience. No other profession besides medicine gives me that chance to advocate health on such a raw level of humanity.

This past spring, I had the opportunity to meet Dr. Julie Gerberding, director of the CDC, and she had a simple mandate. From her standpoint, health professionals have the unique opportunity to enter the world with this skill in hand - the ability to apply preventative approaches while treating the individual all in an effort to hold that fine line stable so we can improve our health while helping to alleviate many of the burdens thrown on our health care system. I would be honored to be a clinician, to combine my skills and knowledge, and help carry out this endeavor.

See page 253 to find out where this student got in.

JEAN PEARCE

Jean received a Merck Undergraduate Science Research Scholarship and studied the effects of seizure medication on inflammation in rheumatoid arthritis. She also volunteered at a cancer ward and studied abroad in Tanzania.

Stats

MCAT: Physical Sciences, 9; Verbal Reasoning, 11; Writing Sample,
P; Biological Sciences, 10

Undergraduate overall GPA: 3.70

Undergraduate science GPA: 3.33

Undergraduate college attended: Gustavus Adolphus College

Undergraduate graduation year: 2001

Gender: Female

Race: Caucasian

Applied To

George Washington University, School of Medicine and Health
Sciences

Michigan State University, College of Human Medicine

Tulane University, School of Medicine

University of Connecticut, School of Medicine

University of Maryland, School of Medicine

University of Michigan, Medical School

University of Minnesota—Twin Cities, Medical School

University of North Dakota, School of Medicine and Health Sciences

University of Oklahoma, College of Medicine

University of Wisconsin—Madison, School of Medicine and Public
Health

Vanderbilt University, School of Medicine

AMCAS Personal Statement

I clung to the clumps of grass, afraid that I would fall. I looked around at my friends. They were as dirty, tired, and scratched as I imagined I was. It didn't bother me. I had climbed a mountain. Me, the girl who had always been petrified of heights had actually climbed a mountain. Oldonyo Lengai, "mountain of the gods." I finally understood the name. As I lay flat against the side of the mountain I chanced a look down. I forgot about the fact that I was over 7,000 feet above the ground. The view was unbelievable. I scanned the endless green plains of Tanzania for the Land Rover we had arrived in, but it was only an unrecognizable dot on the landscape. I was overcome by a feeling of great achievement. The previous six hours of climbing in the dark in order to avoid the midday heat were worth this feeling. That day in Africa I realized something about myself. I can accomplish whatever I put my mind to.

I have never let the mountains that have come up in my life stop me from achieving my goals. Rather, I welcome challenges. Academically, I have challenged myself with a double major in Biology and Classics with Honors and taken on summer research in Immunology. My demanding course load has pushed me to develop better time management and organizational skills that I feel will be invaluable to me in my future. I further challenge myself by taking on leadership responsibilities. I am an officer in the Gustavus Adolphus chapter of Eta Sigma Phi, the national Classics Honors Fraternity. When I began this position I was embarking on unfamiliar territory. Previously I had not been put into many leadership roles. I was afraid that I lacked the experience needed to be successful in such a position. I have learned, however, that often the path that appears most intimidating can be the most rewarding and that when I am thrown into unfamiliar situations I adapt quickly. I adapted very quickly when I began volunteering at a local elementary school as a tutor and mentor to children. This role has allowed me to develop into a more patient and persistent individual. I found that trying to persuade twenty kindergarten children to focus on anything for longer than ten minutes requires an immense amount of patience.

Perhaps the most emotionally challenging experience that I have tackled was my volunteer work in a cancer ward for terminal patients. During the course of my work there I grew to appreciate the difficult role of a physician and the empathy and compassion that she must possess. One of the main jobs I helped the staff perform was simply talking with and listening to the patients. I remember an elderly patient in particular who was unable to speak. On one occasion while the nurse was changing his bandages I simply held his hand to comfort him. The look in his eyes changed as some of his fear disappeared. That experience stuck with me, that such a simple action could help someone so much. I truly understood that being a doctor is not just about curing bodily ailments and illnesses. I realized there that I wanted to become a doctor not only because I love science but also because I love interacting with people.

Africa not only made me realize that I can take on any challenge, but also instilled me with a new curiosity and sense of purpose. We had been prepared before the trip for the inevitably large culture difference. I thought I was prepared. I was wrong. The people I met there were not sad, or angry, or to be pitied by any means. I was immediately struck by the energy and appreciation for life of people who appeared to have so little. Africa changed me. While studying there immersed among the people I developed an interest in healthcare in underserved areas. I found that I want to work where people most need my help. I want to give something back to the people who helped to open my eyes.

In addition, my study abroad experience stimulated an interest in infectious disease. I was amazed by the fact that such tiny organisms could decimate nations. I pursued this curiosity when I arrived home by following an infectious disease doctor. The physician I shadowed cared for mainly AIDS and Hepatitis patients. I immediately admired his commitment, intelligence, and empathy. He is the kind of doctor that I hope to become. Through this experience I learned that I want to be involved in long-term care. I feel that as a physician I can have the most impact and career satisfaction by caring for patients who require intensive and prolonged care.

I view the career path I have chosen much like the mountain I climbed. At the top of the mountain is the goal I have aspired to for years. At the top is a career in which I can combine my interests of problem solving, science and human interaction. It's a steep and difficult climb to the summit, however, and in order to get there I must brave many obstacles and overcome many challenges. I must grow and develop as a person individually and as part of a team. I am confident, however, that I will reach the top of the mountain though the climb will perhaps be the most difficult challenge yet.

See page 253 to find out where this student got in.

JILL HUDGENS LEE

Jill participated in several medical mission trips to Kenya. She was also a member of her school's Division I soccer team.

Stats

MCAT: Physical Sciences, 10; Verbal Reasoning, 10; Writing Sample, Q; Biological Sciences, 10

Undergraduate overall GPA: 3.65

Undergraduate science GPA: 3.20

Undergraduate college attended: Samford University

Undergraduate graduation year: 2004

Gender: Female

Race: Caucasian

Applied To

University of Alabama—Birmingham, School of Medicine

University of South Alabama, College of Medicine

AMCAS Personal Statement

It was January 2003, and there was a long line of people outside our humble clinic in Mombassa, Kenya. Although the temperature had risen over 100 F, and the humid air made it difficult to breathe, the people continued to line up with hope in their eyes that they would be able to see an American doctor and receive free medicine. As I observed the crowd, I noticed a young woman cradling an infant in her arms. Immediately, I was drawn to the placid nature of this little one. As I walked closer to the woman, I noticed the baby in her arms was undisturbed by the intense heat, virtually motionless-too motionless. My experience on the maternity ward of a hospital at home had taught me enough to know that something was wrong with this baby. Immediately, I led the mother through the line of people and into the clinic. My father was inside examining a patient, but when he caught a glimpse of the distress in my eyes, he rushed over to take a look at the infant. As he examined him, I tried to offer comfort to the worried mother. Even though my father and I did not speak this woman's language, our faces said more than our words ever could. As my dad looked up to tell me that the child was deathly ill with diphtheria, I was unable to contain the sympathy that I felt for this mother. Tears flowed freely down my face as I told her, through an interpreter, that we would have to take her baby to the hospital in order for him to have a chance of surviving the illness.

During the time that I have spent in Kenya, I have found myself in many situations similar to one that I have just described. At times, I feel frustrated because of my knowledge of medicine at this point in time provides me with little ability to provide medical care to those who need it. However, assisting the medical professionals in many procedures and comforting and reassuring the patients made this volunteer experience my most satisfying yet. Providing free medicine and medical care to the underpriveleged people of Kenya, communicating compassion and concern for their welfare, and subsequently seeing their profound gratitude for our services has completed my understanding of why I want to become a physician. Not only will my interest in science and healthcare be satisfied, but a career in medicine rewards my interests in counseling and provides a deep sense of fulfillment for playing an integral role in the lives of others.

I have prepared myself to pursue a career in medicine in many ways. My volunteer experiences at Baptist Montclair Hospital and Children's Hospital have given me the opportunity to interact directly with patients. The medical missions trips I have gone on have also provided me with substantial contact with patients. I have volunteered at Easy Street Rehabilitation Unit, where I assisted physicians, physical therapists, and occupational therapists in patient rehab after strokes and surgeries. My internships with Dr. Duane Randleman in cardiothoracic surgery, Dr. Mary Louise Guerry-Force in pathology, and Dr. Maura Carter in neuropsychology, as well as my work-experience with my father in neurology have allowed me to view many perspectives in the medical field. As a physician, it is imperative that I demonstrate good leadership skills. The past three summers, I have served a leadership role at Kanakuk Kamps in Colorado, where I was allotted responsibility for counselors and campers, as well as planning daily activities for the camp.

Understanding that a career in medicine requires hard work, dedication, and time, I have further prepared myself for the rigorous demands by maintaining a busy schedule throughout my college career. I have consistently participated in athletics, volunteer activities, and extracurricular hobbies, while maintaining a rigorous academic curriculum. I have been successful with these activities because I budget my time among all of them.

See page 254 to find out where this student got in.

JIMMY WU

As an undergraduate, Jimmy was an emergency room volunteer, a tutor, and a residential assistant. He was also involved in Wushu, a martial arts organization. He devoted considerable time to each of his extracurricular activities and attained leadership positions in many of them.

Stats

MCAT: Physical Sciences, 11; Verbal Reasoning, 9; Writing Sample, Q; Biological Sciences, 11

Undergraduate overall GPA: 3.40

Undergraduate science GPA: 3.30

Undergraduate college attended: Stanford University

Undergraduate graduation year: 2004

Gender: Male

Race: Asian American

Applied To

Medical College of Wisconsin

University of Wisconsin—Madison, School of Medicine and Public Health

AMCAS Personal Statement

One moment, my then-ten-year-old sister was quietly watching television. The next, she was screaming. I ran to her aid and realized that she had developed an abrupt difficulty in movement with her arms and legs. It was not until the following day when I heard the bad news – the doctors had diagnosed my younger sister with systemic lupus. At the time, I was unable to fathom how my previously healthy sister now lay vulnerably on the hospital bed with IVs inserted all over her. As I watched the doctors and nurses work over her frail body, I felt frustrated that there was nothing I could do to help my sister. Although she would eventually recover from that particular episode, life would never be the same for her. Dealing with daily doses of medication, sensitivity to sunlight, and occasional relapses became a way of life for my sister. Being by her side in her struggle with the illness led me to a fascination with the intricacies of the human body and how her doctors and how medicine have kept her as healthy as possible. Through my sister's experiences, I discovered the wonders and fragilities of life, and I now know I want to engage in a career that allows me to be involved with both on a daily basis. Aspiring to become a professional empowered with the knowledge and compassion to help people like my sister, I have found that I would best fulfill this desire by becoming a physician.

Through science classes in high school and college, I solidified my attraction to the intellectual challenges that a doctor faces on a daily basis. It was, however, activities such as volunteering in various medical care settings that confirmed my aspiration to pursue a life devoted to helping alleviate others' sufferings. Through the times spent holding the hands of dying hospice residents or through moments like comforting a young emergency room patient needing a lumbar puncture, I was able to experience the powerful difference that I could make on people's lives as a physician. Volunteering at the ER, at a local free clinic, and at a hospice residence has given me various perspectives on the importance of embracing the humanistic aspect of medicine. I found the extensive patient interaction extremely rewarding because I was able to help people through difficult emotional, mental, and physical periods, thereby strengthening my desire to enter medical school and become a doctor.

In addition to giving me an intimate idea of how I could impact people's lives through medicine, volunteering, especially at the free clinic and in the Stanford ER, introduced me to a culturally diverse group of patients. Working in such environments galvanized my interest in culture-related issues that increasingly pervade the medical profession. At the free clinic, I once spoke with a Chinese female patient visiting from Wisconsin who explained that she traveled to San Francisco for the sole purpose of seeing a gynecologist who could effectively communicate with her. Such interactions demonstrate to me that much of the inequity in health care access can be resolved by the medical field focusing more on how to provide culturally competent care to its ever-diversifying patient population. As a person who has worked in a Stanford cultural psychology lab for many years and is currently working on a master's thesis focused on the relationship between health and culture, I hope to utilize this knowledge to become a doctor who can practice medicine effectively in cross-cultural situations.

Also related to my interest in medicine and culture has been my exploration of Eastern medicine. I first became intrigued with the possibilities of integrating Western and Eastern medicine when my sister began to receive combined treatments from her Western doctor and from a traditional acupuncturist. Watching the two seemingly different medical systems cooperate in improving my sister's condition fascinated me. Whenever the side effects from her anti-inflammatory drugs became too severe, she would then receive acupuncture treatment to relieve the pain. In order to understand more about Eastern medicine's increasing role in the mainstream medical field, I helped conduct a clinical research project that examined how acupuncture can be best used for analgesic purposes. In addition, I successfully initiated an introductory traditional Chinese medicine course at Stanford. The class is now offered every year, and I continue to help as a teaching assistant. Learning about how the benefits from both systems could complement each other in patient care has provided me with further motivation to pursue medicine.

In what began as some of the most trying times for my sister and family, my curiosity in medicine has been enriched by college courses and by the various clinical endeavors I have undertaken. Whether it was a young child having respiratory problems, a 30-year old Mandarin-speaking patient, or a hospice resident riddled with liver cancer, I have treasured the opportunities to improve each person's quality of life in any way possible. However, these experiences only proved to me that I still desire the capability to effect a greater impact on people like my sister, solidifying my aspiration of making a difference in a multicultural community as a physician.

See page 254 to find out where this student got in.

JOHN FAILING

John worked with the California Department of Health Services to develop, design, and distribute a pamphlet entitled Surfers: Block Those Harmful UV Rays, *which warns of the dangers of unprotected sun exposure. He received several academic honors, including the Robert C. Byrd academic scholarship, and was a member of the Sigma Pi Sigma physics honor society. He also worked as a research assistant on a project concerning the Florida panther. He volunteered for over a year in hospital and clinical settings and spent several months assisting developmentally disabled adults with their daily tasks. Lastly, he worked as a tutor for over four years.*

Stats

MCAT: Physical Sciences, 12; Verbal Reasoning, 10; Writing, S; Biological Sciences, 10

Undergraduate overall GPA: 3.50

Undergraduate science GPA: 3.50

Undergraduate college attended: Duke University

Undergraduate graduation year: 2003

Gender: Male

Race: Caucasian

Applied To

Dartmouth College, Dartmouth Medical School

Stanford University, School of Medicine

University of Colorado, School of Medicine

University of Hawaii, John A. Burns School of Medicine

University of Maryland, School of Medicine

University of Washington, School of Medicine

West Virginia University, School of Medicine

AMCAS Personal Statement

Instead of entering college with a concrete career plan, I left the answer to the omnipresent question, "Where will I be in four years?" blank; intending to let my collegiate experiences and undertakings dictate the theme of the next chapter in my life. My academic career focused on a central dogma consisting of the most basic, albeit by no means "simple," sciences. I chose to submerge myself whole-heartedly into classes in all of the fundamental sciences so that I could understand how the phenomena of the world unravel. My broad collegiate education made it apparent to me that my post-collegiate career had to combine many of the fundamental sciences in a manner that would regularly stimulate and challenge my mind in the years to come. This realization has encouraged me to pursue a career in medicine.

My interest in the sciences is equaled only by my desire to pursue a life of service, where I can contribute to society by helping others. My stringent academic life was balanced by a personal life filled with volunteering and service. At Duke and beyond, I spent valuable time volunteering in medical settings. My taste for medicine was stimulated while volunteering and interacting with patients in the General Medicine Wing of the Duke University Hospital. Unable to satiate my interest in medicine, I supplemented my hospital experience by shadowing a variety of medical professionals as they administered office visits and performed surgeries pertinent to their field of expertise. In all of these situations, I was impressed with the level of respect and appreciation that patients showed their doctors. I was equally impressed with the amount of enjoyment and enthusiasm that the physicians displayed while treating their patients. The breadth of the doctor's influence and depth of their knowledge amazed and inspired me.

Looking back on my life, I now realize that events have occurred on every page of my life's biography that have unknowingly directed me towards a career in medicine. I initially learned first aid while attaining the rank of Eagle Scout and have advanced these skills throughout my life. I have called upon my first aid knowledge in a variety of situations involving everything from participating in a swift-water rescue, where I saved a father and son from drowning in class IV rapids, to dressing and attending to deep lacerations suffered by a fellow surfer. Using first aid in real-world situations made me realize and appreciate the resourcefulness of doctors and strengthened my ambition to become a doctor.

Upon graduating from Duke, I took some time off to explore, and learn about both the world and myself. During this period, I have worked in several positions that have all reinforced my aspiration to pursue a career that combines learning with aiding others. Tutoring showed me how much I enjoy educating and working closely with others. Research experience gained while working to preserve the last prairie stronghold in Montana and helping to promote bison conservation reinforced my aspiration to make learning a part of my life. Aiding developmentally disabled adults with their daily tasks made me realize how fortunate I am to be able to make decisions on my own. I have decided to enter the medical field so that I can combine my passion for the sciences, my objective to work in an ever-evolving field, with my desire to serve others into the most rewarding career possible.

I deeply enjoyed the one-on-one interaction garnered from teaching ski lessons for a winter. Being able to interact with students on such an intimate basis and watching them progress as athletes filled me with a sense of pride that I could help others have a more rewarding life. Yet even in this situation, medical knowledge proved to be useful as I witnessed several injuries on the slope and had to help attend to everything from a bloody nose to a broken ankle. Teaching skiing was a great experience, but I am prepared to help people on another level and this experience furthered my interest in medicine.

After graduation, I exercised the opportunity to live in numerous diverse locations throughout the country. Being able to explore America, live in distinct towns of different sizes, and considering where I grew up have convinced me to live and practice medicine in a rural environment. Growing up in a small town in Appalachia afforded me a front row seat to observe how the doctor-patient relationship evolves in a small town. The intimacy of this relationship and the fact that the bond went beyond the hospital walls further impressed me and has convinced me that my niche lies in practicing medicine in a rural setting.

In my life, I have not been associated with a single mentor, studied a specific subject, or experienced a singular event that has led me towards my decision to matriculate to medical school. Instead, the combination of my life's experiences has propelled me towards the field of medicine, a field that I hope to pursue for the rest of my life.

See page 254 to find out where this student got in.

JULIE KATZ

Julie spent several summers doing clinical work and research. The summer after her sophomore year she worked as a volunteer for the acute-care psychiatric unit at New York Hospital—Cornell Medical Center in White Plains, New York. The following summer she conducted research at the National Institute of Mental Health in Bethesda, Maryland.

Stats

MCAT: Physical Sciences, 12; Verbal Reasoning, 11; Writing Sample, P; Biological Sciences, 12

Undergraduate overall GPA: 3.94

Undergraduate science GPA: 3.80

Undergraduate college attended: Cornell University

Undergraduate graduation year: 2002

Gender: Female

Race: Caucasian

Applied To

Columbia University, College of Physicians and Surgeons

Cornell University, Weill Medical College

Duke University, School of Medicine

Harvard University, Harvard Medical School

Johns Hopkins University, School of Medicine

New York Medical College

New York University, Mt. Sinai School of Medicine

New York University, NYU School of Medicine

Northwestern University, Feinberg School of Medicine

State University of New York—Downstate Medical Center

State University of New York—Stony Brook University, School of Medicine

University of Pennsylvania, School of Medicine

Yale University, School of Medicine

Yeshiva University, Albert Einstein College of Medicine

AMCAS Personal Statement

Cup your left hand with your palm facing upwards. Take the tip of your right middle finger and place it perpendicular to the cupped palm of your left hand. Wiggle your hand from left to right, while maintaining contact between your finger and your palm. This is how one signs the word "medicine" in American Sign Language.

The first time I ever used this sign was during my first week as a volunteer on an adult, inpatient, acute-care psychiatric unit. That week was particularly unsettling for me. In addition to being thrown into the world of the mentally ill, I soon learned that unit on which I was working was the hospital's unofficial deaf and hard-of-hearing unit. I was assigned to work with patients who heard voices in their heads or nothing at all.

Since I know no sign language, the nursing staff provided me with a crash course. After learning how to say nothing more than "medicine," I was sent out to test my new sign on Leah, a deaf patient who was sleeping and needed to take her medication. Down the hall I went, anxiously practicing the one sign I knew by wiggling my finger in my palm. Upon entering Leah's room, and realizing that an auditory cue would not wake her from her slumber, I nudged the mattress of the bed. Leah awoke. With her attention established, I signed, "Medicine." Leah smiled, took the pills, and signed what I later learned to be, "Thank you." I returned to the nurse's station with a deep sense of satisfaction. I had made contact.

During those first few weeks on the unit, I acquired enough signs to interpret the patients' medical complaints. I made careful note of the symptoms and side effects that plagued the patients on the unit and dutifully reported these complaints to the unit's medical staff.

As the summer progressed, my sign language skills improved modestly. Leah's signs, however, were still too fast for me to process. One day, my frustrations prompted a practical alternative. I signed, "Wait," and grabbed a legal pad and two pens. With our supplies, Leah and I sat at a table and talked, using only our hands and our pens to communicate.

We discussed her frustrations with mental illness, the side effects of the medications she hated so much, and her impatience to rejoin her friends and family. Leah was tired of cycling in and out of the hospital and tired of trying to explain the voices no one else heard. The conversation proceeded with ease, and I found myself enjoying my time with Leah. She was so engaging and open, and her sharing nature allowed me to gain a deeper understanding of who she was and the challenges she faced.

It was through this exchange, and others that followed, that I realized the value of my volunteer experience. Leah and the other patients on the unit taught me to be a better listener, an essential skill of a successful physician. I also realized that the patients' symptoms were more than the sum of their conditions. For example, Leah's mental illness was not purely biological in nature, but rather it was also influenced by her isolation from the hearing world.

It is my hope that my career in medicine will allow me to listen ever closer, so that I will always appreciate the patient as an individual and not as a medical condition. For as the noted physician Francis Peabody once remarked, "the secret of the care of the patient is in caring for the patient."

Secondary Essay #1

Julie used the following essay in her application to Duke University, School of Medicine.

Describe a difficult moral or ethical situation that you have encountered and how you dealt with it. What personal strengths, values, and beliefs helped you deal with this challenge?

The physics lecture ended as so many others had before it. Beth and I capped our pens, closed our notebooks, and prepared to brave the bitter March winds.

As we descended down the stairs, Beth asked anxiously, " Hey Julie, could I come over tonight and copy your physics problem set? I'm swamped, and there's no way I'm going to finish it in time."

I was unsure of how to respond. Beth and I had been friends for several years, and we had occasionally consulted one another about various different assignments. We had never plagiarized off of one another, however. Beth knew that I was uncomfortable with any form cheating, and I was surprised that she would even think to ask me to be her accomplice.

On the other hand, the look on Beth's face was one of desperation. She was overwhelmed by her many exams, her MCAT preparations, and her less than complete understanding of magnetic flux. Beth was counting on me to relieve her of this one task that was pushing her over the edge.

Realizing the dilemma with which I was now faced, I was even less sure of how to respond to Beth's request. Not wanting to agree or disagree outright, I said instead, "Come over. We'll talk about it."

That night, Beth stopped by my room, looking even more stressed than she had earlier in the day. She was out of breath and visibly exhausted.

As Beth unpacked her physics books on to my desk, I explained the predicament she had put me in. "Listen," I said, "We've been good friends for a long time, and we've been through a lot together. And while I hate to see you so overwhelmed, I can't, in good conscience, hand you my physics problem set to copy as your own. Just the idea of doing that makes me very uncomfortable, and I hope you understand."

Beth's expression was one of combined understanding and distress. While she accepted my decision, she was also keenly aware that her physics problem set was still incomplete. Beth was clearly starting to panic.

"But," I continued, "What I will do is help you through the problem set. I'm feeling pretty confident with what we've been discussing in class, and hopefully I can help you out. I won't let you copy my work, but I will certainly try to help you with anything you don't understand."

For the first time that day, Beth looked relaxed. She smiled, and said, "That would be fine. Thanks."

Beth and I worked on the problem set for several hours. I explained the questions I was sure that I understood, and we worked through the ones that we both found confusing. Beth even found several mistakes I had made, and together, we corrected them. Soon enough, Beth's problem set was complete, and I understood magnetic flux better than I had just a few hours previous.

As Beth packed up her books, she thanked me for my time. "Julie, I really appreciate this," she said. "I wasn't expecting to spend this much time on the problem set, but at least I understand it now." She paused, and then asked, "Would you mind doing this again next week?"

Without hesitation, I responded in the affirmative. I had enjoyed teaching Beth as much as I enjoyed teaching my chemistry students, and, in this case, my student had helped me to better understand the subject at hand. Instead of Beth mindlessly copying my problem set, we had worked together, and we had both benefited by it.

Needless to say, Beth and I made our problem set review sessions a weekly event. We found that working together was more effective and more fun than struggling alone. My preference for compromise and my love of teaching helped to transform a difficult moral situation into one that was mutually beneficial.

Secondary Essay #2

Julie used the following essay in her application to Northwestern University, Feinberg School of Medicine.

Develop a profile of a good physician. Choose descriptive attitudes and behaviors you think a physician should possess. How closely do you fit the profile?

The first time I considered becoming a physician was while in synagogue one Saturday morning in the eighth grade. After assisting the rabbi with a portion of the service, and returning to my seat, a classmate tapped me on the shoulder.

"Do you want to be a doctor?" she whispered.

"What?" I replied, rather puzzled.

"Do you want to be a doctor?" she repeated.

"Maybe," I said. "I never really thought about it."

"Well, I think you'd make a really good doctor," she said, quite matter-of-factly.

I thanked her for her compliment and then tried to resume my prayers. However, I could not stop thinking about what my classmate had said. How could she know I would be a good doctor? What had she seen that had made her so sure of this fact?

To this day, I do not know what prompted my classmate's comment, but I do know that she was right. After years of course work, several clinical experiences, and just getting to know myself better, I know that I will be a good doctor.

I now know what a good doctor is and what a good doctor is not, and I am confident that I most resemble the former. Beyond the requisite technical skills and scientific knowledge, a good physician needs to possess a certain demeanor. Among many other things, a doctor must be calming, throrough, mature, and approachable.

First and foremost, the good physician is a calming figure in a patient's life. When a patient is faced with the emotions and uncertainty of birth, illness, injury, or death, the doctor is there to congratulate, comfort, or console. A good doctor is one who attends to a patient's feelings just as quickly as he or she makes a diagnosis.

Likewise, a physician ought to be thorough in his or her examination and observation of the patient. The good doctor is sure to gain a complete understanding of the patient's lifestyle and environment, before deciding on a treatment plan. The patient's health is viewed in a broader sense and not hastily reduced to an impersonal diagnosis.

Third, the good doctor is mature in action and in thought. He or she is able to handle difficult situations with professional ease and is able to relate to patients much different from themselves. The physician is aware of the importance of his or her responsibilities and completes them accordingly.

Lastly, a good doctor is approachable. Patients often trust their physician with their most personal questions and concerns. This type of open doctor-patient communication is crucial to the delivery of effective medical care. However, should the doctor be, in some way, unapproachable, the patient's concerns might never be voiced, and their ailments might never be treated. The good physician always makes a conscious effort to be approachable and available to their patients and their needs.

With these characteristics clearly outlined, I am even more certain of my future success in medicine. As a rule, I have always been an even-tempered individual. My emotions rarely go to extremes, and I am usually the first person to attempt to calm or soothe a friend. As a student and as an employee, I am known for being a perfectionist. Spending the extra time to make sure a task is done correctly and completely is, for me, time well spent. My maturity has never been questioned, and friends and family often joke that I am a forty-year old woman trapped in a twenty-one year-old body. I am also extremely approachable, with my petite build and my ever-present smile.

But, then again, my smile has not changed since the eighth grade. The smile that makes me approachable today, made me approachable then, and perhaps this is what my classmate saw so many years ago. Perhaps she caught a glimpse of my developing personality and saw the beginnings of a good doctor.

Secondary Essay #3

Julie used the following essay in her application to Northwestern University, Feinberg School of Medicine.

What processes have you used to explore your commitment to a career in medicine? Describe in detail your evolution of thought and discovery experiences that led to your decision. Be specific .

At the end of my freshman year of college, I began to seriously consider a career in medicine. With my first year at Cornell successfully completed, I was now confident that, if nothing else, I had the academic ability to become a physician. However, while I was sure I could study medicine, I was unsure if I could someday practice it. And so, I began looking for clinical opportunities that would allow me to experience medicine in its true form.

My first clinical experience came to me over the winter break of my sophomore year when I shadowed a Cornell alumna who was a dermatologist in private practice. For one week, I observed patient consultations and gained a greater appreciation for the challenges of being a physician. Most importantly, however, I realized how much I enjoy clinical work. Despite the long hours, I reveled in the parade of patients. I loved the idea of meeting new people every day and helping to relieve whatever it was that ailed them.

I continued to explore clinical work the following summer as a volunteer on an acute, adult, inpatient psychiatric unit. Although extremely different from my previous clinical experience, my two months on the unit confirmed my love of clinical work. Every day I learned more about each patient and their specific struggles, and I loved the idea that I was in a position to help ease their pain.

By the end of my summer on the unit, I was certain that medicine was the career path I wanted to follow. However, while I had sufficiently dabbled in the world of clinical medicine, I had almost no experience in clinical research. Thus, I set out to find a position that would allow me to sufficiently explore this area of medicine.

I found such a position this past summer at the National Institute of Mental Health where I assisted with research on selective visual attention. While I found my work at the NIMH to be extremely interesting, I did not find myself as engaged as I had been the previous summer at the psychiatric hospital. I quickly learned that my interests lie more in clinical medicine than in clinical research.

With my interests now well established, I am even more committed to a career in medicine. I feel I have done justice to both branches of medical science, and I am confident that I will spend my career primarily as a clinician, and not as a researcher. Clinical medicine has given me some of my greatest challenges and satisfactions, and the prospect of building a career on similar experiences is one that truly excites me.

Secondary Essay #4

Julie used the following essay in her application to SUNY—Stony Brook University, School of Medicine.

What is the most pressing contemporary medical issue in the U.S. health care system?

As a result of my many volunteer hours on an acute-care psychiatric unit, I believe that the most pressing contemporary medical issue in the U.S. healthcare system is the effective funding and delivery of mental health services.

Despite decades of progress, mental illness is still affected by social stigmas. Many believe that mental illness is not a truly biological disorder, and that those who suffer are somehow at fault for their troubles. Possibly reflecting this belief, insurance companies may provide limited mental health benefits. Inpatient stays may be restricted to a period of time that is too short-lived for lasting psychiatric stabilization, and outpatient care is often confined to a time frame that is unsuitable for effective clinical practice.

Unlike many other diseases and disorders, mental illness is one that cannot be cured or controlled on a prescribed schedule. It may take weeks to stabilize a patient, and relapses can occur suddenly and seemingly without warning.

Although there have been recent advances in educating the public about the needs of the mentally ill, there are still many obstacles to overcome. Until insurance companies recognize the unique character of mental illness through changes in their health policies, the mentally ill will be consistently denied the quality care they need.

See page 254 to find out where this student got in.

JUSTIN FINCH

Justin was a research assistant in Interventional Radiology (IR) at the University of Minnesota and published research on Peripherally Inserted Central Catheters (PICCs). He volunteered for the Humane Society, worked as a tutor in the Student Transition and Retention (STAR) program, and spent a week in Juarez, Mexico with his church building a school playground.

Stats

MCAT: Physical Science, 13; Verbal Reasoning, 10; Writing, M; Biological Sciences, 13

Undergraduate overall GPA: 3.94

Undergraduate science GPA: 3.94

Undergraduate college attended: University of Minnesota

Undergraduate graduation year: 2003

Gender: Male

Race: Caucasian

Applied To

Boston University, School of Medicine

Cornell University, Weill Medical College

Duke University, School of Medicine

Finch University of Health Sciences, Chicago Medical School

George Washington University, School of Medicine & Health Sciences

Harvard University, Harvard Medical School

Johns Hopkins University, School of Medicine

Loyola University Chicago, Stritch School of Medicine

New York Medical College

New York University, Mount Sinai School of Medicine

Northwestern University, Feinberg School of Medicine

Rush University, Rush Medical College

Stanford University, School of Medicine

Temple University, School of Medicine

Thomas Jefferson University, Jefferson Medical College

Tufts University, School of Medicine

University of California—Los Angeles, David Geffen School of
  Medicine

University of California—San Diego, School of Medicine

University of California—San Francisco, School of Medicine

University of Chicago, Pritzker School of Medicine

University of Maryland, School of Medicine

University of Minnesota—Twin Cities, Medical School

University of North Carolina—Chapel Hill, UNC School of Medicine

University of Pennsylvania, School of Medicine

University of Virginia, School of Medicine

University of Washington, School of Medicine

Yeshiva University, Albert Einstein College of Medicine

AMCAS Personal Statement

I vividly remember being six years old, sitting beside my grandmother as she battled her breast cancer into remission. I was too young to understand why Grandma's hair was falling out, but I was keenly aware of the trust she and I placed in the ability of her doctors to provide the best care possible. This memory is the seed from which my passion for medicine blossomed. My grandmother is still alive today, and she is very proud of my commitment to medicine.

In college, I excelled in all of my premedical courses, and my focus on medicine also developed from experiences outside of the classroom. During my sophomore year I received a research grant to study alcoholism. My research required creative ideas to develop innovative animal models of this human disease. This rapid flow of ideas enthralls me, but animal research lacks the opportunity to help people through direct contact, leaving me yearning for more. I filled this void through volunteering. Whether it's seeing the smile on an elderly woman's face when I bring a Humane Society pet to her nursing home, or helping one of the first-generation minority students in the STAR program work through a difficult new chemistry concept, volunteering gives me a sense of personal fulfillment that research alone cannot.

The most rewarding experiences for me are helping people through education. Teaching the organic chemistry lab to fifteen of my peers each semester and tutoring for the STAR program have refined my talent as a teacher and honed my leadership skills. My language and culture studies have taught me to embrace multiculturalism, and my Spanish proficiency has prepared me to serve an increasingly diverse population. In 1999 I spent a week in Juarez, Mexico with Crown of Glory Church building a school playground. I am extremely excited to begin volunteering this fall through the Minnesota Literacy Council as an English tutor for adult Hispanic immigrants.

Two years ago I began working as a research assistant in Interventional Radiology (IR) at the University of Minnesota. I quickly saw how medicine could combine the problem solving challenge of research that is so important to me with the personal satisfaction I receive from helping people. The research projects that I work on in IR give me significant patient contact in clinical settings, including the opportunity to scrub in and assist in some of the procedures in the operating room. I play an integral role in a study of Peripherally Inserted Central Catheters (PICCs): from watching procedures in the OR and recording data, to reviewing medical records and scheduling follow-up exams. I manage all of the data and employ appropriate statistical tests to uncover important trends and demonstrate the effects of the catheters. I worked with one of the fellows to draft a research paper entitled "The Effects of PICC Lines on Upper Extremity Veins," which will soon be published in *Archives of Pediatrics & Adolescent Medicine*.

When the PICC abstract was accepted for a poster presentation at the 2003 Pediatric Academic Society meeting, one of the faculty provided funds for me to go to Seattle to present the poster. At the conference I attended lectures on pediatric cardiology and participated in discussion groups on the complex ethical challenges faced by medicine today. I am currently incorporating additional data into the poster before bringing it to the 2003 Radiologic Society of North America conference in December. My experience at the conference and in the hospital has introduced me to the intellectual challenges I will face as a doctor, but it could not prepare me for the intense emotional struggle of dealing with severe illness.

In 2001 my aunt Kim became ill and slipped into a coma before being diagnosed with diabetes. I was again in the position of seeing a critically ill relative in the hospital, and this was more difficult than any exam. While the doctors cared for Kim, they also kept my family and me informed of her condition and helped us to remain optimistic. Kim's eyes opened for the first time six days after she entered the hospital, but she remained in critical condition for almost two weeks. When Kim was finally released from the hospital, ending the terrifying experience, I was even more confident in my decision to devote my life to acquiring the tools necessary to cure people and help them heal.

One year ago I began applying to medical school. By the time I finished my final essays I was newly engaged to a beautiful woman who shared my passion for education and healing, but Maran had one more year of education before she could begin her PhD studies in biomedical ethics. I made the difficult decision of postponing my applications so that my fiancée and I could carefully plan for our future together and prepare for the responsibilities of a happy lifelong relationship.

Now, after beginning a happy marriage and gaining another year of invaluable research experience and patient contact, I am eager and well prepared to continue my medical education. My volunteer work, patient contact, research, and teaching experience have not only prepared me to be a doctor; they have made me confident in and passionate about my commitment to a lifetime of learning, teaching, and healing.

See page 255 to find out where this student got in.

KARIN ELISABETH WITTE

Karin played varsity volleyball and was captain of the team her senior year. She also tutored elementary school children. After college she worked in a research lab for two years and volunteered at a free clinic.

Stats

MCAT: Physical Sciences, 9; Verbal Reasoning, 10; Writing Sample, N; Biological Sciences, 11

Undergraduate overall GPA: 3.60

Undergraduate science GPA: 3.40

Undergraduate college attended: University of Pennsylvania

Undergraduate graduation year: 2000

Gender: Female

Race: Caucasian

Applied To

Medical College of Wisconsin

Stanford University, School of Medicine

Temple University, School of Medicine

University of Chicago, Pritzker School of Medicine

University of Wisconsin—Madison, School of Medicine and Public Health

AMCAS Personal Statement

Growing up in the Midwest means many things, one of which is a thorough familiarity with Garrison Keillor. He once said, "Some luck lies in not getting what you thought you wanted but getting what you have, which ... you may be smart enough to see is what you would have wanted had you known." Few statements more succinctly describe the circuitous manner in which I came to choose medicine.

I can, like many, trace my curiosity about medicine to my early childhood. Admittedly, medicine is a profession to which I was preferentially exposed, having a physician father; I spent far more hours in hospitals and doctors' offices than were necessitated by my near-perfect health. I remember particularly fondly the evenings during which my medical skills were first tested. While I sat upon his desk eating pistachios, my father reviewed charts, slid up chest films - and had me identify the patient's sex. I was occasionally wrong, though only with elderly women mistakenly assumed to be male. "Look lower" was his droll advice.

Medicine has not, however, always been my career of choice; in truth, I delivered several speeches to my parents and school counselors expounding my adolescent distaste for it. After consciously rejecting it, some years passed before I recognized that my scholastic and personal pursuits aligned with the medical profession. My interest began anew in high school biology, with my enthusiasm for dissections; I was fascinated by the relationship between the anatomical and the physiological. In my later studies of sociology, I was chiefly concerned with how one's place in society affects health; to that end, I aided my professor in her project addressing the prevalence of pre-term births in minorities. I also became convinced of the relevance of worldview, and consider an awareness of those cultural mores a *sine qua non* of professionals working with a heterogeneous population - whether patients, clients, or students. Still, my decision to pursue medicine felt naggingly passive: it seemed too obvious. Consequently, I dedicated the years after graduating to broadening my clinical and basic science experience.

My duties at the free clinic, though simple, revealed themselves to be of some importance. In the process of greeting, weighing, and discussing with the patient the reason for the visit, I learned that a kind word of comfort and concern has tremendous power. One woman, a diabetic so devoted to caring for her ailing husband that she often forgot to eat, simply needed someone to gently fuss over her for a change; ironically, I am certain only that doing this for her made me feel wonderful. My lab work, though seemingly antithetical to that of the clinic, has been similarly engaging and edifying. Naturally, I now more keenly understand research as an evolutionary process, and am confident managing my clinical project alone. Furthermore, with clinicians directing the aims of the research, the lab work has cultivated and contextualized my philosophy that the endpoint of medical research is its clinical application: its motive, the benefit the patient derives.

What I least expected to gain from the lab, however, was a close relationship with a young mentor. As a female third-year surgery resident, Debby has been a propitious source of valuable insight. In addition to serving as an impartial sounding board, she has encouraged me to observe surgeries and attend physician interviews, go to grand rounds and sit in on journal clubs, while over lunch we discuss science as well as semantics. As a result, the lingering doubts - which successfully derailed my application last year - have been eradicated.

Life is an unpredictable adventure, and I am grateful for the path mine has taken, as I have had the blessing of variety. In the same year, I realized a dream of playing collegiate volleyball but also learned the painful lesson that anything less than full attention to my academics would neither produce sterling marks, nor demonstrate my capability; these are the precious experiences that make me a complete person. As Keillor suggests, we often do not recognize how circumstances are beneficial until after the fact: had I never taken time to test my interest in medicine, I might always have wondered if I had made the right decision. Had I matriculated to medical school directly from Penn, I would not have met Debby, nor been enriched by the volunteers and patients at the free clinic. As such, though I wanted other things along the way, what I have is a profound love of medicine; I earnestly believe my decision to pursue it is both instinctive and deliberate, and that my lifetime of experiences will contribute to a fruitful, fulfilling medical career.

See page 256 to find out where this student got in.

KATIE WILLIHNGANZ

Katie worked at the University of Wisconsin Hospital as an electrocardiogram technician and did research in the university's microbiology lab. She was a student proctor for peers with learning disabilities, a teaching assistant in the Anatomy department, and a peer leader in the Physiology department. She also volunteered for the Red Cross and conducted dance therapy for developmentally delayed adolescents and elementary school children.

Stats

MCAT: Physical Sciences, 8; Verbal Reasoning, 10; Writing Sample, Q; Biological Sciences, 11

Undergraduate overall GPA: 3.80

Undergraduate science GPA: 3.80

Undergraduate colleges attended: University of Wisconsin—Madison

Undergraduate graduation year: 2004

Gender: Female

Race: Caucasian

Applied To

Mayo Clinic College of Medicine, Mayo Medical School

Pennsylvania State University, College of Medicine

Saint Louis University, School of Medicine

University of Minnesota—Twin Cities, Medical School

AMCAS Personal Statement

Childhood dreams to be great can be realized as true possibilities and reachable goals as long as hard work and determination are used as vehicles to get there. My dreams have continually changed as I have aspired to be everything from an actor to a lawyer to an astronaut to a doctor. The final decision to truly become a doctor did not come until I reached college. Growing up in Rochester, Minnesota, where the Mayo Clinic is a major influence in most everyone's lives, I was regularly surrounded by people working in the medical profession, including members of my family. My mother is a nurse and nurse educator, my aunt is a physical therapist, and many of my friends' parents in town are physicians and surgeons. Through these contacts, I have had ample exposure to what life as a medical professional entails. However, my interest in medicine has primarily stemmed from my passion and curiosity for learning about biology. An exceptional high school biology teacher inspired me to learn about all aspects of biology, from bacteria to plants to human physiology. Thus my true calling to study biology in college focused my future. Though a biology degree in college could prepare me for a variety of professions in the medical field, the healthcare career I would choose was still undecided.

One passion that has led me toward the altruistic field of healthcare is my love for helping people. Throughout high school I volunteered at a nursing home, tutored fellow students in different classes, and worked as a customer service sales associate at JCPenney. I knew that whatever career I undertook had to include daily contact with people where I could give help, advice, or just a listening ear. My first year in college, I sought out positions where I would be helping people in one way or another. I started donating blood to and volunteering as a donor aid or the Red Cross blood drives with Youngblood on campus. Donating blood is an important part of giving life back to the community, and I enjoy volunteering with the Red Cross because it gives me a chance to interact with other individuals that feel the same. Additionally my freshman year, I began a job as a proctor for students with disabilities in which I helped them take exams by writing or reading for them. I have continued to work this job throughout my college career because I enjoy helping others and making a difference in their life by providing a service to them to make their life easier.

A variety of experiences my sophomore year in college allowed me to explore the medical field in greater detail. Through some of my personal connections, I received a job as an Electrocardiogram (ECG) Technician at the University of Wisconsin Hospital, through which I gained exposure to many different fields of medicine as well as the different roles physicians can play in people's lives. Exposure to the many areas of medicine and positions available in those areas really allowed me to solidify my desire to become a physician. I have been a part of emergency room situations, traumas, codes, and preoperative clinical settings. I have enjoyed both the personal contact I have experienced with patients and the knowledge that the work I am doing is important to their health. This job has also been personally rewarding by allowing me to care directly for my Great-aunt Bea, 89, while she was in the hospital. I personally performed ECGs for her diagnosis and was able to be there to support her emotionally before and after her angioplasty and stent placement.

To better explore the role of physician better, I shadowed an anesthesiologist at the Mayo Clinic's St. Mary's Hospital the summer after my sophomore year. During that experience, I was thrilled to witness my first open heart surgery, and was glad able to interact with both the anesthesiologist and cardiac surgeon. I enjoyed gaining knowledge about the similarities and differences between these roles. I liked the aspect of autonomy in each specialty as well as the team work necessary to complete the goal of the surgery. On another shadowing day, I was able to do night rounds with a fourth year anesthesia resident and witnessed an emergency fistula repair. This was incredibly exciting because of how quickly the surgery team reacted in the emergency. Overall, this shadowing experience has showed me how life as an anesthesiologist is tied to surgery, and has helped me realize that although that lifestyle is appealing to some, I prefer patient contact outside the surgical setting. This experience was valuable for me to decide what kind of situation would best suit me as a future physician.

I have continued to learn about different types of physicians through the pre-medical organization Alpha Epsilon Delta which I have been a member of since my sophomore year. Twice a month a physician is invited to our meetings to talk about their career in medicine, how they got there, and what the pros and cons are about being a doctor. These meetings are very informative and have sparked my interest in a variety fields such as pediatrics, primary care, obstetrics/gynecology, and cardiology. Specifically, I am drawn toward roles that are more medically based versus surgically based fields. I am excited to explore these options further in medical school.

I know without a doubt that a career as a physician in medicine is right for me because it offers everything I want in a career: patient contact, advising, challenges, autonomy and life-long learning. I feel that my experiences in the medical field continue to solidify that decision. Through hard work and determination my dream of being a doctor can come to life. As a physician I will aspire to help people attain their health goals in life, be an advisor and friend to those of all ages, sexes, and cultures, and enjoy knowing that I have made a difference in people's health and lives.

See page 256 to find out where this student got in.

LOUIS LIN

As an undergraduate, Louis held several internships at molecular biology labs. He also taught a class titled "Biotechnology Today" and earned a minor in business administration from the Haas School of Business at University of California—Berkeley. Following college, he worked at a medical device start-up company.

Stats

MCAT: Physical Sciences, 10; Verbal Reasoning, 10; Writing
   Sample, M; Biological Sciences, 11
Undergraduate overall GPA: 3.45
Undergraduate science GPA: 3.30
Undergraduate college attended: University of California—Berkeley
Undergraduate graduation year: 1999
Gender: Male
Race: Asian American

Applied To

Louis applied to all public U.S. medical schools either in California
   or reading out-of-state applications. He also applied to all private U.S. medical schools without religious affiliation. According to Louis, he applied to about 50 schools.

AMCAS Personal Statement

I have to admit that for most of my life, attending medical school was just an afterthought. Being a child whose formative years were spent in the roaring 80's, I firmly believed a career in business was the way to go. It also did not hurt that my father, a research biologist, insisted that I head toward a career in corporate America, flush with income tax loopholes, generous expense accounts, and substantial year-end bonuses.

Shadowing an otolaryngologist in high school only reinforced my suspicions that medicine was not the way to go—after a few short days I contracted a severe cold from one of my mentor's patients. By this time, the excesses of the 1980's gave way to the internet boom of the 1990's. With managed care deeply entrenched, it was clear to me that medicine was taking a backseat to corporate America.

I cannot say that there was any single event that led to my decision to pursue a career in medicine, but that my life experiences, consciously or not, have been inexorably linked to the field. Even as a business minor in college, I never lost sight of my interest in medicine. Whether it was the summers I spent working for biopharmaceutical firms that were attempting to unlock the secrets of human illness or creating a new course at Berkeley covering the role of biotechnology in science and healthcare, many of my activities have been based on the premise that medicine and the biological sciences will improve humanity.

Despite my initial role in marketing and business development at a start-up medical device firm, I found myself drawn to the medical research aspect of the company—developing a new device platform to remove cardiovascular calcification. From my work experience I have learned to appreciate the interdisciplinary opportunities physicians have to directly and indirectly impact many lives through patient care and entrepreneurial therapeutic development. I can now also appreciate how my interest in business has not gone to waste, for medicine's new emphasis on cost-effective yet compassionate care will require a new business sense if physicians are to successfully navigate the managed care environment and create the next generation of efficient medical technologies. With this in mind, it is clear to me now that medicine appeals to me because it is a combination of science and business that offers a wide range of meaningful career opportunities.

Although I reside in Silicon Valley, where young people like myself seem increasingly flush with internet riches, I choose medicine. My experiences as a volunteer at the Veterans Hospital involving chronic care has made me realize that although I am surrounded by materialism, the look of relief on a patient's face cannot be purchased. I choose medicine because I know I can make a real difference—not just one that lasts until the next product cycle.

See page 256 to find out where this student got in.

MEKEISHA GIVAN

MeKeisha worked as an operating room assistant at Baptist Montclair Hospital in Birmingham, Alabama and shadowed physicians in a variety of fields. She also worked for Habitat for Humanity and volunteered for two years at Birmingham's Ronald McDonald House.

Stats

MCAT: Physical Sciences, 7; Verbal Reasoning, 9; Writing Sample, O; Biological Sciences, 9

Undergraduate overall GPA: 3.58

Undergraduate science GPA: 3.38

Undergraduate college attended: University of Alabama at Birmingham

Undergraduate graduation year: 2001

Gender: Female

Race: African American

Applied To

Meharry Medical College, School of Medicine

AMCAS Personal Statement

The black pill bugs slowly crept along the cardboard maze that led them on a predetermined journey. At the end of the straightaway, one of my seventh-grade students shined a flashlight on each of the small crustaceans; we hoped to teach the pill bugs to pick the left path over the right turn. After several trials—many of which resulted in the pill bugs rebelling and choosing the wrong path—the crustaceans began to follow the course that we had selected for the roly polies. This science project for the University of Alabama at Birmingham-Arrington Middle School Connection taught me perseverance, strength, and determination while also training me in the art of having patience with others. Furthermore, I learned that like the pill bugs, I also have a path to follow in order to complete my goals; this course is the path to a career in medicine.

Throughout college, I had certain medical experiences that enabled me to see the facets of medicine. Although these experiences often demonstrated both the positive and challenging sides of medicine, it was these inside views of the profession that piqued my interest. While in college, I took classes in addition to working at Children's Hospital, volunteering, and participating in other extracurricular activities. I have participated in the Alpha Epsilon Delta, Phi Kappa Phi, and Sigma Tau Delta honor societies and been a member of the Orientation Leaders Team for my university. I have also attended the Summer Medical Education Program as well as the Joint Leadership Conference of the University of Alabama at Birmingham. I am a member of the Minority Scholars Program and participate in community activities with my church, Habitat for Humanity, and the Girl Scouts. One of my most meaningful activities—my work at the Ronald McDonald House—intensely shaped my perspective of medicine.

At the Ronald McDonald House, I performed chores for the families living at the home. These families, all of whom had young relatives who were patients at Children's Hospital, had to perform chores at the house in exchange for free room and board. At the time, my job at the Ronald McDonald House seemed like such an insignificant amount of work; nevertheless, I realized that sweeping, vacuuming, and other duties that I performed eased the stress placed on these families. Furthermore, this experience enabled me to realize the tremendous strength that families of the ill must exhibit.

During my first semester of college, I had to face many challenges as I adjusted to life at the university. In the months of August and September, my mother—the sole provider of our home—had to have both foot and heart surgery that had resulted from serious circumstances; it was at this time that I gained first-hand experience into what families of the sick deal with during times of illness. Because my mom was indisposed, I had to take on the responsibilities at home in addition to my duties related to school. Learning to manage my time was difficult; however, I persevered and made the Deans' List the following semester.

Although this trial greatly challenged my journey to becoming a physician, other tests were just as significant in my path to medicine; it was these tests that enabled me to better handle the later tribulations that I would face. Throughout life, I had to deal with the sicknesses of not only my mother, but other close relatives and friends. As a small child, I often visited the home of my grandmother and great-grandmother. During one visit to my grandparents' home, my great-grandmother went into shock. As my grandmother panicked, I calmly dialed 911 and requested that an ambulance be sent to the house. As the medics arrived, I watched in wonder as they carefully took care of my grandmother and healed her of her sickness. This experience opened my eyes to the wonders of medicine and strongly provoked my interest in the profession.

As a result of the many experiences that I had during my lifetime, I was able to experience the good, bad, and personal aspects of medicine. In my later years, the realistic features of the medical profession personally affected me; early on in my life, I learned the wonderful, life-saving side of medicine. It was this multi-faceted view of medicine that shaped my journey to becoming a doctor. While these experiences coursed the expanse of my lifetime, the journey truly began at the time of my birth. Although no one on earth knew of the physician that I would become, it was at the time that I took my first breath that I, like the pill bugs, had a path that was set into motion. My course is the path to becoming a physician.

See page 256 to find out where this student got in.

MICHAEL CULLEN

As an undergraduate, Michael participated in a variety of re-
search, volunteer, and leadership activities. He studied gene expres-
sion in cancer cells and completed a senior honors thesis in the
Biochemistry department. He volunteered over 150 hours at his
hometown hospital during summer and winter breaks and logged
over 50 hours of volunteer work at a local center for developmentally
disabled individuals. He was also president of the Undergraduate
Biochemistry Student Organization and was a charter member of his
school's AED chapter.

Stats

MCAT: Physical Sciences, 14; Verbal Reasoning, 9; Writing Sample,
    T; Biological Sciences, 15

Undergraduate overall GPA: 4.00

Undergraduate science GPA: 4.00

Undergraduate college attended: University of Wisconsin—Madi-
    son

Undergraduate graduation year: 2002

Gender: Male

Race: Caucasian

Applied To

Duke University, School of Medicine

Mayo Clinic College of Medicine, Mayo Medical School

Medical College of Wisconsin

University of Iowa, Roy J. and Lucille A. Carver College of Medicine

University of Wisconsin—Madison, School of Medicine and Public
    Health

Washington University in St. Louis, School of Medicine

AMCAS Personal Statement

It was a warm summer's evening. I had just arrived home from a tennis match with a good
friend to find the house wide open and eerily dormant. There was a note from my mother on
the counter: "Mike, call Grandma Jean's." On the phone, my mother informed me that my
grandfather had collapsed and been taken by ambulance to the hospital. I rushed out of the
house, leaving it as wide open as I had found it. Thirty minutes later, I was standing

apprehensively in a side room of the local hospital's ER. With its comfortable chairs, soothing colors, and numerous tissue boxes, I could tell that this room was often used for delivering "the bad news." My parents, aunts, uncles, and grandmother surrounded me. I was the youngest person in the room by 15 years, but I found myself surprisingly calm. A young physician opened the door, closed it gently behind him, and began, in a clear, deliberate, yet empathetic manner, to inform us that my grandfather had suffered an abdominal aortic aneurysm, leaving his condition as "grave" (he died later that night). I was the first to speak, asking the doctor to clarify that the aorta was in fact the main artery leaving the heart. While I knew this to be the case, I wanted to convince myself that I could remain analytical and clear minded in such an emotional situation. It was at this moment that my intuition confirmed what my brain had considered for years: medicine was the career for me.

Medicine provides the unique opportunity to meld two prominent facets of human existence: the desire to build relationships on an intimate and personal level and the desire to learn more about science and human biology. Medicine also presents a slight paradox by directly applying cutting-edge scientific technology to fundamental human problems. I am motivated to pursue a career in medicine in order to fulfill mankind's most basic need of physiological health and to satisfy my own desire for emotional and intellectual self-actualization.

For more than two years, I have performed volunteer work at Mercy Hospital in Janesville, Wisconsin. In addition to acquainting me with the inner workings of a health care facility, my work has allowed me to view the human condition in sickness, its most vulnerable state. For example, working as a dietary aide has shown me that the ill typically appreciate small and simple favors such as the help I am able to provide in completing their daily food selection process. The satisfaction I gain by noting their appreciation inspires me to be more helpful to the next patient I encounter. Consequently, medicine offers the opportunity to help and interact with individuals on the intimate matter of personal health, giving doctors the opportunity to influence others in unique and consequential ways. Communicating with and caring for the ill is a terrific responsibility, but my volunteer work has helped me realize its importance and its benefits, to both the patient and myself.

Two years ago, I was attending a graduation party for the sister of a close friend. My friend's father is a respected surgeon. We had begun making small talk when he pulled me aside into his office. For the next hour, he proceeded to tell me why, under no circumstances, would he recommend a career as a physician. As he reeled off a list of grievances ranging from a hectic call schedule, conflicts with medical administrators, and sacrifices in his personal life, his utter frustration became clear. Medicine, to this surgeon, had clearly not developed into the career he envisioned. While acknowledging that the massive changes in medical administration in the last twenty years might have the current generation of physicians bitter about their loss of autonomy, I had never been confronted with such a heartfelt and emotional plea *not* to enter the field of medicine. However, after thoughtful consideration, I concluded that my desire to affect people on such an intimate and personal level as their health outweighed the long nights of call and other personal sacrifices. Furthermore, I reasoned that waking each morning knowing that I was using my God-given talents to help those with truly fundamental needs to improve their quality of life would ultimately provide for a satisfying and fulfilling career.

Despite my youth, my experiences have allowed me to develop a definite appreciation for the dynamics of medicine. The emotional gamut that physicians encounter challenges one's heart to appreciate life's simple pleasures. The cherished relationships cultivated with patients provide interpersonal connections not possible in other careers. Finally, the intellectual and scientific problems that medicine presents challenge the mind to reach new heights of reasoning and creativity. In an effort to find the optimal blend of scientific and professional humanitarianism, I choose to pursue a career in medicine. It is with honor, dignity, and an unwavering faith in the human spirit that I anticipate becoming a medical doctor.

See page 257 to find out where this student got in.

MICHAEL CURLEY

During his college years, Michael volunteered at an AIDS shelter in Madrid, Spain and worked on an ambulance serving inner-city St. Louis, Missouri. He also volunteered at a health clinic for uninsured members of St. Louis's Latino community. He was involved in Micah House, an academic, community service, and housing program that incorporated themes of peace and social justice in the urban community.

Stats

MCAT: Physical Sciences, 10; Verbal Reasoning, 10; Writing Sample, P; Biological Sciences, 11

Undergraduate overall GPA: 3.91

Undergraduate science GPA: 3.80

Undergraduate college attended: Saint Louis University

Undergraduate graduation year: 2002

Gender: Male

Race: Caucasian

Applied To

Creighton University, School of Medicine

Loyola University Chicago, Stritch School of Medicine

Medical College of Wisconsin

Saint Louis University, School of Medicine

Tulane University, School of Medicine

University of Wisconsin—Madison, School of Medicine and Public Health

AMCAS Personal Statement

I was born into wealth. The youngest of five children raised on the income of a social worker, this wealth was that afforded to those fortunate enough to be born into a close-knit, supportive and loving family in which respect and sensitivity, education and service to others were deeply valued. The benefits reaped from this advantage molded my early personal growth, influenced my perspectives on others, encouraged me to explore, to risk, and to challenge myself, and to work to attain that which I value. Ultimately, it shaped me into the person that I am and will guide me in the pursuit of the person I strive to be.

Many of my earliest memories are of my siblings working diligently on their schoolwork at the kitchen table, of their investment in extracurricular activities, and of their involvement with community programs serving children and adults with cognitive and physical disabilities. With a natural tendency to imitate the behavior of those I admired, I developed a special love of learning, an interest in participating in a wide variety of activities, and an appreciation for the importance of working for the good of others with a spirit of compassion. These values were reflected in the effort that I invested in my schoolwork, the opportunities I took advantage of to develop my talents and leadership qualities and, in later years, by my work with some of the very individuals with autism, cerebral palsy and Down Syndrome that my siblings had enjoyed serving.

By the time I entered high school, my siblings' pursuit of college and graduate studies had taken them hundreds of miles from home, but we remained very close and their influence remained strong. With their support and that of my parents, I developed confidence to take on meaningful leadership roles in the arts, athletics, my school community, and employment. Theatrical performances provided me with an opportunity to develop strong communication skills; positions on the cross country and basketball teams impressed upon me the importance of physical and mental endurance as well as the critical nature of working effectively within a group; an opportunity to develop a classroom-based program celebrating student diversity taught me that one effective leadership tool was to encourage others to share the talents of which they felt proud; employment with children and adults with special needs stimulated empathy, patience, and creativity.

The lessons learned through these opportunities and my family experiences helped me to develop a personal philosophy regarding the value of human life and the importance of actively pursuing social justice. I was able to further investigate, develop and act on these beliefs as a student at Saint Louis University involved in Micah House, a community service and social justice program. An opportunity to study at Saint Louis University's Madrid, Spain campus allowed me to face new challenges such as utilizing my foreign language skills and adapting to and embracing a culture quite different than my own. While in Madrid, my dedication to volunteerism took me to the Ermita Del Santo AIDS Shelter. While further developing empathy and an appreciation for my own health, I witnessed and was touched by the intense resolve and love of life demonstrated by the shelter residents despite their serious health conditions.

Today I realize that the wealth stemming from my family, compounded over the years through the rich opportunities and experiences I have had, has formed my foundation. Qualities such as introspection, integrity, determination, compassion and maturity are the building blocks of this foundation, and are respected by my friends, acquaintances, teachers, work colleagues and those I have had the opportunity to serve. I look forward to the challenges ahead as I continue to develop the attributes, knowledge and skills necessary for me to fulfill my desire to be of service to others.

See page 257 to find out where this student got in.

MICHAEL FRANCO

Michael took time off from college to attend culinary school and worked at various high-end restaurants in Philadelphia. After returning to college, he volunteered at the emergency department of Cooper Hospital in Camden, New Jersey.

Stats

MCAT: Physical Sciences, 11; Verbal Reasoning, 13; Writing Sample, Q; Biological Sciences, 10

Undergraduate overall GPA: 3.96

Undergraduate science GPA: 3.90

Undergraduate college attended: Rowan University

Undergraduate graduation year: 2004

Gender: Male

Race: Caucasian

Applied To

Cornell University, Weill Medical College

Harvard University, Harvard Medical School

Johns Hopkins University, School of Medicine

Temple University, School of Medicine

Thomas Jefferson University, Jefferson Medical College

UMDNJ, New Jersey Medical School

UMDNJ, Robert Wood Johnson Medical School

University of Pennsylvania, School of Medicine

AMCAS Personal Statement

It is around 7:00 o'clock AM, and the workday begins. Vegetables must be chopped, meat must be butchered and fish is to be filleted. Suddenly, without warning, it is noon; lunch is upon me. Orders line up in an endless stream. The temperature rises to a stifling, sauna-like level in front of the heavy, iron flat-top grills, and commands are being barked into my ear by a French chef who seems to think that the volume of his voice must be ten times that of the banging pots. In the kitchen of the French restaurant where I worked after leaving culinary school, the intensity level was always high. A delicate balance between speed and finesse was the rule, and sustained efficiency was paramount. The culinary world is still a field I truly enjoy; however, I always knew there would be a point when I would return to the academic arena and pursue my passion for learning.

Upon returning to college, medical school was not made my official target until relatively late. This decision did not come as an after-thought, nor as a result of procrastination. I had grappled with the idea of becoming a physician since the sixth grade; however, I always thought it to be beyond my reach. My notion of the medical school applicant was someone who was the child of a doctor (or at least the child of a college graduate), and someone from an upper-class family. I am neither. After much research, and with the support of the faculty at Rowan University, I was able to dispense with my misconceptions. Throughout my time in college, I had always maintained an excellent academic track record. Now, i just needed to be sure that a career in medicine was best for me.

To gain a better understanding of the medical profession, I obtained a volunteer research position with Cooper Hospital's Academic Associates Program. Working in the emergency department, I am able to witness doctors treating patients with ailments that range from serious traumas to the common cold. I see how the stress level increases with high patient volume. Yet the staff continues to provide quality care for the constant stream of sick and injured people. I appreciate the professional yet compassionate manner with which these doctors conduct themselves despite working long, strenuous hours. Working at Cooper, I see a similarity between my past work experience in restaurants and the emergency department. Like the French kitchen from which I came, a career in medicine would provide me with daily challenges that need to be overcome with proper organization, intensity and a wide breadth of knowledge. Unlike the kitchen, I am confident that my satisfaction with this profession would be far greater. Receiving thanks for serving a beautiful preparation of lamb is nice. However, there is much deeper meaning in receiving a smile from a previously tearful child who has had a laceration sutured and pain ameliorated.

Working as a physician will afford me the opportunity to harness my knowledge and skill to obtain substantive results. The idea that treating a patient with a medication, or with a specific operation can make a difference in the quality of a person's life buttresses my commitment to this path. I am confident that my education at Rowan University has provided me with the framework to succeed in medical school, and my years in the restaurant setting have given me a maturity that would not come with general college courses. Providing sustenance for a hungry diner comes with its own rewards; however, my need for scientific knowledge, and my desire to contribute to society can best be satisfied by embarking on a career in medicine. I know that upon obtaining my undergraduate and graduate medical training, I will be capable of fulfilling my potential as a physician as well as a compassionate human being.

See page 257 to find out where this student got in.

MICHELLE JONELIS

Michelle volunteered at a rare dementias clinic for a summer and did basic science research for two summers. Throughout college she danced at least five days a week and was involved in various dance performance groups.

Stats

MCAT: Physical Sciences, 14; Verbal Reasoning, 13; Writing Sample, S; Biological Sciences, 13

Undergraduate overall GPA: 3.76

Undergraduate science GPA: 3.80

Undergraduate college attended: Stanford University

Undergraduate graduation year: 2005

Gender: Female

Race: Caucasian

Applied To

Columbia University, College of Physicians and Surgeons

Cornell University, Weill Medical College

Harvard University, Harvard Medical School

New York University, Mt. Sinai School of Medicine

New York University, NYU School of Medicine

Stanford University, School of Medicine

University of California—Irvine, College of Medicine

University of California — Los Angeles, David Geffen School of Medicine

University of California — San Diego, School of Medicine

University of California — San Francisco, School of Medicine

University of Pennsylvania, School of Medicine

AMCAS Personal Statement

Did it all start with moles? Yes, when I look back, I think it did. When I was in 6th grade, I did my science fair project on malignant melanoma. After presenting the information I'd learned about the different types of melanoma, how to recognize them, and various treatment options, several of my classmates approached me with questions about moles that either they or their family members had and what they should do about them. I think that is when I first realized what it would mean to be a doctor and how much I wanted to be one. I wanted to be able to actually answer their questions and help them, rather than having to simply listen and then tell them that I couldn't help them and they should talk to their doctor.

I had always known I wanted to be a doctor though. My parents are both doctors and from as early as I can remember they would tell me about their work. I was fortunate in that once they realized that I was interested in what they did, they never assumed that what they said would be too complex. Instead, they told me what I wanted to know, and the more questions I asked, the more I would learn. As early as 5th grade I remember hearing about xeroderma pigmentosa, epidermolysis bullosa and other rare skin disorders from my dermatologist father. From my psychiatrist mother I learned about schizophrenia, bipolar disorder and some of the ethical dilemmas associated with clinical research. I would remember the things my parents told me for years to come.

The summer after my junior year of high school I had my first direct experience with basic science research and medicine when I worked in a neurosurgery research lab at Boston Children's Hospital. Because I was only in high school and had no research or upper level biology training, the project that I was given was very simple – staining rat retinal slices for an axon guidance molecule. When I was not working on my project, however, I spent my time talking to the other people in the lab about their research. The focus of the lab was neuronal regeneration in the CNS and there were many different projects, ranging from surgeries on rats to mimic strokes and spinal cord injuries, to studies using a mouse model for ALS, to molecular biology using radioactive tracers. I was fascinated by everything going on and felt privileged to get a taste of what it's like be on the cutting edge of science. A few of the people working in the lab were neurosurgeons, and through them, I was able to observe two neurosurgeries. The neurosurgeries allowed me to see how basic science research could be

Applied To medicine. I left Boston having gained a fascination with the human brain and neuroscience that has only continued to grow.

To experience what clinical research and medical practice were like, I spent the summer after my sophomore year of college working in a dementia clinic at the West Los Angeles Veterans Hospital and UCLA. While there, I had the opportunity to observe patients with all different types of dementia, from Alzheimer's disease to primary progressive aphasia to various occipital lobe disorders. The experience was both fascinating and emotionally trying. It was incredibly interesting to be actually witnessing the disorders I had read about in Oliver Sacks' *The Man who Mistook his Wife for a Hat*. On the other hand, I was saddened that there was so little medicine seemed able to do to help those with the disorders other than diagnose them. Diagnosis, however, is important, and did seem to provide relief to family members in the sense that they now at least knew what was going on. One unexpected thing that I learned that summer was about families and the different types of relationships that exist within them. I realized that dementia, and any disease affecting the personality, affects the entire family and not just the patient. I was incredibly touched by the patience, tolerance and unconditional love shown by some family members, and I found myself slightly angered by those family members who did not seem to care as much about the patient. More than anything, I realized how trying the situation must be and had nothing but the utmost respect for the family members trying to deal with it. Consequently, whereas in Boston I gained a fascination with the brain and neuroscience, in Los Angeles, I learned what it means to experience the complexity of the brain in the context of a person. I learned that medicine is not just about the science and the disease; it is about the people afflicted by the disease, and trying to improve their lives a little, even if there is no cure.

Now I am finally to the point where I am actually applying to medical school and I feel as if I have been anticipating this moment my entire life. I know that it is cliché to say that I want to go to medical school because I want to help people. I really believe that almost any field one goes into can offer the opportunity to help others. It's just a question of how a particular individual is best suited to help. I believe that medicine is my way to help others, not only because I am and have always been good at science, but also because it is what I have wanted to do, and felt I was meant to do, for as long as I can remember. I truly believe that medicine is my passion.

See page 258 to find out where this student got in.

RADHIKA LU BAUER

Radhika volunteered at the maternity ward of a local hospital. She also spent several years as an MCAT and LSAT instructor for The Princeton Review.

Stats

MCAT: Physical Sciences, 10; Verbal Reasoning, 12; Writing Sample, S; Biological Sciences, 9

Graduate school GPA: 3.90

Graduate school attended: University of Pennsylvania

Graduate school degree earned: Doctor of Anthropology (PhD)

Graduate school graduation year: 2005

Undergraduate overall GPA: 3.97

Undergraduate science GPA: 4.00

Undergraduate college attended: State University of New York at Binghamton

Undergraduate graduation year: 1998

Gender: Female

Race: Asian American

Applied To

Cornell University, Weill Medical College

New York University, NYU School of Medicine

Northwestern University, Feinberg School of Medicine

Rush University, Rush Medical College

Saint Louis University, School of Medicine

State University of New York—University at Buffalo, School of Medicine and Biomedical Sciences

State University of New York—Upstate Medical University, College of Medicine

University of Illinois at Chicago, UIC College of Medicine

University of Pennsylvania, School of Medicine

University of Wisconsin—Madison, School of Medicine and Public Health

Yale University, School of Medicine

AMCAS Personal Statement

Within the academy, various realms of human experience are segregated and presented as separate entities. Studies of social theory are relegated to the social sciences, while the integral mechanisms of biology and chemistry are taught in the natural sciences. Unfortunately, this separation potentially obfuscates critical aspects of both socio-cultural and biochemical realms of knowledge. My academic record and secondary experiences evidence a background which effectively bridges these seemingly disparate fields.

Before entering medical school in the fall of 2005, I will have both earned a PhD in Anthropology from the University of Pennsylvania, and have completed fundamental course work in chemistry, physics, and biology. As these achievements suggest, my intellect has been shaped towards the sciences since childhood. In high school, I was able to earn 3 semesters of science credit with advanced placement classes in Biology and Physics. Furthermore, while in school I worked as an assistant in an ophthalmologist's office. For nearly two years, I administered visual field tests, confirmed appointments, and updated patient files, and more recently I have been working with patients as a volunteer in the maternity ward at St. Joseph's Hospital. As such, my intellectual interests were stretched tremendously when I also chose to tackle the obtuse fields of philosophy, anthropology, and social theory. This decision, coupled with my inherent desire for empirical, uniformitarian data, drove my interests towards the intersections of socio-cultural phenomena with human nutrition, osteology, hominid evolution, and population biology. These concerns were manifested in my independent research on vertebrate osteology, primatology, as well as my strong background within prehistoric archaeology, and physical and biological anthropology. Thus, my desire to study medicine is a result of the need to integrate the natural and social sciences. Rather than contemplate humanity on a theoretical or epistemological level, I am determined to impact human lives in a practical manner as a teacher, researcher, and - more directly - as a physician.

This desire is driven by, and emerged out of, my extensive travels in developing nations and throughout the United States. Since childhood, I have been fortunate to visit and live in India, China, and Taiwan. In addition, my undergraduate and graduate anthropological fieldwork has taken me to the developing countries of Bolivia, Mexico, Costa Rica, and India. These travels have exposed me to the inequities of the modern human condition; specifically, I have been able to witness disparities in access to health care, nutrition, and education. With my broad understanding of social theory and forthcoming medical training, I am determined to explore the socio-cultural nexus of these problems and apply the insights of scientific knowledge in order to ameliorate these conditions. For example, it is important to consider how diseases are locally perceived, which in many ways influences how they are contracted, spread, and treated. However, it is also necessary to understand how disease actually affects the body. In other words, it is imperative to couple germ theory with cultural knowledge as it innervates aspects of subsistence, interpersonal relations, socio-economy, religious practice, and the effects of political forces. Hence, it is obvious that the study of medicine is central to understanding human life, and it is the interdigitation between the social and the biochemical which will represent the focus of my intervention as a physician. Thus, while distinctive from other medical school applicants, I would argue that my educational background is advantageous for becoming an effective doctor in today's global community.

I was drawn to the field of anthropology as it allowed me to explore and experience firsthand the complexities of human behavior as imbedded in historical, political, and socio-economic contexts. My desire to broaden the scope through which I understand and impact the lives of others can only be fulfilled through the articulation of anthropological and medical realms of knowledge. For example, diseases such as polio and tuberculosis continue to plague developing nations - although they have been generally eradicated from Western countries - primarily because adequate treatment and prevention requires an understanding of local practices, circumstances, and social relations. This is particularly important in terms of effective health education and the promotion of sanitary living conditions. In other words, it is necessary to marry local, contingent, and cultural variables to overarching scientific frameworks in order to ensure that all humans are afforded the basic health standards that modern scientific research has established. As a medical doctor, I intend to dedicate my career towards the pursuit of this goal - which I am uniquely and superbly qualified to undertake given my ability to integrate the diverse realms of socio-cultural and biochemical knowledge - and thereby improve the quality of life worldwide.

See page 258 to find out where this student got in.

REBECCA SHARIM

Rebecca was in the Pool Premedical Program at Lehigh University, which allowed her to hold summer internships and conduct research at the start of her sophomore year. She co-published two papers, presented research at two national conferences, and composed a senior thesis on stigma and liver disease. She was the recipient of multiple academic awards, including the George Lemmon Award for Research and the Contribution to Student Life Award. She was a 2005 Donald T. Campbell Social Science Research Prizes Finalist.

Stats

MCAT: Physical Sciences, 10; Verbal Reasoning, 9; Writing Sample, R; Biological Sciences, 9

Undergraduate overall GPA: 3.98

Undergraduate science GPA: 3.98

Undergraduate college attended: Lehigh University

Undergraduate graduation year: 2005

Gender: Female

Race: Caucasian

Applied To

Temple University, School of Medicine (applied early decision)

AMCAS Personal Statement

"Never be a doctor if you're going to have any loans to pay back." "Don't do this to yourself." "You'll never have a family if you go to medical school." "The two worst jobs in America belong to physicians and teachers." Without even soliciting their advice, physicians noticed my "Pre-medical Volunteer" nametag, and immediately approached me with words of discouragement. I participated in a volunteer summer internship at St. Mary Hospital in Langhorne, Pennsylvania, following my sophomore year of college, in an effort to gain more experience in the medical field and solidify my lifelong desire to become a physician. Throughout the eight weeks, I spent mandatory hours in both the Emergency Room and the Operating Room, made contacts with physicians in specific areas of interest, and spent time shadowing them. In addition, each of us in the program attended weekly business meetings in which administrators of the hospital and local physicians spoke to us about their particular positions and experiences. Unlike the many years of high school I spent volunteering at a hospital and a nursing home, where I was limited to carrying around food trays and refilling cups of water, I was able to gain hands-on and more intimate experience. Initially uneasy at the site of the blood gushing into plastic sheets draped around the orthopedic surgeon's patient in the OR, it took only a few days to grow accustomed to the images on the television screen during a laparoscopic procedure and the shocking way the neurosurgeon drilled into the patient's brain. By the end of the internship, I was ready to begin my junior year and the application process, with a newfound confidence in my abilities and chosen path. No longer shocked by the procedures or stresses I witnessed, I was only amazed at the lack of encouragement I received, and these quotes still ring sharply in my ears whenever I envision my future. However, instead of discouraging me, the experience only inspired me to pursue my goals further. After that summer, I learned that nothing would deter me from my plans, and that I could still say with conviction that this is what I want to do with my life, despite however much negative feedback I may receive.

As a member of Lehigh University's newly created Pre-medical Pool Scholar's Program, I have been given a variety of opportunities. Despite my strong affinity for the sciences and mathematics, I have always had a keen interest in a liberal arts education. Whenever I am not studying for an organic chemistry class or completing the science requirements, the ultimate treat is to read a good novel, take a religion or literature course, pursue artistic endeavors, or sit down at the piano, which I have been playing for fifteen years. Coming from a diverse family, with parents from different cultures and religious faiths, sociological issues stemming from these types of differences have always intrigued me. Having the opportunity to do additional research has been a wonderful experience for me. I knew that I did not want to spend my elective research in a laboratory, but rather wanted to focus on more personal concerns of medicine. Working with Dr. Lasker, a medical sociologist, has been an eye-opening experience. Together, we study the emotional side of diseases, rather than the biological. We have worked on and completed several projects that study the biomedical, socioemotional, and organizational aspects of concern for individuals with Primary Biliary Cirrhosis. My research focuses on one online support group for these people, and together, Dr. Lasker and I have identified different areas of concern. As an aspiring physician, this research has helped me to recognize the compassion and emotional support that patients desire and physicians should offer. In August 2005, Dr. Lasker and I will travel to San Francisco to present our research at the annual conference of the Society for the Study of Social Problems. We will travel to Washington, D.C. again in November to present this research at the annual conference for the American Public Health Association. I am also looking forward to the upcoming year, in which I will interview patients with different forms of hepatitis and learn about the stigma they experience. This will culminate in a senior year thesis and presentation, as a part of another honors program, the College Scholar Program, of which I am a member. My research has been an inspiring marriage of two of my interests, medicine and socioemotional issues, and through it I have learned valuable lessons about the impact that physicians can have on the mental health of patients.

I also recognize the importance of proper listening, guiding, and teaching, learned through six years of employment. I work full time every summer as a Teaching Associate at a private tutoring center in Morrisville, Pennsylvania. Opened as a center for educational therapy, this space now serves a wide variety of students, each with lessons tailored to their personal needs. My growth there has been invaluable. It has given me the opportunity to work with children and adolescents on a one-to-one basis, proving to me the power of cooperation and discovery. I am able to directly influence my students, whether they are exceptional learners, or simply need personal attention, by illustrating to them not only the mechanics of reading, writing and math, but also the sheer joy of accomplishment. I am a people person and cherish the moments I spend with others. Through this experience at the tutoring center, I have learned that I also value sharing the benefits of education through instruction. One of the lessons I have learned is how important it is for a physician to be a good listener, a patient teacher, and a caring human being. I am eager to apply the interpersonal skills I have mastered throughout my experiences to my future in the medical field. I look forward to a lifetime of learning, exciting new challenges, and the ability to positively affect the lives of others.

See page 259 to find out where this student got in.

RYAN NOVAK

Ryan was Vice President of the Rho Chi pharmacy honor society and Class Representative to the College Board. He received several scholarships and financial awards to do research and shadowed three physicians to get exposure to primary, secondary, and tertiary care in a hospital.

Stats

MCAT: Physical Sciences, 11; Verbal Reasoning, 10; Writing Sample, O; Biological Sciences, 13

Graduate school GPA: 3.71

Graduate degree earned: Doctor of Pharmacy (PharmD)

Graduate school attended: University of Minnesota—Twin Cities

Graduate school graduation year: 2004

Undergraduate overall GPA: 3.68

Undergraduate science GPA: 3.82

Undergraduate colleges attended: Riverland Community College, Florida Atlantic University, University of Minnesota—Twin Cities

Undergraduate graduation year: 2000*

Gender: Male

Race: Caucasian

* This is the year Ryan's graduate course work began at the University of Minnesota—Twin Cities. He did not receive an undergraduate degree before earning his PharmD.

Applied To

University of Minnesota—Duluth, Medical School*

University of Minnesota—Twin Cities, Medical School*

* Ryan completed a single application for both schools.

AMCAS Personal Statement

My first memorable life experience as a child was the Hormel union strike in Austin, MN. I can still remember hordes of men and women huddling in the basement of the local Armory demonstrating support for one another. Even though I was only six years old, I could feel the passion and emotion evoked by the strike. I learned several important life lessons from this early experience. I watched my parents and family persevere with limited resources. My parents upheld their moral convictions with courage despite the economic and social hardships we endured. These were the first life lessons that molded my character, and they have helped guide me toward my goal of being a rural family-practice physician.

At an early age I showed academic promise, but I lacked direction. My parents finalized their divorce during my junior year in high school. This was a very difficult time for me as I was confused and angry. During my senior year, I opted to learn a trade at the local technical college by enrolling in machining technology courses. It wasn't long before I realized this was not the right decision and I needed something more intellectually challenging.

I began my first year of college optimistic. It was in this setting where I met many people who helped me find direction and taught me about perseverance. Within a few weeks of beginning my first year of college, I began tutoring a nontraditional student. Jeremy was a high school dropout but a recent graduate of a GED program. He struggled with his math competency test and was placed in a yearlong review program. We began a consistent regimen of meeting two times a week to improve his math skills. I had the pleasure of watching him grow into a proficient student, and by the next year he was excelling in college algebra.

Because of my valuable experiences at RCC, I tutored a student at Florida Atlantic University. Her name was Jennifer, and she was recovering from a near-fatal car accident. Her mobility was impaired, and she needed physical assistance in the laboratory and tutoring in chemistry lecture class. Despite her difficulty with daily activities, Jennifer managed to successfully complete her class.

My intent at Florida Atlantic University was to enter the biological sciences program and specialize in ichthyology. During this time, I realized my future career allowed for minimal opportunity for doing the things I enjoyed, namely interacting with other people. Because of this, I changed my career path to pharmacy, a profession where I could have more direct impact on people's lives. Also, when I transferred to Florida, I left an important person in Minnesota. As a result, I came home to the University of Minnesota to be close to my future wife.

We encountered a major obstacle during the pharmacy program but one that has made me more compassionate. My wife required two spinal fusions in as many years, and although this was a difficult time for us, our interactions with her physicians contributed immeasurable insight toward my future career. This experience has allowed me to fully appreciate the widespread impact of health on an individual and family.

I entered pharmacy expecting to continue building my personal and professional character, conduct independent research, expand my pharmaceutical knowledge, and personally impact the lives of patients. I am confident I will continue to improve upon the former ideas, although the latter idea is the fundamental driving force for my desire to be a physician. Pharmacists often don't have the opportunity for long-term relationships with patients to the extent that I desire. The rural family-practice setting will allow me to become more integrated with my patients and the community.

My decision has matured through extensive patient interactions. My first contact occurred when I worked as a Lab Care Technician at a local hospital.[1] My primary responsibility was phlebotomy for the inpatient population. This allowed me to experience one-on-one interactions in a setting where I was the caregiver. Most, if not all, patients detested daily blood draws, so I attempted to create the best experience possible.

My years working in pharmacy have contributed to my experience with patients through clinical rotations, the EPhECT project, and working as a pharmacy intern at FUMC. I have also shadowed physicians in a variety of settings. Specifically, it was by shadowing a rural family-practice physician that I experienced the practice setting I find most stimulating. Not only was I exposed to this physician's clinical knowledge, but more important, I had the opportunity to witness the extraordinary relationships that he had cultivated with his patients. He will serve as my benchmark for building personal and professional relationships with my patients.

I plan to enter the M.D. program and continue to excel as I have done in various settings in the past. Ultimately, I plan to serve a rural community as a family-practice physician. Because of my valuable experiences in my hometown, I understand the unique challenges of rural medicine. These underserved areas would benefit greatly from a physician with the pharmacy knowledge I have acquired during the last four years.

[1] At the author's request, the names of certain locations and individuals have been removed from his personal statement and secondary essay.

Secondary Application Essay

You have listed your postsecondary experiences on your AMCAS application. Describe here two (2) separate experiences, what you learned from them, and what they have meant to you.

While on pharmacy rotations at a local hospital, I often attended the core curriculum lectures and daily morning case presentations. These experiences have allowed me to better understand the physician's approach to appropriately diagnosing and treating patients. I realize the importance of a global perspective and completely exhausting all possibilities in order to properly diagnose and treat a patient. While completing medical school I will focus on developing a comprehensive understanding of the many different aspects of medicine in order to better serve my patients.

During a shadowing experience with a physician, we encountered a patient who had schizophrenia. The patient was a previous acquaintance of mine. After completing our interaction with the family, we discovered the patient had been threatening family members with violence. This situation was very complicated because our communication between the patient and the family needed to be carefully executed. The family was afraid their family member, who is the patient, would become increasingly violent if he discovered the true reason for his appointment with his physician. I witnessed the physician serving as more than a medical doctor. He also served as emotional support, a caring friend and confidant for the family. Ultimately, the patient was taken to a psychiatrist for long-term treatment. Without him serving as the intermediate between the patient and appropriate treatment, the patient would never have been willing to visit a psychiatrist. I also learned the importance of confidentiality, especially in a rural town. Information travels fast in this type of setting where most people know each other, and any breach of trust between the patient and physician would destroy my future clinical relationships.

See page 259 to find out where this student got in.

SAMANTHA L. PACE

Samantha traveled extensively as an undergrad. She studied abroad in Haiti and Denmark and lived on the Pine Ridge Reservation in South Dakota. She taught courses—including labs—in undergraduate biology and was actively involved in her school's newspaper. She is also a skilled pianist.

Stats

MCAT: Physical Sciences, 11; Verbal Reasoning, 11; Writing, R; Biological Sciences, 11

Graduate school GPA: 4.00

Graduate school program: University of Minnesota—Twin Cities

Graduate school : Master of History of Medicine (MA)

Graduate school graduation year: 2005*

Undergraduate overall GPA: 3.75

Undergraduate science GPA: 3.73

Undergraduate college attended: University of Minnesota—Twin Cities

Undergraduate graduation year: 2001

Gender: Female

Race: Asian American

* Samantha aims to complete her master's thesis by the end of medical school.

Applied To

Case Western Reserve, School of Medicine

Cornell University, Weill Medical College

Duke University, School of Medicine

Georgetown University, School of Medicine

Harvard University, Harvard Medical School

Medical College of Wisconsin

Stanford University, School of Medicine

University of California—San Francisco, School of Medicine

University of Cincinnati, College of Medicine

University of Minnesota—Twin Cities, Medical School

University of North Carolina—Chapel Hill, UNC School of Medicine

University of Rochester, School of Medicine and Dentistry

AMCAS Personal Statement

Steeped in a liberal arts background of music and philosophy, I am constantly bombarded with the question, "Why do you want to be a doctor?!" Although I could explain why my desires, personality and abilities have tailored me into a future physician, I would rather let the rest of my application answer that question and instead focus my words on my passion for international medicine.

I was born in Seoul, South Korea, on September 5, 1978 - a Virgo by the astrological calendar, a Horse by the Chinese calendar, and a Korean by anyone's calendar. When I was younger, I remember honestly surprising myself when I would catch a casual glimpse of my reflection while walking past a mirror. Constantly surrounded by my Caucasian family and living in Minnesota, I completely identified with American culture and was vaguely disturbed that my physical appearance failed to match. Home-schooled by my mother from age 8 to 18, I trained for 12 years to become a concert pianist, developing a discipline, concentration and love for all music that remains even today. The summer before my freshman year, however, I veered from a future in piano to major in philosophy and ultimately pursue medicine. Little did I know then that my developing self-identity, my choice of major and my travel experiences would unconditionally lead me to international medicine.

Initially, my desire to become a doctor was raw and unrefined. Motivated by a naive altruism, I wanted "to make the world a better place," and medicine represented a field that combined the dedication demanded by music with the beneficence music had lacked. In college, though, a more sophisticated sense of self-in-world emerged when I first grasped I was an *Asian*-American. From hearing the simple question "So where are you from?" to the childhood taunts of "Chink!" I had always felt as if I should be an American but somehow was not. Once at the university, however, a newly discovered multi-cultural world greeted and welcomed me, and I finally learned how to appreciate my own reflection in a mirror. Never feeling at home anywhere yet somehow living comfortably everywhere, I knew the cosmopolitan must somehow figure into my medical career. Being an adopted Korean has also refined my sense of subtle discrimination. For patients, illness not only compromises their health but also transforms their entire sense of self. Growing up in Minnesota has enabled me not only to sympathize but also to empathize with those who feel set apart from the majority.

Studying philosophy also fostered my newfound love of the international. Philosophy is what you make of it and unfortunately, thinking deep thoughts about being unemployed can only take you so far. I originally chose philosophy because I admired the Renaissance figure. Obviously, the pre-medical courses would develop the analytical scientific rationale, but when faced with a vulnerable patient, a chemical equation can offer neither solace nor sympathy. Philosophy, though, encourages one to look beyond anatomy and biology and to embrace the existential and ethical questions that concern all humankind. Although Heidegger famously stated, "Every man dies alone," ethical philosophy dictates that such apathy is unacceptable. I have seen a patient die because there was no blood bank to provide a simple blood transfusion, and I once cradled a baby girl with orange-tinted hair because of chronic malnutrition. In both instances, my outrage and frustration were futile. Although one person cannot change a country (let alone the world), I sought to channel my feelings into a career that could share the wealth and privilege with which I have been freely granted.

Seizing any opportunity to learn more about my prospective career, I traveled as much as I could during college. Volunteering at hospitals in Haiti and the Pine Ridge Indian Reservation, researching traditional Haitian health beliefs, and studying European medical practice, policy and bioethics in Denmark dispelled any romantic notions I had about working abroad, yet strengthened the resolve to continue. Constantly challenged to adapt and survive in foreign cultures, I quickly learned the value of flexibility, tolerance and communication. Observing cross-cultural health care and the accompanying ethical dilemmas inspired me to write my honors thesis on non-traditional medical ethics, and seeking out advice from medical personnel with extensive experience in international health has given me invaluable personal perspectives to the career. My master's degree is in the history of medicine, from which I learned about the social and historical aspects to not only the U.S. medical system, but to healing and sickness around the world.

Directly experiencing health care in three different settings - Haiti, the Pine Ridge Reservation and Denmark - has committed me to global medicine and constantly reminds me of the flip side of the health care coin. Most global health crises occur in developing nations, and as an international health worker, I can never take for granted the vast medical advances of the US and Europe. Rather, I hope to contribute my efforts toward lessening the gap between the two worlds.

See page 259 to find out where this student got in.

SAMANTHA VIZZINI

Samantha did neuroscience research at the Medical University of South Carolina and had the opportunity to be a student observer at the Center for Pain Management in Atlanta, Georgia. She was a member of the Alpha Epsilon Delta premedical honor society, a peer tutor, and involved in Greek life.

Stats

MCAT: Physical Sciences, 10; Verbal Reasoning, 10; Writing Sample, Q;
   Biological Sciences, 10

Undergraduate overall GPA: 3.30

Undergraduate science GPA: 3.50

Undergraduate colleges attended: Tulane University

Undergraduate graduation year: 2005

Gender: Female

Race: Caucasian

Applied To

Emory University, School of Medicine

Medical College of Georgia, School of Medicine

Tulane University, School of Medicine

AMCAS Personal Statement

The summer before my senior year at Tulane I thought I knew exactly what I wanted out of life, but that was the summer I realized how little I actually know about life and about myself. I had always dreamed of becoming a doctor but until then I did not understand why. It was always a feeling I had and could never really explain. Becoming a doctor just made sense to me. But that summer, after filling out my Medical School applications for the first time, I learned why I truly want to be a doctor.

I spent the entire summer working in a pain management clinic, following the Doctor around picking up after him while trying to pick up any knowledge possible. I was so excited to be in a real Doctor's office, observing patient examinations and procedures, but I had no idea that the real lesson I would learn would be about myself. Not that I didn't learn a great deal that summer observing Dr. Kabakibou, but I learned much more talking with his patients.

There was one patient in particular that I remember more than anyone I met in those few months. She was an older woman, divorced, and in her late fifties. She was a hair dresser running a school and a business out of her home with her daughter who was also a patient of Dr. KK. Like most of Dr. KK's patients they lived far from the metro area and drove many hours each month to see him. She was suffering from chronic back pain and was receiving a series of epidural steroid injections. Every month when she came in Dr. KK would send me to the pharmacy to get her a valium to calm her nerves for the procedure. As the valium started to take effect I would often sit in the exam room with her and discuss her life and her family.

We talked about her daughters, one who worked with her and suffered from endometriosis as well as chronic pain, and the other who ran off with her boyfriend, leaving an infant behind. We talked about everything from her court struggle to get custody of her granddaughter to her realization that the women she taught had been stealing her medication as well as her money. It was through these talks that I learned how strong this woman is. How amazing and resilient she must have been to be fighting against all of this and to still be so tolerant and compassionate. She taught me to see the good in people and to forgive the bad. She believed the people who stole from her were obviously fighting against something bigger than themselves and they could not help what they did, therefore we have no choice but to forgive them.

However, through discussions with this woman, and many other patients, I learned that there are many more people in this world fighting against things that seem bigger than themselves yet are succeeding in this struggle everyday. These people are the reason I want to be a doctor. To help those who are fighting for every moment they get in life. The people who refuse to let anything get in their way. These remarkable people inspired me all summer long to see each problem for what it is: an obstacle that I can overcome, even if it requires asking for help. They taught me so much yet at the end of my summer each one thanked me for helping them. I politely said goodbye to each of them and wished them well yet to this day I am still shocked. I should have been the one thanking them for teaching me the most important lessons I have ever learned; lessons that I could never have learned in school; lessons about myself and about life. To these people I will be eternally grateful, for showing me how what seemed like such a small effort on my part could make such a big difference to so many people, and for helping me understand the massive impact the medical profession has on people's lives, including my own.

See page 259 to find out where this student got in.

TARA A. O'CONNELL

Tara worked as a health professions adviser and volunteered at an emergency room and at a dialysis center. She also held a solo photography exhibit and traveled internationally. As an undergrad, she raced at the national level for Cal Poly's mountain bike team.

Stats

MCAT: Physical Sciences, 12; Verbal Reasoning, 9; Writing Sample, P; Biological Sciences, 10

Undergraduate overall GPA: 3.60

Undergraduate science GPA: 3.50

Undergraduate colleges attended: University of California—Santa Cruz, Orange Coast Community College, Saddleback Community College, California Polytechnic State University—San Luis Obispo

Undergraduate graduation year: 2002

Gender: Female

Race: Caucasian

Applied To

Albany Medical College

Boston University, School of Medicine

Dartmouth College, Dartmouth Medical School

Duke University, School of Medicine

George Washington University, School of Medicine and Health Sciences

Georgetown University, School of Medicine

Johns Hopkins University, School of Medicine

Northwestern University, Feinberg School of Medicine

Oregon Health & Science University, School of Medicine

Stanford University, School of Medicine

Thomas Jefferson University, Jefferson Medical College

Tufts University, School of Medicine

University of California—Irvine, College of Medicine

University of California—Los Angeles, David Geffen School of Medicine

University of California—San Diego, School of Medicine

University of California—San Francisco, School of Medicine

University of Maryland, School of Medicine

University of Minnesota—Twin Cities, Medical School
University of Southern California, Keck School of Medicine
University of Washington, School of Medicine
University of Wisconsin—Madison, School of Medicine and Public
   Health
Vanderbilt University, School of Medicine
Yeshiva University, Albert Einstein College of Medicine

AMCAS Personal Statement

A few seconds passed as I sat holding a spoonful of maggots in front of my lips. Finally I unlocked my jaws and shoved the heap pf worms in. The maggots actually tasted quite good and before long I had polished off a small bowl full of the plump critters. My two travel companions sat by my side and the three of us giggled our way through the exciting meal of worms.

While traveling throughout Southeast Asia, my travel companions and I laughed our way through a number of new adventures. We laughed when we realized that at any given moment at least on of us felt like the star of a Pepto Bismo commercial. And my travel companions enjoyed a good laugh as they watched me mistakenly wheelie a motorcycle into a gas station pump in Thailand. Yet, most importantly, the three of us laughed and smiled as a way to share our joy for life with those people whom we meet along our travels.

During my time spent in Southeast Asia, I was actively pursuing a career in photography. So, when I returned to UC Santa Cruz, after having taken fall quarter off to travel, I was delighted to develop the film from my trip. I spent the next few months in the dark room, and after developing seventy-five roles of film and nearly three hundred prints, I began the process of selecting those images that would be hung in my show.

At the time, I remember standing on my coffee table in Santa Cruz with hundreds of black and white images scattered on the floor below. I had utilized this technique before as a way to assess what a group of individual photos meant to me when placed together as a whole. Only this time, as I gazed at the many intimate photographs of people I had meet in Southeast Asia, I began to see more then a cohesive work of art, As I looked at all the images of people scattered on the floor, I began to realize that what I truly enjoyed about photography was the intimate relationships it allowed me to develop with others and myself.

In fact, I slowly became conscience that in general what satisfied me most in my life were those activities that involved being a part of a community. I knew that photography satisfied my desire to participate in a diversity of relationships, but I questioned if there might be a career that would better enable me to help elevate the scaffolding on which communities can be built. I had entered college straight from high school and after two years at UC Santa Cruz, I felt compelled to take a step back in order to reassess where I was headed.

I liken the experience of letting go of a career as a photographer to letting go of a solid grip while rock climbing. Once I had let go, I swung back and forth for a while before I was able to re-anchor myself. During that "swinging" period, I made a few important discoveries in my life. One, I learned how to be comfortable with the fact that I didn't know exactly were I was headed. Two, I discovered that the best way to get anywhere was to take a first step. After working through an important time of confusion, I took my first step to toward a new route in my life. I enrolled in some classes at a local junior college and made sure to keep my eyes wide open.

My first day of chemistry class, the teacher walked in wearing a glow in the dark shirt of the periodic table and proceeded to belt out a song about the elements. By the end of the semester, I too felt so excited about science that if given the chance I would have proudly song out loud tale of rediscovered love. The enthusiasm I felt for science and my passion for health along with my love of people directed me to the new goal of becoming a doctor. With each investigative step I took regarding a career in medicine, I continually reconfirmed that I had appropriately redirected myself on the rock.

Currently, as a health professions peer advisor at Cal Poly, I see many students with anxiety because they are unsure exactly what career they want to pursue. I always enjoy sharing with these students about my transition from pursuing a career as a photographer to my goal of becoming a doctor. I share how important it was to have the courage to question were I was headed. I stress the significance I placed on taking time to discover what made me happy, But most of all, I commend the students for putting forth the energy to search for answers and I remind them that the grandest of dreams is actualized by first taking one step.

See page 259 to find out where this student got in.

TERI MARSH

Teri was a high school teacher after college. She also spent time as a marine conservationist before focusing on medicine. She volunteered with a physician treating HIV-positive individuals the year prior to sending out her medical school applications.

Stats

MCAT: Physical Sciences, 10; Verbal Reasoning, 11; Writing, S; Biological Sciences, 11

Graduate school GPAs: 3.77 (University of Washington), 3.79 (San Jose State University)

Graduate degrees earned: Master of Marine Affairs (MMA) from UW, Master of Physiology (MP) from SJSU

Graduate schools attended: University of Washington, San Jose State University

Graduate school graduation years: 1997 (UW), 2005 (SJSU)

Undergraduate overall GPA: 3.33

Undergraduate science GPA: NA

Undergraduate college attended: University of California—Santa Cruz

Undergraduate graduation year: 1992

Gender: Female

Race: Caucasian

Applied To

Cornell University, Weill Medical College

New York Medical College

New York University, Mount Sinai School of Medicine

New York University, NYU School of Medicine

Ohio State University, College of Medicine and Public Health

Oregon Health & Science University, School of Medicine

Stanford University, School of Medicine

University of California—Davis, School of Medicine

University of California—Irvine, College of Medicine

University of California—Los Angeles, David Geffen School of Medicine

University of California—San Diego, School of Medicine

University of California—San Francisco, School of Medicine

University of Cincinnati, College of Medicine

University of North Carolina—Chapel Hill, UNC School of Medicine

University of Southern California, Keck School of Medicine

University of Vermont, College of Medicine

University of Wisconsin—Madison, School of Medicine and Public
   Health

Wake Forest University, School of Medicine

Yeshiva University, Albert Einstein College of Medicine

AMCAS Personal Statement

I have avoided going to medical school all my life. I grew up in a home of health care professionals, but wanted to find a life beyond my parents and grandparents. I was young, passionate, and smart, so, naturally, easily distracted. I set off to capture something different from life and in many ways I did. Only in the past couple of years have I discovered my own innate desire to become a physician, a culmination of years of experiences and personal growth. I have been a dedicated teacher and student, an intrigued scientist and a frustrated policy-maker, an international wanderer and a decisive leader. I've been a daughter, a sister, a friend, and a favorite aunt. I have not traveled a narrow path, but one that has afforded me wonderful experiences. Now through the wising of time, I realize that I am exactly where I should be.

My love of working with people will make me a great doctor in one-on-one settings; a variety of other skills I have acquired over the years will enhance my contributions to a medical institution and to the field of medicine. As a self-supporting student, I learned time management and critical thinking skills. Working in policy I learned to be diplomatic. I often worked with a variety of stakeholders, assessing the impacts that policies would have on them and integrating their viewpoints into my decision-making. As a teacher I learned patience, leadership and organization.

I am proud of my marine policy work. It was sound, science-based work. I am proud of the organizations for which I've worked. However, trapped in front of a computer screen left me uninspired, not to mention disappointed that my hard work had such seemingly little impact in the snail-paced world of environmental policy.

As a teacher, I got the personal interaction I had been craving. The year I taught at Traveling School International we had 36 students, ranging in age from 12 to 18 years. My smallest class had only two students, and it was this very personal nature of the school, from its design, with one big living room we all shared, to its emphasis on personal growth, that brought me in close contact with each student every day. When we traveled I was teacher, disciplinarian and confidant from our pre-breakfast exercise to our call for lights out. I often augmented my lights-out warnings with a bedtime story. No matter how tired I was, it was this time of day I enjoyed most, when I had the privilege to just be there for and with a room full of sometimes exhausted, often homesick kids. I loved the trust they gave me, whether as a knowledgeable math teacher or an adult to lean on. It was exhausting, but I would never again trade working with and helping people for a desk-tied office job.

Although I loved these aspects of teaching, I also felt a need for greater intellectual challenge and growth. Returning to school was a turning point for me. I absolutely loved the world of physiology. Craving more, I enrolled in a physiology graduate program. In retrospect, it seems inevitable that my curiosity and passion for learning would lead me to seek ways to understand the practical application of all that I was learning. I realized I needed to understand pathophysiology and treatment options as well.

I decided to augment my studies with practical experience. For the past nine months I have been volunteering with a physician who sees primarily HIV-infected and hospice patients. This experience has been deeply gratifying. Not only do I see a great doctor at work, I have also seen the impact he has on his patients' lives. What has made this such a poignant experience is that Dr. Leff was in the process of retiring from his private practice when I began volunteering. The reactions of his patients ranged from disappointment to distress. Through his reflections I realize he is ending this part of his career with tremendous pride. My time working closely with his patients has given me a taste of that world. The small conversations we had while I took their vital signs don't begin to compare to the intimate conversations between patient and doctor. Nevertheless, these moments have given me a taste of a greater, more fulfilling career than I've ever known.

I am indebted to the patients and Dr. Leff for what they've taught me about the doctor's role as a companion and sometimes guide between life and death. I am happy to bring my Spanish language skills to the office; I feel some of the same gratitude and personal connection patients so naturally give to Dr. Leff when I am able to eliminate the impersonality and frustration of the telephone translation service. As much as it gives the patients a sense of comfort, it gives me great satisfaction, and I will continue to serve Spanish-speaking patients throughout my career.

Being a physician will couple my love of physiology with my commitment to working with people. I know now that I will travel this path with the strength, compassion and commitment that will make me a doctor who doesn't just bears the letters M.D., but lives up to all that they imply: a kind, concerned and dedicated health care provider. More than any other profession, the work and human connection as a physician will help me find fulfillment as I help others in ways in which I am skilled.

See page 260 to find out where this student got in.

THAYER HEATH

Thayer was an All-American in track and field. After earning his undergraduate degree, he spent over five years in the financial services industry. He volunteered at the San Francisco Free Clinic and worked at UCSF's Department of Molecular and Cellular Biology prior to applying to medical school.

Stats

MCAT: Physical Sciences, 12; Verbal Reasoning, 11; Writing Sample, Q; Biological Sciences, 12

Undergraduate overall GPA: 3.60

Undergraduate science GPA: 3.60

Undergraduate college attended: Stanford University

Undergraduate graduation year: 1997

Gender: Male

Race: Caucasian/Asian American

Applied To

Columbia University, College of Physicians and Surgeons

Cornell University, Weill Medical College

Duke University, School of Medicine

Georgetown University, School of Medicine

Harvard University, Harvard Medical School

New York University, Mount Sinai School of Medicine

New York University, NYU School of Medicine

Northwestern University, Feinberg School of Medicine

Oregon Health & Science University, School of Medicine

University of California—Davis, School of Medicine

University of California—Irvine, College of Medicine

University of California—Los Angeles, David Geffen School of Medicine

University of California—San Diego, School of Medicine

University of California—San Francisco, School of Medicine

University of Chicago, Pritzker School of Medicine

University of Colorado, School of Medicine

University of Hawaii, John A. Burns School of Medicine

University of Miami, School of Medicine

University of Southern California, Keck School of Medicine

University of Washington, School of Medicine

Yale University, School of Medicine

AMCAS Personal Statement

I formed buck teeth, pulled out my ears, squeaked, and asked, "Rat?" To my dismay, Osa nodded yes. My stomach revolted at the thought of such an unappetizing meal, but I just couldn't offend my starving host. Besides, we had just eaten monkey the night before, and I was still alive. So I bit in. The first bite was full of bones — little rat ribs, to be precise. What a great way to start a day.

I ate this breakfast with Osa's tribe in the Laos highlands during an eight month trek through the back roads of South America and Asia. Along the way, I topped Himalayan peaks, surfed Indonesian waves, samba'd at Carnaval, and soaked up local cultures. Although it was a great adventure, this trek had a higher purpose: it was a soul search for a new direction in life. I was leaving behind the world of Silicon Valley finance that had defined my first six years out of college.

Although I majored in biology and had an ongoing interest in medicine, I also developed an interest in the financial markets during my college years. Financial services firms offered immediate and appealing opportunities, so I joined Cambridge Associates and later Goldman Sachs. Each company provided intriguing responsibilities, intelligent co-workers, high profile clients, and nice promotions. But at the end of the day, I never found the work rewarding or meaningful.

And so I began my trip, hoping to find a more fulfilling path in life. Far from my customary surroundings, I reconnected with my core interests, which led me back to my earlier ambitions of pursuing a career in medicine.

As a student, a medical career seemed to be a strong marriage of my academic interests and my desire to have a career centered on positive and influential relationships. I majored in biology because I was fascinated with the capacity and delicate balances of the human body, most likely from my years as a competitive athlete. Years later, on my travels through third world nations, I began to understand more clearly my potential to have a meaningful impact on the lives of others. I often stayed with local families, sharing meals and exchanging cultures. I was given a glimpse into the tremendous difficulties that were present in their daily lives compared to mine. Soon, it became obvious that a career in medicine would provide the ideal platform for me to improve the lives of individual people by learning and applying a body of knowledge that has always intrigued me.

Naturally, I had some reservations about leaving an established and comfortable career to start anew. So after my trip, I exposed myself to medicine as thoroughly as possible. First, I shadowed several MDs, witnessing the tremendous satisfaction of being able to heal another person and building relationships with patients. My next step, at St. Mary's ER, increased my level of observation, exposing me to trauma and putting me into contact with patients. Although my responsibilities were limited, I enjoyed many of my "gopher" tasks: turning a parched patient into a grateful one with a cup of water, sprinting with a gurney to assist in a code blue, or consoling a mentally ill woman until her son arrived. However, I was eager to expand my patient interactions.

I found a rewarding solution at the San Francisco Free Clinic where I volunteer. When a patient arrives, I document their medical history and concerns, perform simple procedures (e.g. drawing blood, ear irrigation) and administer basic tests (e.g. urinalysis, lung capacity). I enjoy establishing relationships with our patients and watching them progress. It is wonderful to be involved with an institution of motivated professionals that provides quality health care to people in need.

To continue this trend of increased clinical responsibility and exposure to the underserved, I will spend the month of July on Utila Island in Honduras, volunteering with an American MD. As the island's only physician, he provides all the medical care for the 1500 residents.

To supplement my clinical pursuits and feed my inquisitive nature, I work in UCSF's Orthopaedic Dept. Our group explores craniofacial development using quail/duck chimeras. My work spans the process, from creating a "quck" via a neural crest transplant to developing figures for publications. I view research as an excellent way to nurture my interest in lifelong learning. After a seven year hiatus, it feels good to wear a lab coat again.

As I reflect on my circuitous path from biology classrooms to corporate offices to the corners of the world and finally to the medical field, I am thankful for the breadth of my experiences. At the end of this unconventional path, I have found a sense of purpose that I had been missing for so many years. I am excited to pursue a medical career and am grateful to have found my calling.

Recently, I saw a patient at the free clinic with a history of unsuccessful blood draws and a fear of needles. She was relieved to see me because I had previously drawn her blood on the first try. But she was still nervous. I calmed her down, struck a vein on the first attempt, and filled the vials. "Wheeeew," she sighed, and a big smile spread over her face. Now that is the type of contagious smile that can stay on my face all day long — even on a day that starts with rats for breakfast.

See page 261 to find out where this student got in.

ANONYMOUS 1

For two years after college, the applicant worked as a registered dietitian and attended school full-time to meet medical school prerequisites. She also did research on food intake in low-income populations and taught for the local office of the American Heart Association.

Stats

MCAT: Physical Sciences, 9; Verbal Reasoning, 11; Writing Sample, R; Biological Sciences, 9

Undergraduate overall GPA: 3.86

Undergraduate science GPA: 3.66

Undergraduate college attended: University of Minnesota—Twin Cities

Undergraduate graduation year: 2003

Gender: Female

Race: Caucasian

Applied To

Medical College of Wisconsin

Tufts University, School of Medicine

University of Illinois at Chicago, UIC College of Medicine

University of Iowa, Roy J. and Lucille A. Carver College of Medicine

University of Minnesota—Duluth, Medical School

University of Minnesota—Twin Cities, Medical School

University of North Dakota, School of Medicine and Health Sciences

University of Wisconsin—Madison, School of Medicine and Public Health

AMCAS Personal Statement

He looked like he was dead and it scared me. Four hours before I was a carefree college freshman away from home for the first time and loving it. That was until I got the call from my mom to come home…soon. I was now in the ICU, watching my dad, his eyes shifting back and forth, his hands in restraints, his body yellowed and drenched in iodine solution. At the age of 44 my father my lie on a gurney after an emergency triple coronary bypass procedure. He had finally gone in for a routine check-up after 15 years of avoiding doctors and was told the surgery was imminent. As I stood there in that stuffy room, my mind racing, my ears numbed by the humming of strange machines, I wondered, "What happens next?"

What happened next was my father recovered and my family came to realize that a family history of heart disease was not something to be taken lightly. In the past family members had not suspected anything more than the obvious when three of my grandparents passed away in their fifties. Many of my aunts and uncles who were tested dismissed concern when their cholesterol levels came back in the 300's and 400's. Things were different now. Within a year my extended and immediate family members all had their lipids drawn. About half of us were advised to begin statins, myself included. About half of those advised actually did.

Coming from Northern Minnesota it frustrates me to know that many residents dismiss the need for regular medical care. I heard my own father say it many times. "I'll be fine. I'll go in if I'm really sick." The truth is he was. He just didn't know it. Seeing a physician regularly could have prevented it from going as far as it did.

My dad's surgery made me think harder about what I wanted to do for a career. I was taking a basic nutrition course and became extremely interested in the effect nutrition had on health. I set out to become a dietitian.

I took classes in many areas including counseling, food safety, and even management. I was, however, fully engrossed in my biochemistry and core science courses. The human body was incredible. I would rattle off interesting facts to my friends and family and stay up until 2 AM reading physiology. There was a period when my roommate started calling me the human medical dictionary. With all of this information, I wanted to know more.

Over next three years I interned at two large hospitals in the Twin Cities area. I came to love the medical setting. I caught on quickly to the terminology and came to thrive on the pace of the day. The work was interesting and challenging. At the county hospital I remember hearing five different languages in the same waiting room. I recall helping a homeless diabetic man find a steady source of food to help control his blood sugars. I also took a job with the government program WIC (Women, Infants and Children) in Ramsey County. There I provided health education and distributed food to low-income mothers and their children. At the clinic I met a little girl, tired and anemic, hemoglobin 6.5, who we rushed to a doctor. I counseled a Hmong woman and her 70 pound four year-old on childhood obesity. My experiences an intern and as a professional opened my eyes to the unfulfilled need for medical care in Minnesota.

Currently as a dietitian at St Luke's, a hospital in my hometown, I realize that need is especially crucial in greater Minnesota. I've seen patients from the Iron Range who come in for hip surgery and end up being diagnosed with diabetes, after living with the disease and complications for years. I've treated patients in their eighties who have fallen and lay on their floor at home for days because they have no one to check in on them while living alone. I am grateful when I can really help a patient. However, I can't help but think of the vast area of people that rely on Duluth for medical care. How many people are out there that the current hospitals and clinics are not seeing? Could there be someone missing from the cardiac rehab classes I teach that is just as stubborn as my own father was?

I want to go to medical school and become a primary care physician in Minnesota because I feel I can fill the gap between patients receiving no medical care at all and patients with an immediate need for care. I would like the opportunity to treat those people, like my dad, that need medical attention but do not know it; to be the first line of intervention and education for those in underserved areas.

I help patients everyday in my profession now but I know I have the potential to do more than that. I wish to show patients how to improve their health before their family members are left wondering, "What happens next?"

See page 262 to find out where this student got in.

ANONYMOUS 2

The Applicant earned a BFA in studio art and taught for two years with Teach For America. She also worked as a waitress, led a high school study abroad program in Ireland, and volunteered at a women's health clinic.

Stats*

MCAT: NA

Graduate school GPA: 3.93

Graduate degree earned: Masters of Education (MEd)

Graduate school attended: Loyola Marymount University

Graduate school graduation year: 2002

Undergraduate overall GPA: 3.83

Undergraduate science GPA: NA

Undergraduate college attended: University of North Carolina — Chapel Hill

Undergraduate graduation year: 2000

Gender: Female

Race: Caucasian

* During the 2002–2003 academic year, the applicant was enrolled in a post-baccalaureate premedical program at Bryn Mawr College. This is where she fulfilled all of her medical school prerequisites. Students in the program had the option of applying early to one of several medical schools partnering with the college. If they were accepted to that school and maintained a high GPA in the program—the applicant's cumulative GPA was 3.77—the MCAT was not required.

Applied To

Brown University, Brown Medical School (early decision)

AMCAS Personal Statement

Jocie Cortez, thirteen, stares down at the 12" by 17" sheet of drawing paper. Her blank look matches the empty page in front of her. Two weeks into the semester, the class works steadily on their first drawing project. The assignment, titled "My Walk Through Life Drawing," involves students drawing their shoe surrounded by images about their past, present, or future. Noting Jocie's hesitancy to begin, I approach her and squat down at her table.

"You're stuck," I say, asking and declaring at the same time.

Jocie nods, and a shy smile replaces the empty gaze on her plump yet beautiful face.

"Well," I say in my practical teacher voice, "Let's keep it simple: Do you want to focus on your past, your present, or your future?"

A clouded look passes over Jocie's face. Then Sandy, her outspoken tablemate, blurts out, *"Jocie tiene un hijo."*

Jocie has a child.

"Well that's something to draw about," I say, attempting to regroup and mask my disbelief. Then I proceed in Spanish, asking Jocie questions about her child as if taking an elaborate patient history.

Jocie's son, ironically named Angel, is now seven months old. He was born premature, weighing under five pounds at delivery. Jocie had no prenatal care: In fact, she managed to disguise her pregnancy from her family until the third trimester. Jocie now spends afternoons looking after her baby, while her homework is forgotten. Now an eighth grader, she is failing every class except art.

Jocie begins her drawing, sketching a baby bottle and some booties next to her larger shoe. Angel's welfare has become Jocie's past, present and future. I watch Jocie work, but I want to *take charge*. I want to be her doctor, to provide the essential health care her situation requires as she continues on a difficult walk through life.

Given that my father is a gynecological oncologist and my mother a pediatrician, I have had longstanding exposure to both academic medicine and community private practice work. My parents provided a window into the stimulating and complex responsibility of their positions. Nonetheless, they encouraged me to explore college studies outside of a route pre-medical course work track. With my interest in cultures and talent in visual arts, I pursued opportunities to travel and make art in and about diverse communities. While living in Ireland, I worked with domestic violence victims in a Dublin slum, using art as a vehicle of therapy, expression, and empowerment. I assisted community artists in Belfast who were providing workshops for troubled youth, focusing on peace-making and multicultural education.

My own art emphasized themes of metaphysical and physiological pain and healing. College projects included an installation and photographic work about breast surgery and post-op psychological issues, a series of paintings about the healing powers of Holy Wells in Ireland, and large-scale mixed-media works showing abstracted brain function. Human figure drawing and photography were also foci of my independent artwork. My senior thesis project was a public installation piece depicting suburban development as a surgical procedure invading rural land in my home community.

After graduating from the University of North Carolina with a BFA in Studio Art, I moved to Los Angeles as a Teach For America Corps member. Teach For America enlists high-achieving college graduates with no background in education to commit two years to teaching in our nation's neediest public schools. Because of my fluency in Spanish and previous experience working with Latino populations, I was placed in East Los Angeles, a historic Mexican-American *barrio*. As a teacher in this impoverished community, I am a front-line witness to the lack of decent, sustained health care and its impact on children's education. Untreated health problems like asthma, poor nutrition and obesity, attention deficit hyperactivity disorder, and fetal alcohol syndrome impede many of my students from evolving as educated adolescents. By working with these students and volunteering at White Memorial Hospital in East LA, I have had many experiences that have made me appreciate the complexity of a community's health care needs. While teaching art to these students gives me a unique window into their joys and concerns in life, I seek a more involved and immediate role in their healthy development.

Recently, I shadowed third year medical students at Duke Medical Center's cervix clinic, helping take patient histories and learning about the role of the medical student in the clinical environment. The clinic provides treatment for low-income women from public satellite clinics who have mild to severe cervical dysplasia. One of our patients was a twenty-three year old, HIV positive, Honduran woman who had recently delivered her second child. Like my student Jocie, she had no prenatal health care. She was in the cervix clinic for a follow-up visit after having an abnormal pap smear. The medical student and I worked with a translator to take her medical history. She listened and responded, rubbing her belly and focusing her worried gaze on the linoleum floor. At the end of the interview, we asked for her remaining questions or concerns.

Her eyes looked up, clearly overwhelmed. "*¿Me digaís que es cáncer?*" Are you telling me I have cancer?

Through the translator, the medical student proceeded to explain the difference between dysplasia and cancer, and how, with follow-up visits and regular pap smears, her condition should never reach the cancerous stage. The woman's face relaxed, and she nodded along enthusiastically. But I was concerned: Are these woman's other doctors effectively communicating her medical problems to her? Does she have consistent access to preventative health care information and services? Will she take a proactive role in her and her children's health care? I fear that for her and her young family's case, "follow-up treatment" and "preventative health care" are more abstract concepts than necessary realities.

From rural North Carolina to East Los Angeles, populations of Americans lack the basic health awareness and services necessary to grow as healthy and productive individuals. I seek the urgent challenge of becoming a doctor, leader, and agent of change in our nation's disadvantaged communities.

See page 262 to find out where this student got in.

ANONYMOUS 3

The applicant was awarded a Pfizer Fellowship in molecular biology and had her research published in Archives of Ophthalmology. She volunteered as a patient assistant in the Radiology Department at the University of Wisconsin Hospital and was named Volunteer of the Month in September 1998. She was also on UW's lightweight crew team, which was undefeated during the 1999–2000 season. After she received her undergraduate degree, she left school for a year and worked as an associate research specialist on the Childhood Origins of Asthma (COAST) project, an ongoing study testing whether there is a critical time in a child's life when genetic and environmental factors, primarily viral infections, come together to cause asthma and other allergies.

Stats

MCAT: Physical Sciences, 10; Verbal Reasoning, 7; Writing Sample, Q;
   Biological Sciences, 11

Undergraduate overall GPA: 3.78

Undergraduate science GPA: 3.77

Undergraduate colleges attended: University of Wisconsin—Madison

Undergraduate graduation year: 2002

Gender: Female

Race: Caucasian

Applied To

Loyola University Chicago, Stritch School of Medicine

Medical College of Wisconsin

Ohio State University, College of Medicine and Public Health

University of Iowa, Roy J. and Lucille A. Carver College of Medicine

University of Minnesota—Twin Cities, Medical School

University of North Carolina—Chapel Hill, UNC School of Medicine

University of Virginia, School of Medicine

University of Wisconsin—Madison, School of Medicine and Public Health

AMCAS Personal Statement

When I was 14 years old, my mother was diagnosed with a brain tumor. I saw how greatly she suffered, and I quickly committed myself to learn more about the possible causes and treatments of her disease. I helped by caring for my younger brother, but I also wished to assist medically. My mother's surgeon successfully removed the tumor without any complications, and while no indication of the tumor has been detected during her subsequent MRI scans, headaches persist. Living through this incident showed me the power as well as the limitations of medicine. In spite of her overall success, I realize that many others in similar situations are not so fortunate.

The summer following my mother's surgery, I began my apprenticeship as a medical researcher. I was accepted into the University of Wisconsin Medical Research Apprenticeship Program from 1995-1997. Beginning in the summer of 1995, I worked under the direction of Dr. Michael Fiore at the Center for Tobacco Research and Intervention, where I was part of a team working to establish smoking as a health vital sign, such as heart rate and blood pressure, to be documented during every clinic visit. My part in the project consisted of administering questionnaires to patients concerning their smoking status as they left their appointments, in order to determine whether they would view physician intervention positively in their efforts to quit.

I began laboratory research in 1996 in the Department of Ophthalmology and Visual Sciences under the supervision of Dr. Daniel Albert and subsequently Dr. Arthur Polansthis work ultimately laid the foundation for my senior honors thesis. The focus of my thesis was whether the expression of the putative angiogenic factor, Tissue Factor, correlates with blood vessel density in uveal melanoma, the primary malignancy of the eye. In the summer of 2000, I was one of fifteen students nationwide awarded a Pfizer Fellowship in Molecular Biology, enabling me to conduct my studies in ocular oncology. I presented my results at Pfizer Inc. and a manuscript describing out laboratory's finding is in the Archives of Ophthalmology press. It was through my research that I was able to apply material I was learning in class to the experiments I was conducting in the laboratory, and I learned to be persistent when the experiments in lab did not progress as they did in class. Research also taught me to act independently, and to evaluate many parameters in order to make educated guesses based on what I knew.

In addition to laboratory research, I interacted with patients in diverse settings. I volunteered at the University of Wisconsin Hospital, where I spent a portion of my time as a patient assistant in the Radiology Department. There, I helped prepare patients for their appointments and assisted in making their visits easier. There were many nights when I would stay past my scheduled shift to talk to patients or take them to their rooms; this commitment earned me the UW Hospital Volunteer of the Month award in September 1998. Currently, I volunteer weekly at the Ronald McDonald House, where I entertain ill children and talk with family members. These children remind me regularly of the importance of hope and determination in life. My volunteer experiences have taught me that time spent listening can help patients and their families tremendously.

As an undergraduate, I also became involved in athletic activities. I began rowing with the Mendota Rowing Club and participated in local bike rides to raise money for charities. Being a member of the University of Wisconsin lightweight crew team reinforced the values of teamwork and setting goals that I initially learned from research. I learned to push myself both physically and mentally, and my commitment to crew was based on the high standards set by our team. Joining the crew team taught me a great deal about perseverance and follow-through, and these values carried me through many tough, sometime, non-stop, days of training. Our dream to be first in the nation was realized when we became the undefeated lightweight crew team for the 1999-2000 school year. I was subsequently honored at the UW Athletic-Academic Banquet in April 2000 for my academic accomplishments and athletic performance. The award validated the efforts of my teammates both during and after crew practice.

My mother's surgery and the improvements in her life first inspired me to become a physician. Her physicians gave her tremendous care and attention, and I hope to provide the same quality of care and treatment to my patients. My experiences have taught me to accomplish multiple tasks and to be confident in my decision-making abilities. My academic and personal experiences have strengthened my resolve to become a physician and have helped prepare me for future training.

See page 262 to find out where this student got in.

ANONYMOUS 4

The applicant participated in the Vagelos Scholars Program at the University of Pennsylvania, which allowed her to earn a bachelor's degree in biochemistry and a master's degree in chemistry in four years. As part of the program, she did two summers of research, completed a significant amount of laboratory work in her junior and senior years, and took graduate courses. While at Penn, the applicant sang in an a cappella group and earned various leadership positions within the group. A Phi Beta Kappa member, she graduated summa cum laude and received an award of distinction from Penn's biochemistry department.

Stats

MCAT: Physical Sciences, 12; Verbal Reasoning, 10; Writing Sample, Q; Biological Sciences, 12

Graduate school GPA: 3.80

Graduate degree earned: Master of Science (MS) in Chemistry

Graduate school attended: University of Pennsylvania

Graduate school graduation year: 2004

Undergraduate overall GPA: 3.82

Undergraduate science GPA: 3.75

Undergraduate college attended: University of Pennsylvania

Undergraduate graduation year: 2004

Gender: Female

Race: Caucasian

Applied To

Boston University, School of Medicine

Columbia University, College of Physicians and Surgeons

Cornell University, Joan & Sanford I. Weill Medical Center

Emory University, School of Medicine

Harvard University, Harvard Medical School

New York University, Mount Sinai School of Medicine

New York University, NYU School of Medicine

Stanford University, School of Medicine

Tufts University, School of Medicine

University of Massachusetts, Medical School

University of Pennsylvania, School of Medicine

Washington University in St. Louis, School of Medicine

AMCAS Personal Statement

I had an appointment, a gig, in another world, only ten minutes and a half-dozen blocks away. I left my lab early and walked quickly through the Friday afternoon rain to meet up with my a cappella group, Dischord. The eleven of us met at my house on the edge of Penn's campus, and walked past dilapidated houses to an old church. This was the home of New Beginnings, an after-school program for low-income West Philadelphia families. As strangers, we entered a room overflowing with children and set up on a small makeshift stage at the front. I played an "A" on the pitch pipe, bringing Dischord to the ready and silencing the crowded room. We led off with Jenny, an upbeat tune—one of our best arrangements. After the second verse, the room lit up with smiles and wide-eyed excitement. Some children even danced! We performed three more songs and then divided the children into groups to teach them our different voice parts. A chorus of eight little hands grabbed me, pleading: "Can you please teach me your part?" We crowded into a tight circle and sang the soprano line to Jenny over and over again. In no time they had it mastered. Together we made music. While they learned a new song to hum on the way home, I learned something about myself that lent a new clarity to my future goals. For me, the greatest sense of fulfillment would come from using the passions that drive me, as a vehicle to reach others.

While I truly enjoyed the challenge of my undergraduate research experience, this exchange at New Beginnings made me better understand what was lacking. No matter how many new techniques I mastered or how many problems I solved, there was always a void. How could investigating interesting and challenging scientific problems not bring me the sense of fulfillment I expected? Not understanding the answer, I worked harder and became a better, more independent scientist. Experiments grew easier to plan, and my work involving the crystallization trials of lambda integrase moved closer to completion. Despite my progress, something important was still missing.

The challenge of research needed the same sharing of passion I experienced at New Beginnings. This to me is the essence of the medical profession—a passion for science and problem solving, coupled with the emotional satisfaction derived from caring for and interacting with people. These two important aspects of medicine became more apparent to me when I recently spent some time shadowing a medical geneticist. The doctor I followed explained her thinking processes and dealings in regard to patient risk, benefit, and available therapeutic options. What I appreciated about this doctor was not only her ability to think critically and scientifically, but also her ability to communicate this information to her patients in a compassionate and clear manner. The combination of all of these experiences brought me to the realization that practicing medicine would best synthesize my love of science with my desire to share my passions with others.

Specifically, I am most interested in pursuing pediatrics or oncology. Pediatrics is appealing because I love interacting with children, and appreciate their fresh world perspective. Oncology also interests me, because it is an intellectually stimulating, quickly evolving field, requiring ongoing education to remain current. Learning about cancer has become increasingly important to me in the past few years, as I witnessed firsthand its affects on the lives of so many people for whom I have cared. I watched helplessly as lung cancer took the life of my grandmother, and as many of my mother's friends underwent lumpectomies, chemotherapy, and radiation for breast cancer. I want to become empowered to help make a difference in people's lives, and the medical profession is a challenging and fulfilling way to do so.

See page 263 to find out where this student got in.

ANONYMOUS 5

The applicant worked on three emergency medicine research studies that allowed her to interact with patients, conduct basic animal research, and learn the fundamentals of clinical research. Apart from her scientific and medical activities, the applicant was captain of her varsity swim team in college and studied abroad at Oxford University.

Stats

MCAT: Physical Sciences, 9; Verbal Reasoning, 11; Writing, R; Biological Sciences, 11

Undergraduate overall GPA: 3.58

Undergraduate science GPA: 3.48

Undergraduate college attended: Macalester College

Undergraduate graduation year: 2003

Gender: Female

Race: Caucasian

Applied To

Boston University, School of Medicine

Cornell University, Weill Medical College

Georgetown University, School of Medicine

Loyola University of Chicago, Stritch School of Medicine

Stanford University, School of Medicine

Tufts University, School of Medicine

University of Chicago, Pritzker School of Medicine

University of Minnesota—Duluth, Medical School

University of Minnesota—Twin Cities, Medical School

University of Virginia, School of Medicine

AMCAS Personal Statement

I stared at that record for a year. During morning practice. During lifeguard shifts. During swim meets. I had missed the 100-meter butterfly record by two-tenths of a second the year before, and I was not about to miss it by that much again. And one year later, I decided I was ready. I dove into the water and smashed the record set nine years before by over a second.

Tenacity is one of my defining character traits. I love a good challenge. My determination has inspired me to study at Oxford University, pick a major where I knew I would have to work hard, and attempt *The New York Times* crossword puzzle every day. I see my hard-working personality as my underlying driving force to become a physician, because determination is essential for studying and practicing medicine.

There is no one concrete reason why I want to become a physician. Instead, there are many little reasons that led me to realize that I wanted to dedicate my life to medicine. One factor is my love of science. For example, my favorite course in my academic career so far has been my high school anatomy and physiology class. Strangely enough, I thoroughly enjoyed drawing detailed pictures of epithelial tissues in my lab notebook and dissecting and memorizing fifty-odd muscles of a cat. The physiology part was even better. When I first started physiology, I never really thought about the concept of blood pressure. Then I learned the body had this intricate and marvelously designed system all to maintain a desirable blood pressure. It is hard to believe that various human systems work together so perfectly to make up a healthy human being. This past semester, I learned that hemoglobin binds oxygen over carbon dioxide based on one hydrogen bond. Such a small thing that makes such a big difference! That one hydrogen bond allows our tissues and muscles to get what we need and let us live happy lives. These small and seemingly arbitrary interactions make up our world and I love learning about them.

Despite my appreciation of chemistry and biology, I need something more. There is no place for emotion in scientific fact. I appreciate the value of laboratory work, but at the same time, I know that I cannot spend the rest of my life in a laboratory. I like people too much. Designing and synthesizing a new drug is an incredible feat, but the whole process is too abstract for me. Even if a researcher does get note-worthy results, it takes years to get a drug on the market, and she does not get to see the direct results and rewards of her work. The researcher does not work with the patients taking the drug every day. I want the focus of my work to be people, not some product.

I came to this realization when I started comparing my experiences in the organic chemistry laboratory with my experiences as an emergency department volunteer and emergency department research intern. Working in the organic laboratory was fun, and I will continue organic research throughout my senior year. There is a certain satisfaction in synthesizing and analyzing an organic molecule that few people in the world have made before. But the hours in the organic lab do not fly by like they do in the emergency department. In the emergency department, a new face and a new challenge come in the door every fifteen minutes. A team of people is responsible for figuring out what is wrong with this particular patient and fixing him. That pressure and responsibility is exciting. Knowing you have a chance to make a person's life better or even saving his or her life is exciting.

My love of science and people draws me to the medical profession. My fascination with medicine is what pulls me away from being, for example, a veterinarian, social worker, chemist, or science teacher. Interning in the emergency department has strongly re-enforced my decision to go into medicine. In the department this past weekend, I forgot to eat until the eight-hour shift was nearly over. For a person who thinks about food every ten minutes, this is a rare occurrence. That day I was busy interviewing patients in regards to their quality of care, monitoring a trauma patient's level of consciousness while they were being intubated, taking arterial blood gases from a pig, and asking overdose patients if they would consent to being in a study investigating the effects of ondansetron as an anti-emetic. This work is motivating. The studies we are doing will have a relatively immediate effect for many sick people. And I get to watch, learn, and interact with doctors at work, which is the best part.

The basis of medicine is commitment to others. Of course I want a happy and worthwhile life, but I want the same for others as well. I feel that I have an obligation to leave a positive impact on society. Medicine bridges the gap between personal and social fulfillment. I would like to be a part of it.

See page 263 to find out where this student got in.

ANONYMOUS 6

The applicant conducted Micro-Electro-Mechanical Systems (MEMS) research at UC Berkeley, presented at an Optical MEMS conference in Hawaii, and coauthored a paper while interning at Agilent Laboratories. He completed his medical school prerequisites as a post-baccalaureate at San Jose State University, where he maintained a 4.0 GPA. He interned at the Parkinson's Institute and later worked at National Semiconductor. He is an avid tennis player and runner.

Stats

MCAT: Physical Sciences, 14; Verbal Reasoning, 10; Writing, R; Biological Sciences, 11

Undergraduate overall GPA: 3.97

Undergraduate science GPA: 4.00

Undergraduate college attended: University of California—Berkeley

Undergraduate graduation year: 2003

Gender: Male

Race: Asian American

Applied To*

Albany Medical College (MD only)

Baylor College of Medicine

Boston University, School of Medicine

Columbia University, College of Physicians and Surgeons

Cornell/Sloan-Kettering/Rockefeller Tri-Institutional MD-PhD Program

Dartmouth College, Dartmouth Medical School

Drexel University, College of Medicine

George Washington University, School of Medicine and Health Sciences (MD only)

Georgetown University, School of Medicine

Johns Hopkins University, School of Medicine

Mayo Clinic College of Medicine, Mayo Medical School

New York University, Mount Sinai School of Medicine

New York University, NYU School of Medicine

Northwestern University, Feinberg School of Medicine

Stanford University, School of Medicine

University of California—Davis, School of Medicine

University of California—Irvine, College of Medicine

University of California—Los Angeles, David Geffen School of Medicine

University of California—San Diego, School of Medicine

University of California—San Francisco, School of Medicine

University of Michigan, Medical School

University of Pennsylvania, School of Medicine

University of Pittsburgh, School of Medicine/Carnegie Mellon University
    Joint MD-PhD Program

University of Rochester, School of Medicine and Dentistry

University of Southern California, Keck School of Medicine

University of Washington, School of Medicine

Washington University in St. Louis, School of Medicine

Yale University, School of Medicine

Yeshiva University, Albert Einstein School of Medicine

* All MD/PhD programs unless otherwise noted.

AMCAS Personal Statement

"Come on, let's get the saline and try again," my partner urged me as I tried soldering some wires on the digital controller together. We had not slept in 36 hours and hoped that our 276th effort would not go unheeded by the electrical engineering gods. As we got the saline, we flipped the switch and saw static. Then, for a second, we captured an image on our screen – a near perfect topical image of frog cardiac tissue. For the last 7 months, we rebuilt a controller that controlled the ability to extract current and voltage data over living tissues. Using this data, we tried to algorithmically reconstruct an image of that tissue, rivaling MRI-quality at less than 25% the cost. Our success had been marginal, but with this slight image, our first in 40 trials, we knew the technology – Electrical Impedance Tomography (EIT) – was viable. Never before had any of my research been aimed at benefiting people directly. As fatigued as I was, I shrieked in excitement at the thought that EIT would one day make cancer screening cheaper and more accessible to people worldwide. It was then that I thought I could do more than be an engineer.

I started working on this project the beginning of my senior year, hoping to enter the emerging field of biological microelectromechanical systems (MEMS). I had worked on various MEMS-related projects in industry and at school. In summer 2002, I worked at Agilent Labs, a company whose culture was all about independent research and forging your own path in your work. I immersed myself in the culture and worked with a manager to collect data on common MEMS chemical etchants, while he tutored me on the basics of MEMS processing. I greatly enjoyed this learning experience whetting my appetite for basic research.

Returning to UC Berkeley, I worked for EE Professor Richard Muller on an optical MEMS project, concurrently with my other BioMEMS EIT project. Both projects allowed me to grow as I improved my library research, lab technique, and group work, while maintaining my independent research goals. As I built a novel polarization beam splitter for Dr. Muller, I had to learn about optics, develop my own theory, and manufacture beam splitters. Within 1 academic year, I went from knowing little about optics to presenting an optical MEMS research project at an international conference in Hawaii. However, of all my research experiences – the EIT project affected me the most. I felt connected to my test subjects, hoping to give more purpose to my work other than a glittering publication or conference presentation. I, also, was intrigued by oncology since much of our work dealt with cancerous tissue from other animals. Indeed, even my graduate student advisor commented that my goals might best be served in a clinical, not just a research setting.

As he planted the idea of a medical career in me, I took his advice about finding clinical experience. At the Parkinson's Institute (PI), my main role was to analyze motion data from Parkinsonian and dyskinetic monkeys. Working with 2 others, we tried to classify the random motions we observed. Dr. Daniel Togasaki, the primary investigator on the project, took me under his wing allowing me to observe the animal test subjects and human patients in the clinic. The researchers lesioned monkeys for Parkinson's Disease, and I saw their erratic motor behavior "in the flesh." Those severely affected could hardly stand still. One week after seeing the monkeys, I sat in on a patient appointment. The patient, an older woman, had trouble walking but otherwise appeared normal. Dr. Togasaki evaluated her motor skills with tests like clapping her hands to a constant rhythm and timing how fast she walked on a set path. Her performance indicated she was worsening. Although still relatively early in the disease, I could not help but shudder at the thought that this woman might one day lose motor control. In the exam room, Dr. Togasaki's main role did not come from his ability to quote and prescribe medication. Instead, as patients react to their treatment, he examines their progress while keeping them informed of all their options. I realized that Dr. Togasaki's greatest task is to keep the patient abreast with knowledge of new and old drug treatments available to them. He inspired me to become a researcher and a clinician like him, as I realized that I want to interact with patients and offer guidance in their treatment.

Now, I want to study oncology to improve cancer screening. During my time with Dr. May Chen, an oncologist I recently have begun shadowing, cancer patients who go beyond stage II cancer have a low chance for full recovery. Let the challenge of universal early detection be mine as I make screening cheaper and more accessible. My goals are clear: I want to treat patients directly, while studying BioMEMS and oncology and teaching students the fundamentals behind the engineering and the medicine. Ideally, I see myself at an academic institution splitting my time between research, clinical work with patients, and teaching. As ambitious as that sounds, I believe I will be an oncologist who can make differences in patient lives, particularly in imaging technologies, and in educating patients and the next generation of doctors.

See page 264 to find out where this student got in.

ANONYMOUS 7

After college, the applicant served as an investigator on legal defense teams representing death row inmates, volunteered at an inner-city family practice clinic, assisted in research on schizophrenia and bipolar disorder, and started a nonprofit organization providing mental health services to Rwandese genocide survivors.

Stats

MCAT: Physical Sciences, 12; Verbal Reasoning, 12; Writing Sample, O;
   Biological Sciences, 11

Undergraduate overall GPA: 3.44

Undergraduate science GPA: 4.00

Undergraduate college attended: Harvard College

Undergraduate graduation year: 2002

Gender: Female

Race: Caucasian

Applied To

Columbia University, College of Physicians and Surgeons

Cornell University, Weill Medical College

Emory University, School of Medicine

Harvard University, Harvard Medical School

New York University, Mount Sinai School of Medicine

New York University, NYU School of Medicine

Northwestern University, Feinberg School of Medicine

Oregon Health and Science University, School of Medicine

Stanford University, School of Medicine

Tulane University, School of Medicine

University of California—Davis, School of Medicine

University of California—Irvine, College of Medicine

University of California—Los Angeles, David Geffen School of
   Medicine

University of California—San Diego, School of Medicine

University of California—San Francisco, School of Medicine

University of Chicago, Pritzker School of Medicine

University of Miami, School of Medicine

University of Southern California, Keck School of Medicine

University of Washington, School of Medicine

Yeshiva University, Albert Einstein College of Medicine

AMCAS Personal Statement

The attorney-client conference room at North Carolina's Guilford County Jail has three gray plastic chairs. They are old chairs, the kind that have been warped by humidity and wear such that that they never sit evenly on the floor. Miguel and I sat in those chairs together all day every day for three straight weeks. Miguel liked to switch every few hours from his chair to the empty one. He liked to rock the uneven chairs back and forth on the cement floor. When we talked about his involvement with East LA gangs, he rocked harder. When we talked about the execution of his family by guerilla terrorists in El Salvador, he rocked even harder. When we talked about his methamphetamine addiction, he picked up the chair underneath him and began dragging it around the room. Sometimes Miguel made so much noise the guards outside came to make sure everything was all right. One of the first phrases Miguel learned to say in English was, "We're fine, thank you."

Miguel was not fine. He was facing a first-degree murder charge and capital punishment. He was actively psychotic and was diagnosed with bipolar and post-traumatic stress disorders. Moreover, the unclean needles Miguel had used to shoot meth had left him, years later, with an advanced case of Hepatitis C.

As an investigator assigned to Miguel's case, I had spent the last six months traveling between North Carolina, San Francisco and Los Angeles uncovering all this. Because I spoke Spanish, I was the first professional to whom Miguel had been able to communicate his symptoms and experiences since coming to the United States. I worked feverishly with physicians, psychiatrists and defense attorneys to prepare a bio-psycho-social case history for the Guilford County Court, with the hope that the court would come to see the degree to which Miguel required both medical and mental health care. When the Guilford County district attorney's office at last offered a deal for life in prison, with a clause ensuring adequate mental and physical health facilities, I flew once more to North Carolina to meet with Miguel. It took us three weeks of sitting all day in those gray chairs before Miguel was able to take in what he was facing and make a decision to save his life.

When Miguel finally accepted the deal, I rose from my plastic chair for the last time, exhausted by all I had been through, still coming to terms with what I had experienced. My time with Miguel led me to understand the inextricability of physical and mental illness, and the complexity of the skills required in their treatment. I realized I wanted to learn these skills, to appreciate better the origin and consequence of conditions such as Miguel's. Additionally, I realized how critical personal connection is in being able to help people like Miguel. The research and investigation I had been able to do for Miguel's case, the final plea bargain— all of that resulted from the relationship that Miguel and I had built.

Though my work with Miguel crystallized these ideas, they had been growing in me for a number of years. They traced back to my junior year in college, when my mother became critically ill with intestinal scleroderma. I know that the hours I spent sitting by my mother's bed, working with her to manage the physical realities of her illness, steered me towards the hours I later spent sitting in those gray chairs with Miguel. My mother died not long after Miguel's life was spared. Though my mother's situation couldn't have been more different from Miguel's, both relationships left me with a clear vision of the work I wanted to pursue.

Other experiences I have had— traveling solo through rural Bolivia, discussing trauma care with Rwandese genocide survivors, communicating with doctors in Zanzibar who treat malaria-induced epilepsy— have confirmed my understanding of medicine as an emotionally rewarding and socially active career. They have also confirmed my belief that the skills involved in achieving good medical care are numerous, complicated, and critical to master. This past year, working at the Contra Costa Center for Health and the San Francisco VA hospital, I have seen these skills in action. I have been inspired to see patients outside of the terrifying context of criminal defense and third world conditions, patients at ease with their doctors and their treatments. I think about Miguel and try to imagine what might have been different had he received treatment before his crime. I think about someday having the resources and expertise to treat the potential Miguels. Whether I end up a free-clinic internist, a Doctors Without Borders obstetrician, or a jail psychiatrist, I cannot envision a more rewarding or important career.

Secondary Essay #1

The applicant used the following essay in her application to Columbia University, College of Physicians and Surgeons.

What satisfaction do you expect to receive from being a physician?

There are many ways in which I expect to find a career as a physician satisfying. I expect that the science and the daily problem solving will be interesting and exciting. I expect that my relationships with patients will be instructive and affecting. I expect to be challenged, both emotionally and intellectually, by my efforts to improve the medical, social, and psychological well being of the communities in which I work. In fact, what I expect to find rewarding about a career as a physician is precisely that it offers an array of intellectual, emotional, and social-political satisfactions.

I've come to learn that a complex combination of satisfactions is important to me. I spent much of college trying to achieve a balance among them—how to be stimulated intellectually without becoming too self-involved, how to help others without losing sight of my own needs. My senior thesis as an English major became a quest to solve this very dilemma. I wrote my thesis on the poetry of Robert Hass because I was fascinated by Hass's unique ability to explore political and theoretical issues through a personal and phenomenological framework, pulling large and important ideas out of the abstract and into a more intimate and empathic realm. Hass's poems use various literary devices to demonstrate that seemingly disparate political and personal spheres can coexist and inform one another. Hass makes clear how the capacity for self-understanding is what gives rise to the capacity for compassion, and how capacity for compassion is what drives political idealism.

My decision to pursue medicine arose in the context of my study of Hass's poetry. In medicine, I believe I can find what Hass describes: intellectual excitement and interpersonal engagement driving social-political accomplishment. Hass's poetry fit well with my efforts to find my way out of my senior year quandary, and I believe that a career in medicine fits well with what I know I want to do in my life. I'm sure that there will be times of heart-ache— dying patients, long hours, working with inadequate resources—and I expect to falter in some moments just as I expect to soar in others. But even in those times of complete exhaustion I think that I will maintain a deep and personal investment in my work that I already feel fortunate to have found.

Secondary Essay #2

The applicant used the following essay in her application to Northwestern University, Feinberg School of Medicine.

Describe the distinguishable characteristics you possess and tell us how you think these characteristics will enhance your success as a FSM medical student and future physician.

My beliefs in social justice and helping others have always been very important to me, and working diligently and competently to follow these beliefs has always been something I have found myself able to do as well as enjoy. I am able to remain calm in chaotic situations, whether I am talking down a psychotic patient or managing a group of summer interns assisting our legal team during a death penalty trial. I can successfully mediate between parties in conflict, whether I am working with an angry mother and her terrified daughter who has recently received a positive pregnancy test or with an inmate and a prison guard, each of whom insists the other is out to get him. I don't tire easily, and when passionately invested in a project I will work until its completion. I am a fast learner, and I am inspired and eager to learn from people with experience greater than my own in order to more efficiently and effectively achieve my goals. Lastly, I am a competent Spanish speaker, and find it extremely satisfying to communicate successfully with people in need who have been isolated and intimidated by an existing language barrier.

I expect these skills to prove useful in medical school and in my career as a physician. In medical school I anticipate being challenged by long hours, difficult material, and clinical inexperience. I will need to be eager, unassuming, and dedicated in order to meet these challenges successfully. I will need to call upon the skills I already possess and be open to learning from the skills of others, mentors and peers alike. I believe the experience I have had working with various medical, legal, and research teams will help me to strike this balance effectively. I also believe that my unremitting dedication to helping others and achieving social justice will only get stronger as I acquire the skills needed to become a physician. I hope that the combination of my passionate beliefs, enthusiasm, and willingness to learn will make me a devoted and effective health care provider.

Secondary Essay #3

The applicant used the following essay in her application to University of California—Davis, School of Medicine.

Who would you consider to be the most influential person in your life and why?

My mother was, and continues to be, the most influential person in my life. My mother gave me a sense of security and empowerment in the world that is fundamental to the choices I have made and the paths I intend to follow. One of my earliest memories is of the two of us sitting together in our bathroom when I was three. I was in the tub, dressed in my bathing suit, swim cap and goggles. She was just outside the tub, reaching her arm over the side so her hand was flat at the bottom. I remember holding my breath, ducking my face in the water, kissing my mother's fingers, and spluttering back up for air. Years later my father explained this puzzling recollection to me. Apparently, I wanted to learn to swim but was terrified of putting my head under water. Kissing my mother's hand, however, was something I loved to do. So, night after night, my mother helped me practice kissing her hand at the bottom of the bathtub until I was comfortable putting my head underwater and could join my friends in swim class.

My mother's love for me and her belief in all I could accomplish have enabled me to do so much more than learn to swim. My ability to work hard, follow my passions and expect success is directly linked to those early days in the tub and the many variations of those days that followed.

My mother died this past January of intestinal scleroderma, an illness she had been battling for almost twenty years. She got sick when I was a little girl, and lived on powdered food and IV-feeding for much of my childhood. It wasn't until I was in college, however, that I realized how sick she was. I remember being a teenager and describing my mother's condition to people by saying, "Oh, it's not life-threatening; she just can't always eat." I had no idea of the magnitude of her daily struggle with pain and deprivation. I knew the details of her illness — the circumference of her G-tube, the antibiotics she rotated through — yet I never connected these facts with the reality that my mother was slowly dying. Talking to other family members, friends, my mother's colleagues, and even the physicians who treated her, I've come to realize that we were all living with a positive and hopeful view of my mother's condition that she constructed, for us and for herself. My mother taught me the powerful lesson that we can define our own realities. Her optimism and her refusal to live as an invalid defined her world and mine as I was growing up. Today, my life is filled with excitement, a sense of opportunity, and a belief that I can make a difference. I know I would be a very different person had my mother raised me in a climate of fear and suffering.

I learned from my mother that one's approach to a problem defines the problem. I learned from her what truly excellent care-taking can be. I remember the absolute trust I had in my mother, the encouragement I felt when I saw her hand at the bottom of the tub. If I can give my patients one ounce of that encouragement, if I can communicate to them the same courageous optimism that informed my childhood, I know I will become an effective physician.

Secondary Essay #4

The applicant used the following essay in her application to University of California—Davis, School of Medicine.

Each applicant brings with them goals of what they want to accomplish as a physician. They also have their larger dreams with regards to what they hope to accomplish in their lifetime. In a brief paragraph, please describe how you would want to be remembered at the end of your life.

The final line of Shakespeare's "Sonnet 73"— "Love that well, which thou must lose ere long"—captures how I would like to be remembered at the end of my life. I want to be remembered not just as somebody who loved her community, but as somebody who loved it well, somebody who didn't just take but also gave back, somebody who put attention and effort toward following her ideals. Shakespeare deliberately includes the word "well" at the end of his sonnet to avoid a clichéd statement about love and loss, to convey that the idealized notion of love being all that matters is false. He indicates that love alone is not enough; it must be accompanied by dedication and hard work. I think these are crucial words of advice for a future doctor. They help me understand that my strong desire to help my community is not, in itself, enough to make me an effective health care provider. I will need to read article upon article as research progresses. I will need to deliver bad news to patients in a calm and encouraging manner. I will need to work long hours when I'm tired. I look forward to medical school as a place in which I can apply Shakespeare's instructions to my life as a physician and continue to construct a legacy of one who loved well the world in which she lived.

See page 265 to find out where this student got in.

ANONYMOUS 8

The applicant held several jobs in the medical field, including a nursing assistant position at the transplant unit of the University of Wisconsin hospital. He was also a behavioral therapist for an autistic child. Aside from his science-related accomplishments, the applicant was a member of his college tennis team and took classes in guitar performance.

Stats

MCAT: Physical Sciences, 10; Verbal Reasoning, 10; Writing, S; Biological Sciences, 10

Undergraduate overall GPA: 3.71

Undergraduate science GPA: 3.90

Undergraduate college attended: Lawrence University

Undergraduate graduation year: 2002

Gender: Male

Race: Caucasian

Applied To

Johns Hopkins University, School of Medicine

Medical College of Wisconsin

University of Iowa, Roy J. and Lucille A. Carver College of Medicine

University of Washington, School of Medicine

University of Wisconsin—Madison, School of Medicine and Public Health

Yale University, School of Medicine

AMCAS Personal Statement

For much of my life, I have felt a desire to work in the field of health care. My father, a pathologist, would occasionally bring me to work and share his medical knowledge by showing me slides of cancerous growths and teaching me anatomy during autopsies. At first it was the wonder of learning the biological complexities of life that fascinated me most. Three years ago, however, that changed. My grandfather died of emphysema. This event evoked countless nights of lying awake, thinking about life, death, and the human condition. I wanted to lead a worthwhile and meaningful life, but how? My mind raced through numerous possibilities. One particularly simple answer, however, intrigued me most: help people. Volunteering and tutoring had always provided me with a certain feeling of well-being that I could achieve through no other means. My grandfather's death provided me with a new, better reason to become a doctor. No longer was I merely fascinated with the textbook world of biology and human medicine. I now felt an emotional connection to much of what I read and reflected upon biology's human impact. The next summer, I was able to experience this impact firsthand as a nursing assistant (NA).

The NAs at the nursing home in which I worked shouldered enormous responsibility and interacted extensively with the residents. One particular resident had lost much of his vision and hearing, and, as a result, tended to become extremely agitated when disturbed. He invariably yelled at us when we assisted him with showering, eating, and using the bathroom, regardless of how accommodating we were. From this experience, I learned that the most one can do for another is to provide his or her best effort, but even one's best effort does not guarantee a desired (or even friendly) response.

One inevitable consequence of working at a nursing home is observing death. Three residents died during my employment, but the death of the oldest resident under my care was by far the most upsetting. Her death was preceded by a constant, agonizing pain throughout her body and the misery of a relentless cold. Her singular request during this time was for someone to kill her, and her request always left me speechless. Everyone tried to make her as comfortable as possible, but the pain persisted, making us very conscious of the importance of quality of life. Eventually, after about one week under these unfortunate circumstances, she died. Her death taught me that although life is very precious, death can also be a blessing.

In that same summer, I worked as a behavioral therapist for an autistic child. He communicated only with single-word sentences and never looked anyone in the eyes. For the first week of therapy, I spent hours and hours saying "hello" and waiting for him to respond with eye contact. Finally, in the middle of the second week, he looked directly into my eyes, said "hello", and was immediately rewarded with three chocolate treats! At no other time in my life had I been nearly as excited to hear anyone utter those two words. It was a great success that taught me the value of persistence and patience and gave me an appreciation for even the smallest of achievements.

That summer provided me with tangible experiences that reminded me of the impact that my studies would have on real people. With each class during the next year, I became increasingly eager to discuss and investigate each topic and its related issues. My grades, as a result, showed steady improvement. At the end of that year, I began my senior honors project, a year long research and thesis-writing experience that abounded with independence and responsibility. During the first six months of laboratory research, nothing worked as I had expected, but after a substantial amount of protocol manipulation, I began to obtain results. This initial project phase taught me the importance of detailed observations when working within the complex world of biology. While researching background information for my thesis, many of the relevant sources concerned developmental abnormalities, the incidence and scope of which were far greater than I had ever imagined, and reminded me that life is truly a great achievement, especially considering all that can go wrong.

While my previous experiences solidified my desire to become a doctor, another experience introduced me to a new goal. In my biomedical ethics course, we engaged in very emotional discussions about health insurance, throughout the course of which I became determined to donate my time and professional knowledge to those who cannot otherwise afford medical care. Through such deeds, I believe that the essential qualities of my most passionate activities will be encompassed, allowing me to lead a fulfilling life of service to others. For the next year, I will be working again as a nursing assistant but this time in a hospital's transplant unit in addition to tutoring local high school students and attending meetings of the coalition for universal health care. My hope is that these experiences will provide me with an even closer and more intimate look at the world of medicine in terms of both provision and policy, while allowing me to share my knowledge with those who need my assistance the most.

See page 266 to find out where this student got in.

ANONYMOUS 9

The applicant volunteered at Stony Brook University Hospital in the Pediatric, Pediatric Intensive Care, and Pediatric Oncology units. She did research on the evolution of pelvic asymmetry in the threespine stickleback—a type of fish—that was presented at several conferences. A teaching assistant for the Biology and Psychology departments, the allpicant was involved in course planning and held review sessions for students. She was a member of the Sigma Beta Honor Society Steering Committee, Phi Beta Kappa Honor Society, Golden Key International Honor Society, and the National Society of Collegiate Scholars. She also assisted physicians in a medical office for four years.

Stats

MCAT: Physical Sciences, 11; Verbal Reasoning, 11; Writing Sample, P; Biological Sciences, 11

Undergraduate overall GPA: 3.92

Undergraduate science GPA: 3.89

Undergraduate college attended: Stony Brook University— State University of New York

Undergraduate graduation year: 2005

Gender: Female

Race: Caucasian

Applied To

Columbia University, College of Physicians and Surgeons

Cornell University, Joan & Sanford I. Weill Medical College

New York University, Mount Sinai School of Medicine

State University of New York—Downstate Medical Center

State University of New York—Stony Brook University, School of Medicine

University of Pennsylvania, School of Medicine

Yeshiva University, Albert Einstein College of Medicine

AMCAS Personal Statement

"What do you want to be when you grow up?" That is the magic question that is most often asked of children. For many youngsters the answer wavers between a lawyer, a teacher, a policeman or an astronaut, and alternates every week. For me, however, the answer has always been a consistent "I want to be a doctor."

The inspiration to become a physician first came when I was eight years old. My two year old brother was ill and no one knew what was wrong with him. He could not explain what was hurting him because he had not learned to speak yet. Sophisticated imaging technology, such as a sonogram, that was necessary to reveal my brother's acute appendicitis was simply not available, and thus neither the pediatrician nor the emergency room doctors were able to come up with a diagnosis. Luckily, a physician family friend correctly suspected appendicitis and encouraged us to take my brother to the hospital before it was too late. Finally, not a moment too soon, my brother was operated on and his ruptured appendix was removed. If any more time had been wasted, he would have died. Watching my little brother go through this painful ordeal, and seeing my family in such distress was extremely difficult for me. I wished I could do something to ease his pain and help him get better. It was frustrating, sitting in the sidelines, witnessing a loved one suffering, and not being able to do anything about it. But the surgeon and the doctor who diagnosed him were able to help him. By telling my parents that their son would be well again, they were able to make a difference. In my young eyes they were real heroes for saving him. After that day I wanted to be just like them, I wanted to be able to at least have the chance to help others deal with their illnesses. I wanted to be some little girl's hero someday too. It was then that I decided that when I grew up I would become a doctor.

At the time, it was probably just a childish dream, but this dream has stayed with me all along, maturing as I matured. As I got older and more knowledgeable, I became even more confident that this was the right path for me. In addition to the healing and interpersonal aspect of being a physician, I am also especially interested in the science of medicine itself. All throughout my scholastic career I was always drawn to the natural sciences. I was very curious about how things work or why certain phenomena take place. The more answers I discovered, the more captivated I became, and that fascination continued to drive my hunger for more scientific knowledge.

In preparation for the future, I attended Brooklyn Technical High School, one of the top three science school in New York City and was part of the Bio-Medical Sciences major. I challenged myself by taking Genetics, Anatomy and Physiology, Organic Chemistry, and Advanced Placement courses in Biology, Physics, and Calculus. Ultimately, I graduated as one of the top ten students with honors in my major and chose to attend Stony Brook University, knowing it was one of the top research universities concentrated on the sciences.

I chose the biology major since it closely fit my interests, and again offered sufficient challenges. In addition to focusing on the sciences, I kept my focus on a future in medicine as well. One of the most rewarding experiences was taking a class in Darwinian Medicine. Learning about this newly emerging field was truly enthralling. The core of this course was centered on the evolution of pathogens and the resulting counter human evolution. For a potential physician, the notions presented were eye-opening and provided me with an improved grasp of, and better perspective on, the prominent health issues of today and tomorrow. Taking this course made me want to strive even harder to achieve my goal and be able to apply my knowledge. Currently, I am working on a study concerning the evolution of loss of bony armor in fish. In the near future this research will lead to the discovery and isolation of a growth factor that is responsible for the growth of bone. This finding has a potential use in the medical field in dealing with bone injuries. I also spend time volunteering in the Pediatrics unit of Stony Brook University Hospital. I have learned a great deal about the doctor-patient relationship by observing doctors and interacting with the patients and their families.

For me a medical profession presents the opportunity to learn continuously throughout my career and to employ my knowledge directly in a beneficial manner. It is an exigent, and yet extremely rewarding field, the rigorous path to which is paved with sacrifice and determination. Without the willpower and a real desire to practice medicine in accordance to its doctrines, this goal cannot be achieved. The aspiration to enter the medical field and make a difference in people's lives has motivated me to do everything I have accomplished so far. That eight year old girl who was inspired by a doctor saving her brother's life is now all grown up and is ready to embark on the first step of the journey that will allow her to make a significant impact on the healthcare of other people.

See page 266 to find out where this student got in.

ANONYMOUS 10

The applicant volunteered at Pattengil Middle School, where she help students in math and social studies, provided after-school homework help, and created activities that encouraged students to be involved in school. She also volunteered at Huron Valley Sinai Hospital in Commerce, Michigan, where she fed, bathed, and took the vitals of patients. Proficient in Indian classical dance, the applicant's performances raised money for the education of under-privileged children in India.

Stats

MCAT: Physical Sciences, 9; Verbal Reasoning, 6; Writing Sample, M; Biological Sciences, 9

Undergraduate overall GPA: 3.67

Undergraduate science GPA: 3.80

Undergraduate college attended: Michigan State University

Undergraduate graduation year: 2006

Gender: Female

Race: Asian American

Applied To

Michigan State University, College of Osteopathic Medicine

Wayne State University, School of Medicine

AMCAS Personal Statement

"That's the last box," my dad said as we just finished loading the truck to be shipped to India. Moving: a word very familiar to me, as I have moved three times during a span of twenty-one years. At the age of five we moved to Curacao, a small island in the Caribbean, at eleven back to India, and again at thirteen to the United States of America. Traveling and living in different communities has taught me how to understand different kinds of people and their unique situations. These experiences have also instilled in me a deep desire to interact with others different from myself and serve my community. As a physician, I want to help, educate and value the needs of people in various situations.

Irrespective of the country, in both developing and developed societies, every individual seeks for help. In India, I watched mothers carrying their kids as they were begging for money when cars halted at stoplights, just to gather a few pennies to feed their children. This made me realize that their role as mothers made them stand in the scorching heat so their kids would not go to sleep on an empty stomach. In America, I have seen homeless people searching for pop cans in the trash bins so they can make a little money to buy dinner. Observing these conditions has made me understand that every person acts according to their situation and they do whatever necessary, within their limits, for survival. My desire to help society awakened in me when I saw these people in these situations and this led me to explore the medical profession. My exploration of the medical field started off in a school setting and progressed further through volunteering at a hospital. These experiences have built my passion towards being a physician.

My determination to educate people is why I decided to volunteer at Pattengil Middle School in East Lansing, Michigan. By volunteering at Pattengil, I hoped to make students aware of the importance of education, the impact it has on one's future, and the role it plays in one's survival. I was paired with a sixth grader who was significantly behind in school, as she did not get the necessary support at home. She did not have anyone to help her with her schoolwork, until I provided her with after school help and made sure she completed her homework for the next day. My role in educating her helped me to understand her situation, as she was just a young child who wanted some love and support when she got home from school.

My Bharatanatyam (Indian classical dance) performances have contributed to raise funds for several organizations to help support the education of the underprivileged. My contribution has helped children to obtain a better education, which ultimately provides them with several options for their future. I feel a doctor's primary role is to educate and promote awareness to patients about various diseases and their treatments. My love of educating and interacting with people enhanced my interest in medicine.

As a volunteer at the Huron Valley Sinai Hospital in Commerce, Michigan, I had an opportunity to observe and value the needs of people in various situations. My experience in the hospital has helped educate me on what being a physician is all about: their driving passion to help people, to be challenged, and to learn throughout their life. It has also given me first hand experience as a care provider. I wanted to assist patients by providing them with a comfortable healing environment so that they could heal faster. I helped Patient Care Assistants in the hospital by taking patient vitals, bathing immobile patients, and feeding those that needed assistance. Even though most of the patients were several generations older than I was, they all looked to me for compassion and comfort. They enjoyed my company, as I would watch television with them, talk to them about their hobbies, and give them a helping hand when needed. I realized that my perfect vision of the hospital environment was distorted, as some patients do die and some act aggressively. I never lost sight of the fact that they are human beings who just want some love and guidance to feel better. These are all experiences that have helped me build a stronger passion for the field of medicine. This passion includes my wish to provide people with the prospect of good health, and my respect for people in various settings and situations. As a doctor I want to work with people and assist them in the healing process.

Observing different societies has made me the person I am today, broadened my horizons, and above all made me realize that my goal is to be a physician. I chose to become a doctor because it is the perfect career in which I will be able to acquire humanistic rewards, which to me are priceless. Living in different countries around the world has shown me the meaning of responsibility, flexibility, cooperation and respect towards different ideas and principles. Most of all it has enhanced my lifelong commitment to better society.

Secondary Application Essay

The applicant used the following essay in her application to Michigan State University, College of Osteopathic Medicine.

Describe a personal experience or ethical challenge you have faced that has influenced the development of your character. How has this experience helped you to develop specific skills and/or abilities that are essential to becoming an osteopathic physician?

My life in general has been different from the life led by the normal American youth. I was born in India and raised with the customs and traditions of a conservative Indian family. We lived in a joint family where my parents lived with their parents and siblings, and their families. Girls did not have the same privileges as boys in several circumstances. For example, girls were not allowed to go out of the house to watch movies and go shopping with friends. We were also constrained in the clothes we are supposed to wear. We were only supposed to wear clothes that cover our entire body. Our house ran in a timely manner, people are not allowed to do as they pleased. Breakfast, lunch and dinner are only served at a certain time, and the schedule had to be followed. Everyone is very disciplined as they all rise early and sleep early. Through this part of my life I learnt discipline that is necessary to make a good osteopathic physician.

At the age of thirteen, we moved to Detroit, Michigan. Moving to the United States has been a big change and almost the turning point of my life. When we first moved here, I was amazed by the American culture. The fact that children get so much independence was something new to me. After living in a joint family for several years of my life, it took me a while to adjust to a house with only four people living in it. When I moved here in the eighth grade, it was hard for me to make friends too. Everyone had already made his or her friends group and I did not quite know which group I belonged to. Everyone was very different from me; in the way they spoke, behaved and presented themselves. I also had to adapt to the different educational systems. In India, we were evaluated solely on our class exam results, but in America, we are encouraged to be well-rounded individuals. It took sometime to get used to the idea of extracurricular activities, volunteering, lab work and sports, which characterize a well-rounded person. After moving to America I have learnt adaptability and flexibility that are essential to becoming an osteopathic physician.

Staying in different parts of the world has allowed me to experience how life differs in a developed nation and a third world society. It has also enhanced my interest in the medical field. Not being able to afford for a medical checkup, millions of people in India are left clueless, not knowing the symptoms of the disease and what needs to be done to control it. Watching mothers carrying their kids and begging for money as cars halt at a stoplight so they can gather a few pennies to feed their children made me realize how fortunate I am for being able to have three meals a day. Not even having enough money to eat a proper meal, they definitely have never gotten a medical checkup. Experiencing all these situations has motivated me to become a physician and provide an opportunity where underprivileged people can turn to physicians for guidance irrespective of their financial status. Seeing the poverty has made me compassionate and wanting to help the underprivileged and the poor.

Having been raised in either of the two hemispheres, I have learnt to adapt and be open-minded about different cultures, educational systems, and different lifestyles. Visiting the world and meeting people of all different backgrounds has built my desire to interact and learn more about people. Living in India has taught me bonding, respect, and responsibility. In America I have learnt flexibility, good judgment and cooperation, which I feel, are qualities that will make me be a better osteopathic physician.

See page 266 to find out where this student got in.

CHAPTER 9

WHERE THEY GOT IN

Adam Douglass Marks
University of Wisconsin—Madison, School of Medicine and Public Health
Applied to:

Emory University, School of Medicine .... accepted

Medical College of Georgia, School of Medicine .... accepted

Ohio State University,

College of Medicine and Public Health .... accepted

State University of New York—University at Buffalo,

    School of Medicine and Biomedical Sciences .... accepted

University of North Carolina—

    Chapel Hill, School of Medicine .... waitlisted, TK

University of Pittsburgh,

    School of Medicine .... accepted

University of Virginia, School of Medicine .... waitlisted, TK

University of Wisconsin—Madison,

    School of Medicine and Public Health .... accepted

Brandon Devers
Baylor College of Medicine
Applied to:

Baylor College of Medicine .... accepted

Duke University, School of Medicine .... accepted

Johns Hopkins University, School of Medicine .... accepted

Stanford University, School of Medicine .... waitlisted, TK

University of California—Los Angeles,

    David Geffen School of Medicine .... accepted

University of California—San Francisco,

    School of Medicine .... accepted

University of Kentucky, College of Medicine .... accepted

Washington University in St. Louis, School of Medicine .. accepted

Caelan Johnson
Rush University, Rush Medical College
Applied to:

Case Western Reserve University, School of Medicin .... accepted

Loyola University Chicago, Stritch School of Medicine .... denied

Northwestern University, Feinberg School of Medicine .... denied

Rush University, Rush Medical College .... accepted

Southern Illinois University, School of Medicine .... accepted

University of Chicago, Pritzker School of Medicine .... denied

University of Illinois at Chicago,

    UIC College of Medicine .... accepted

University of Iowa,

    Roy J. and Lucille A. Carver College of Medicine.............. denied

University of Wisconsin—Madison,

    School of Medicine and Public Health.............................. denied

Washington University in St. Louis, School of Medicine ...... denied

COLLEEN KNIFFIN

University of Minnesota—Twin Cities, Medical School

Applied to:

    Baylor College of Medicine.. denied

    Loma Linda University, School of Medicine .... accepted

    University of California—Davis, School of Medicine......... withdrew

    University of California—Los Angeles,

    David Geffen School of Medicine .... denied

    University of California—San Diego, School of Medicine ..... denied

    University of Illinois at Chicago,

    UIC College of Medicine .... accepted

    University of Minnesota—Duluth, Medical School .... withdrew

    University of Minnesota—Twin Cities, Medical School ..... accepted

    University of Southern California,

    Keck School of Medicine .... withdrew

DAN NAYLOR

University of Southern California, Keck School of Medicine

Applied To:

    Boston University, School of Medicine .... denied

    Case Western Reserve University, School of Medicine ..... withdrew

    Dartmouth College, Dartmouth Medical School .... denied

    Drexel University, College of Medicine .... waitlisted, withdrew

    Duke University, School of Medicine .... withdrew

    George Washington University, School of Medicine

    and Health Sciences .... denied

    Georgetown University, School of Medicine .... withdrew

    Harvard University, Harvard Medical School .... denied

    Johns Hopkins University, School of Medicine .... denied

    Loma Linda University, School of Medicine .... withdrew

    New York Medical College .... waitlisted, withdrew

    New York University, NYU School of Medicine .... denied

    Northwestern University, Feinberg School of Medicine .... denied

    Oregon Health & Science University, School of Medicine .... denied

    Pennsylvania State University, College of Medicine .... denied

    Stanford University, School of Medicine .... denied

    Thomas Jefferson University, Jefferson Medical College ..... denied

Tulane University, School of Medicine .... denied
University of California—Davis, School of Medicine .... denied
University of California—Irvine, College of Medicine .... denied
University of California—Los Angeles,
   David Geffen School of Medicine .... denied
University of California—San Diego, School of Medicine ..... denied
University of California—San Francisco,
   School of Medicine .... denied
University of Chicago, Pritzker School of Medicine .... denied
University of Michigan, Medical School .... denied
University of Southern California,
   Keck School of Medicine .... accepted
University of Vermont, College of Medicine .... denied
Vanderbilt University, School of Medicine .... denied
Yale University, School of Medicine .... denied

EDDIE SILVER
Thomas Jefferson University, Jefferson Medical College
Applied To:
Thomas Jefferson University,
   Jefferson Medical College .... accepted, early decision

ERIC RANDOLPH SCOTT
University of Virginia, School of Medicine
Applied To:
Boston University, School of Medicine .... withdrew
Dartmouth College, Dartmouth Medical School .... denied
Duke University, School of Medicine .... denied
Georgetown University, School of Medicine .... withdrew
Johns Hopkins University, School of Medicine .... denied
University of Chicago, Pritzker School of Medicine .... withdrew
University of Virginia, School of Medicine .... accepted
Virginia Commonwealth University, School of Medicine .. accepted
Wake Forest University, School of Medicine .... accepted
Yale University, School of Medicine .... denied

FAWN LANGERMAN
Ohio State University, College of Medicine and Public Health
Applied To:
Case Western Reserve University, School of Medicine ..... accepted
Georgetown University, School of Medicine .... denied
Johns Hopkins University, School of Medicine .... withdrew

Ohio State University,
    College of Medicine and Public Health .... accepted
Oregon Health & Science University,
    School of Medicine .... withdrew
University of Cincinnati, College of Medicine .... accepted

HEATHER NELSON
University of Minnesota—Twin Cities, Medical School
Applied To:

Creighton University, School of Medicine .... accepted
Emory University, School of Medicine .... waitlisted, withdrew
Medical College of Wisconsin .... withdrew
Pennsylvania State University, College of Medicine .... accepted
Tulane University, School of Medicine .... accepted
University of Illinois at Chicago,
    UIC College of Medicine .... accepted
University of Minnesota—Duluth,
    Medical School .... waitlisted, withdrew
University of Minnesota—Twin Cities,
    Medical School .... accepted
University of North Carolina—Chapel Hill,
    School of Medicine .... denied
University of Pittsburgh, School of Medicine . waitlisted, withdrew

JEAN PEARCE
University of North Dakota, School of Medicine
   and Health Sciences
Applied To:

George Washington University,
    School of Medicine and Health Sciences .... denied
Michigan State University, College of Human Medicine .... denied
Tulane University, School of Medicine .... accepted
University of Connecticut, School of Medicine .... denied
University of Maryland, School of Medicine .... denied
University of Michigan, Medical School .... denied
University of Minnesota—Twin Cities, Medical School .... denied
University of North Dakota,
    School of Medicine and Health Sciences .... accepted
University of Oklahoma, College of Medicine .... denied
University of Wisconsin—Madison,
    School of Medicine and Public Health .... denied
Vanderbilt University, School of Medicine .... denied

JILL HUDGENS LEE

University of South Alabama, College of Medicine

Applied To:

University of Alabama—Birmingham,

School of Medicine .... accepted

University of South Alabama, College of Medicine .... accepted

JIMMY WU

University of Wisconsin—Madison, School of Medicine and Public Health

Applied To:

Medical College of Wisconsin .... accepted

University of Wisconsin—Madison,

School of Medicine and Public Health.......................... accepted

JOHN FAILING*

Applied To:

Dartmouth College, Dartmouth Medical School .... denied

Stanford University, School of Medicine .... denied

University of Colorado, School of Medicine.......................... denied

University of Hawaii,

John A. Burns School of Medicine .... denied

University of Maryland, School of Medicine .... accepted

University of Washington, School of Medicine .... denied

West Virginia University, School of Medicine .... accepted

* At the time of this book's printing the applicant had not yet decided where he would enroll.

JULIE KATZ

University of Pennsylvania, School of Medicine

Applied To:

Columbia University, College of Physicians

and Surgeons .... waitlisted, withdrew

Cornell University, Joan & Sanford I. Weill

Medical College .... waitlisted, withdrew

Duke University, School of Medicine .... waitlisted, withdrew

Harvard University, Harvard Medical School .... denied

Johns Hopkins University, School of Medicine .... denied

New York Medical College .... waitlisted, withdrew

New York University, Mt. Sinai School of Medicine .... accepted

New York University,

NYU School of Medicine .... waitlisted, withdrew

Northwestern University, Feinberg School of Medicine ... accepted
State University of New York—
   Downstate Medical Center .... accepted
State University of New York—Stony Brook University,
   School of Medicine .... accepted
University of Pennsylvania, School of Medicine .... accepted
Yale University, School of Medicine .... denied
Yeshiva University,
   Albert Einstein College of Medicine .... withdrew

JUSTIN FINCH
University of Minnesota—Twin Cities, Medical School
Applied To:
Boston University, School of Medicine .... accepted
Cornell University,
   Joan & Sanford I. Weill Medical College .... denied
Duke University, School of Medicine .... waitlisted, denied
Finch University of Health Sciences,
   Chicago Medical School .... withdrew
George Washington University,
   School of Medicine & Health Sciences .... withdrew
Harvard University, Harvard Medical School .... denied
Johns Hopkins University, School of Medicine .... denied
Loyola University Chicago, Stritch School of Medicine .... withdrew
New York Medical College .... denied
New York University, Mount Sinai School of Medicine .... withdrew
Northwestern University,
   Feinberg School of Medicine .... denied
Rush University, Rush Medical College .... withdrew
Stanford University, School of Medicine .... withdrew
Temple University, School of Medicine .... withdrew
Thomas Jefferson University,
   Jefferson Medical Colleges .... withdrew
Tufts University, School of Medicine .... withdrew
University of California—Los Angeles,
   David Geffen School of Medicine .... withdrew
University of California—San Diego,
   School of Medicine .... withdrew
University of California—San Francisco,
   School of Medicine .... withdrew
University of Chicago,
   Pritzker School of Medicine .... waitlisted, denied

University of Maryland, School of Medicine .... accepted
University of Minnesota—Twin Cities,
    Medical School .... accepted
University of North Carolina—Chapel Hill,
    UNC School of Medicine .... denied
University of Pennsylvania, School of Medicine .... accepted
University of Virginia, School of Medicine........................ withdrew
University of Washington, School of Medicine .... withdrew
Yeshiva University,
    Albert Einstein College of Medicine .... withdrew

KARIN ELISABETH WITTE
University of Wisconsin—Madison, School of Medicine and Public Health

Applied To:
Medical College of Wisconsin .... accepted
Stanford University, School of Medicine .... denied
Temple University, School of Medicine .... accepted
University of Chicago, Pritzker School of Medicine .... denied
University of Wisconsin—Madison,
    School of Medicine and Public Health .... accepted

KATIE WILLIHNGANZ
University of Minnesota—Twin Cities, Medical School

Applied To:
Mayo Clinic College of Medicine, Mayo Medical School .... denied
Pennsylvania State University,
    College of Medicine .... waitlisted, withdrew
Saint Louis University, School of Medicine .... accepted
University of Minnesota—Twin Cities,
    Medical School .... accepted

LOUIS LIN
University of Minnesota—Twin Cities, Medical School

Applied To:
University of Minnesota—Twin Cities,
    Medical School .... accepted
Louis was denied at all the other schools to which he applied.

MEKEISHA GIVAN
Meharry Medical College, School of Medicine

Applied To:
Meharry Medical College, School of Medicine .... accepted

MICHAEL CULLEN
University of Wisconsin—Madison, School of Medicine and Public Health
Applied to:

Duke University, School of Medicine .... denied

Mayo Clinic College of Medicine,

Mayo Medical School .... denied

Medical College of Wisconsin.. accepted

University of Iowa, Roy J. and Lucille A. Carver

College of Medicine .... accepted

University of Wisconsin—Madison,

School of Medicine and Public Health........................... accepted

Washington University in St. Louis,

School of Medicine .... denied

MICHAEL CURLEY
University of Wisconsin—Madison, School of Medicine and Public Health
Applied To:

Creighton University, School of Medicine......................... accepted

Loyola University Chicago, Stritch School of Medicine .... accepted

Medical College of Wisconsin.. accepted

Saint Louis University, School of Medicine....................... accepted

Tulane University, School of Medicine .... withdrew

University of Wisconsin—Madison,

School of Medicine and Public Health........................... accepted

MICHAEL FRANCO
Temple University, School of Medicine
Applied To:

Cornell University, Joan & Sanford I. Weill

Medical College .... waitlisted, denied

Harvard University, Harvard Medical School .... denied

Johns Hopkins University, School of Medicine .... denied

Temple University, School of Medicine .... accepted

Thomas Jefferson University,

Jefferson Medical College .... waitlisted, withdrew

UMDNJ, New Jersey Medical School .... accepted

UMDNJ, Robert Wood Johnson Medical School .... accepted

University of Pennsylvania,

School of Medicine .... waitlisted, denied

MICHELLE JONELIS

University of California—San Francisco, School of Medicine

Applied To:

Columbia University, College of Physicians
and Surgeons .... waitlisted, withdrew
Cornell University, Joan & Sanford I. Weill
Medical College .... denied
Harvard University, Harvard Medical School .... denied
New York University, Mt. Sinai School of Medicine .... denied
New York University,
NYU School of Medicine .... waitlisted, withdrew
Stanford University, School of Medicine .... denied
University of California—Irvine, College of Medicine .... accepted
University of California—Los Angeles,
David Geffen School of Medicine .... waitlisted, withdrew
University of California—San Diego,
School of Medicine .... waitlisted, withdrew
University of California—San Francisco,
School of Medicine .... accepted
University of Pennsylvania,
School of Medicine .... waitlisted, withdrew

RADHIKA LU BAUER

New York University, NYU School of Medicine

Applied To:

Cornell University, Weill Medical College .... denied
New York University, NYU School of Medicine .... accepted
Northwestern University, Feinberg School of Medicine .... denied
Rush University, Rush Medical College .... accepted
Saint Louis University, School of Medicine .... denied
State University of New York—University at Buffalo,
School of Medicine and Biomedical Sciences .... denied
State University of New York—Upstate Medical University,
College of Medicine .... accepted
University of Illinois at Chicago,
UIC College of Medicine .... accepted
University of Pennsylvania, School of Medicine .... denied
University of Wisconsin—Madison,
School of Medicine and Public Health .... denied
Yale University, School of Medicine .... waitlisted, denied

REBECCA SHARIM
Temple University, School of Medicine

Applied To:

Temple University, School of Medicine ...... accepted early decision

RYAN NOVAK
University of Minnesota—Twin Cities, Medical School

Applied To:

University of Minnesota—Duluth, Medical School .... accepted

University of Minnesota—Twin Cities, Medical School ..... accepted

SAMANTHA L. PACE
University of Minnesota—Twin Cities, Medical School

Applied To:

Case Western Reserve, School of Medicine .... denied

Cornell University, Weill Medical College .... denied

Duke University, School of Medicine .... waitlisted, denied

Georgetown University, School of Medicine .... withdrew

Harvard University, Harvard Medical School .... denied

Medical College of Wisconsin .... accepted

Stanford University, School of Medicine .... denied

University of California—San Francisco,

School of Medicine .... denied

University of Cincinnati, College of Medicine .... withdrew

University of Minnesota—Twin Cities, Medical School ..... accepted

University of North Carolina—Chapel Hill,

UNC School of Medicine .... waitlisted, denied

University of Rochester,

School of Medicine and Dentistry .... waitlisted, denied

SAMANTHA VIZZINI
Tulane University, School of Medicine

Applied To:

Emory University, School of Medicine .... denied

Medical College of Georgia, School of Medicine .... denied

Tulane University, School of Medicine .... accepted

TARA A. O'CONNELL
University of Minnesota—Twin Cities, Medical School

Applied To:

Albany Medical College .... denied

Boston University, School of Medicine .... denied

Dartmouth College, Dartmouth Medical School .... denied

Duke University, School of Medicine .... denied

George Washington University,

    School of Medicine and Health Sciences .... denied

Georgetown University, School of Medicine .... denied

Johns Hopkins University, School of Medicine .... denied

Northwestern University, Feinberg School of Medicine .... denied

Oregon Health & Science University, School of Medicine .... denied

Stanford University, School of Medicine .... denied

Thomas Jefferson University, Jefferson Medical College ..... denied

Tufts University, School of Medicine .... denied

University of California—Irvine, College of Medicine .... denied

University of California—Los Angeles,

    David Geffen School of Medicine .... denied

University of California—San Diego, School of Medicine ..... denied

University of California—San Francisco,

    School of Medicine .... denied

University of Maryland, School of Medicine .... denied

University of Minnesota—Twin Cities, Medical School ..... accepted

University of Southern California,

    Keck School of Medicine .... accepted

University of Washington, School of Medicine .... denied

University of Wisconsin—Madison,

    School of Medicine and Public Health .... denied

Vanderbilt University, School of Medicine .... denied

Yeshiva University, Albert Einstein College of Medicine ...... denied

TERI MARSH

University of California—San Francisco, School of Medicine

Applied To:

    Cornell University, Weill Medical College .... denied

    New York Medical College .... withdrew

    New York University, Mount Sinai School of Medicine .... denied

    New York University, NYU School of Medicine .... denied

    Ohio State University, College of Medicine

        and Public Health .... withdrew

    Oregon Health & Science University,

        School of Medicine .... accepted

    Stanford University, School of Medicine .... denied

    University of California—Davis, School of Medicine .... denied

    University of California—Irvine, College of Medicine .... denied

    University of California—Los Angeles,

        David Geffen School of Medicine .... denied

University of California—San Diego,

    School of Medicine .... denied

University of California—San Francisco,

    School of Medicine .... accepted

University of Cincinnati, College of Medicine .... withdrew

University of North Carolina—Chapel Hill,

    UNC School of Medicine .... denied

University of Southern California,

    Keck School of Medicine .... denied

University of Vermont, College of Medicine .... denied

University of Wisconsin—Madison,

    School of Medicine and Public Health .... denied

Wake Forest University, School of Medicine .... denied

Yeshiva University,

    Albert Einstein College of Medicine .... withdrew

THAYER HEATH

University of California—San Francisco, School of Medicine

Applied To:

Columbia University,

    College of Physicians and Surgeons .... waitlisted, withdrew

Cornell University, Weill Medical College .... accepted

Duke University, School of Medicine .... denied

Georgetown University, School of Medicine .... withdrew

Harvard University, Harvard Medical School .... denied

New York University,

    Mount Sinai School of Medicine .... accepted

New York University, NYU School of Medicine .... accepted

Northwestern University, Feinberg School of Medicine .... denied

Oregon Health & Science University,

    School of Medicine .... accepted

University of California—Davis, School of Medicine .... denied

University of California—Irvine, College of Medicine .... accepted

University of California—Los Angeles,

    David Geffen School of Medicine .... denied

University of California—San Diego, School of Medicine ..... denied

University of California—San Francisco,

    School of Medicine. .... accepted

University of Chicago, Pritzker School of Medicine .... withdrew

University of Colorado, School of Medicine .... waitlisted, withdrew

University of Hawaii,

    John A. Burns School of Medicine .... withdrew

University of Miami, School of Medicine .... withdrew

University of Southern California,

    Keck School of Medicine .... denied

University of Washington, School of Medicine .... denied

Yale University, School of Medicine .... denied

Anonymous 1

University of Minnesota—Twin Cities, Medical School

Applied To:

    Medical College of Wisconsin .... accepted

    Tufts University, School of Medicine .... denied

    University of Illinois at Chicago,

        UIC College of Medicine .... accepted

    University of Iowa,

        Roy J. and Lucille A. Carver College of Medicine .... denied

    University of Minnesota—Duluth,

        Medical School .... accepted

    University of Minnesota—Twin Cities,

        Medical School .... accepted

    University of North Dakota,

        School of Medicine and Health Sciences .... denied

    University of Wisconsin—Madison,

        School of Medicine and Public Health.............................. denied

Anonymous 2

Brown University, Brown Medical School

Applied To:

    Brown University,

        Brown Medical School .... accepted early decision

Anonymous 3

University of Wisconsin—Madison, School of Medicine and Public Health

Applied To:

    Loyola University Chicago,

        Stritch School of Medicine .... denied

    Medical College of Wisconsin .... withdrew

    Ohio State University,

        College of Medicine and Public Health.............................. denied

    University of Iowa,

        Roy J. and Lucille A. Carver College of Medicine .... denied

    University of Minnesota—Twin Cities,

        Medical School .... withdrew

University of North Carolina—Chapel Hill,
   UNC School of Medicine .... denied
University of Virginia, School of Medicine .... denied
University of Wisconsin—Madison,
   School of Medicine and Public Health .... accepted

ANONYMOUS 4
New York University, NYU School of Medicine
Applied to:

Boston University, School of Medicine .... accepted
Columbia University, College of Physicians
   and Surgeons .... waitlisted, withdrew
Cornell University, Joan & Sanford I. Weill
   Medical Center .... denied
Emory University, School of Medicine .... accepted
Harvard University, Harvard Medical School .... denied
New York University,
   Mount Sinai School of Medicine .... waitlisted, withdrew
New York University, NYU School of Medicine .... accepted
Stanford University, School of Medicine .... waitlisted, withdrew
Tufts University, School of Medicine .... accepted
University of Massachusetts, Medical School .... accepted
University of Pennsylvania, School of Medicine .... accepted
Washington University in St. Louis,
   School of Medicine .... waitlisted, withdrew

ANONYMOUS 5
University of Minnesota—Twin Cities, Medical School
Applied To:

Boston University, School of Medicine .... denied
Cornell University, Weill Medical College .... denied
Georgetown University, School of Medicine .... denied
Loyola University of Chicago,
   Stritch School of Medicine .... waitlisted, denied
Stanford University, School of Medicine .... denied
Tufts University, School of Medicine .... denied
University of Chicago,
   Pritzker School of Medicine .... withdrew
University of Minnesota—Duluth, Medical School .... denied
University of Minnesota—Twin Cities,
   Medical School .... accepted
University of Virginia, School of Medicine .... denied

Anonymous 6

The applicant is currently enrolled in the University of California—
Los Angeles, David Geffen School of Medicine's MD-PhD (MSTP)
program, which is offered in conjunction with the California Institute
of Technology.

Applied To*:

Albany Medical College .... accepted (MD)

Baylor College of Medicine .... accepted

Boston University, School of Medicine .... withdrew

Columbia University,

    College of Physicians and Surgeons .... waitlisted, denied

Cornell/Sloan-Kettering/Rockefeller,

    Tri-Institutional MD-PhD Program .... denied

Dartmouth College, Dartmouth Medical School .... withdrew

Drexel University, College of Medicine .... withdrew

George Washington University,

    School of Medicine and Health Sciences .... accepted (MD)

Georgetown University, School of Medicine .... withdrew

Johns Hopkins University, School of Medicine .... denied

Mayo Clinic College of Medicine, Mayo Medical School ... accepted

New York University, Mount Sinai School of Medicine .... accepted

New York University,

    NYU School of Medicine .... waitlisted, denied

Northwestern University,

    Feinberg School of Medicine .... accepted

Stanford University, School of Medicine .... waitlisted, denied

University of California—Davis, School of Medicine .... withdrew

University of California—Irvine, College of Medicine .... withdrew

University of California—Los Angeles,

    David Geffen School of Medicine .... accepted

University of California—San Diego,

    School of Medicine .... accepted (MD)

University of California—San Francisco,

    School of Medicine .... waitlisted, denied

University of Michigan, Medical School .... denied

University of Pennsylvania, School of Medicine .... withdrew

University of Pittsburgh, School of Medicine/

    Carnegie Mellon University,

    Joint MD-PhD Program .... withdrew

University of Rochester,

    School of Medicine and Dentistry .... waitlisted, denied

University of Southern California,

    Keck School of Medicine .... accepted

University of Washington, School of Medicine .... denied

Washington University in St. Louis,

    School of Medicine .... accepted (MD)

Yale University, School of Medicine .... denied

Yeshiva University, Albert Einstein School of Medicine ... accepted

*   Accepted into MD-PhD program unless otherwise noted.

ANONYMOUS 7
University of California—San Francisco

Applied To:

Columbia University,

    College of Physicians and Surgeons .... withdrew

Cornell University, Weill Medical College .... withdrew

Emory University, School of Medicine .... accepted

Harvard University, Harvard Medical School .... withdrew

New York University, Mount Sinai School of Medicine .... withdrew

New York University, NYU School of Medicine .... withdrew

Northwestern University, Feinberg School of Medicine ... withdrew

Oregon Health & Science University,

    School of Medicine .... withdrew

Stanford University, School of Medicine .... withdrew

Tulane University, School of Medicine .... withdrew

University of California—Davis, School of Medicine .... withdrew

University of California—Irvine, College of Medicine .... withdrew

University of California—Los Angeles,

    David Geffen School of Medicine .... withdrew

University of California—San Diego,

    School of Medicine .... accepted

University of California—San Francisco,

    School of Medicine .... accepted

University of Chicago, Pritzker School of Medicine .... withdrew

University of Miami, School of Medicine .... denied

University of Southern California,

    Keck School of Medicine .... withdrew

University of Washington, School of Medicine .... denied

Yeshiva University,

    Albert Einstein College of Medicine .... withdrew

ANONYMOUS 8

University of Wisconsin—Madison, School of Medicine and Public Health

Applied To:

Johns Hopkins University, School of Medicine .... denied

Medical College of Wisconsin .... accepted

University of Iowa,
Roy J. and Lucille A. Carver College of Medicine .... denied

University of Washington, School of Medicine .... denied

University of Wisconsin—Madison,
School of Medicine and Public Health .... accepted

Yale University, School of Medicine .... denied

ANONYMOUS 9

Yeshiva University, Albert Einstein College of Medicine

Applied To:

Columbia University,
College of Physicians and Surgeons .... denied

Cornell University,
Joan & Sanford I. Weill Medical College .... denied

New York University,
Mount Sinai School of Medicine .... waitlisted, denied

State University of New York—
Downstate Medical Center .... accepted

State University of New York—Stony Brook University,
School of Medicine .... accepted

University of Pennsylvania, School of Medicine .... denied

Yeshiva University,
Albert Einstein College of Medicine .... accepted

ANONYMOUS 10

Michigan State University, College of Osteopathic Medicine

Applied To:

Michigan State University,
College of Osteopathic Medicine .... accepted

Wayne State University, School of Medicine .... denied